The
Last Baron

Master of the Universe: Baron Édouard-Jean Empain at his company headquarters

Christian Simonpiétri/Sygma via Getty Images

The Last Baron

THE PARIS KIDNAPPING
THAT BROUGHT DOWN AN EMPIRE

TOM SANCTON

DUTTON

DUTTON
An imprint of Penguin Random House LLC
penguinrandomhouse.com

Copyright © 2022 by Thomas A. Sancton
Penguin supports copyright. Copyright fuels creativity, encourages diverse voices,
promotes free speech, and creates a vibrant culture. Thank you for buying an authorized
edition of this book and for complying with copyright laws by not reproducing, scanning,
or distributing any part of it in any form without permission. You are supporting
writers and allowing Penguin to continue to publish books for every reader.

DUTTON and the D colophon are registered trademarks of
Penguin Random House LLC.

LIBRARY OF CONGRESS CATALOGING-IN-PUBLICATION DATA
has been applied for.

ISBN 9780593183809 (hardcover)
ISBN 9780593183816 (ebook)

Printed in the United States of America
1 3 5 7 9 10 8 6 4 2

BOOK DESIGN BY ELKE SIGAL

While the author has made every effort to provide accurate telephone numbers,
internet addresses, and other contact information at the time of publication, neither the
publisher nor the author assumes any responsibility for errors or for changes that occur after
publication. Further, the publisher does not have any control over and does not assume
any responsibility for author or third-party websites or their content.

For my son, Julian Sancton,
who inherits no dynasty
but the brotherhood of writers

CONTENTS

Prelude   *1*

PART I   *The Kidnapping*   *3*

Chapter 1   Pride Before the Fall   *5*

Chapter 2   Your Money or Your Life   *24*

Chapter 3   The Investigators   *34*

PART II   *The Kidnappers*   *53*

Chapter 4   The Making of a Gangster   *55*

Chapter 5   "Make the Money Come to Us!"   *66*

Chapter 6   Planning the Caper   *73*

PART III   *The First Baron*   *83*

Chapter 7   The Founder   *85*

Chapter 8   The Birth of the Métro   *90*

Chapter 9   The Big Dig   *99*

Chapter 10   Opening Day   *104*

Chapter 11   In Leopold's Heart of Darkness   *113*

Chapter 12   A Place in the Sun   *124*

PART IV   *The Showdown*   *133*

Chapter 13   Operation Snowplow   *135*

Chapter 14   On the Move   *144*

Chapter 15   The Fatal Rendezvous   *150*

Chapter 16   "Can't I Call from Here?"   *163*

Chapter 17   From One Prison to Another   *173*

PART V   *The Empain Legacy*   181

   Chapter 18   The Baron's Progeny   183

   Chapter 19   Goldie   191

   Chapter 20   Disgrace   197

   Chapter 21   The Inheritor   207

   Chapter 22   Wado's Triumph   221

PART VI   *Endgame*   227

   Chapter 23   Aftershocks   229

   Chapter 24   Exile's Return   244

   Chapter 25   The Dragnet   251

   Chapter 26   The Reckoning   258

   Chapter 27   Afterlives   270

   Chapter 28   Light and Twilight   281

   Chapter 29   Wado's Adieu   291

   Epilogue   299

Acknowledgments   305

Notes   309

Alas for the affairs of men! When they are fortunate you might compare them to a shadow; and if they are unfortunate, a wet sponge with one dash wipes the picture away.

—AESCHYLUS

God give me the strength to get up when I fall—and the grace to forgive those who gave me the push.

—ANONYMOUS PRAYER

The
Last Baron

PRELUDE

*T*his is the story of the rise and fall of an empire. Not a terrestrial empire, like that of Napoleon or Charles V, but one of the world's great industrial dynasties. It was founded in the late nineteenth century by a Belgian baron who built railroads, created banks, fathered the Paris Métro, dug mines in Africa, and raised a fantastic city on the sands of Egypt. In time, this empire was passed down to the founder's grandson, a dazzling golden boy who expanded its dominion and proclaimed himself a "master of the universe." Then something happened, an almost random event that toppled the dynasty and stripped the last baron of his power. It is a cautionary tale about a man who threw caution to the wind. Some might even see his fate as a kind of karmic retribution for his grandfather's colonial exploitation, his father's alleged Nazi collaboration, and his own unbridled passions. If so, he paid a heavy price.

PART I

The Kidnapping

JANUARY–FEBRUARY 1978

Golden Boy: Wado in 1978

Photograph © Cor/AFP

CHAPTER 1

Pride Before the Fall

*H*is friends called him Wado, but the world knew him as Baron Édouard-Jean Empain. With his longish blond hair, blue eyes, and high cheekbones, he could have been mistaken for a movie star—some people compared him to Paul Newman and Robert Redford. Tall, square-shouldered, and athletic, he had been a champion skier and horseman in his youth. Now, at age forty, he was the head of an industrial empire that comprised 174 companies and employed 136,000 workers in fields ranging from mining and metallurgy to banking, heavy construction, shipbuilding, armaments, and nuclear energy.

Empain was half American and half Belgian, but his headquarters, his sumptuous apartment, and his ancestral château were in France, where he enjoyed a position of almost unrivaled influence. His conglomerate was so central to French economic and security interests that the papers dubbed him *le Krupp français*—an allusion to the Krupp industrial dynasty that supplied armaments to German regimes from the Thirty Years' War to the end of the Third Reich. Hailed as a member of the "international gentry," Baron Empain was the first foreigner to be named a director of Le Patronat, the powerful French employers' association. His personal credo was that of the classic capitalist: "work, family, property."

The stars seemed to be aligning nicely for Empain in this pivotal decade of the 1970s. He had the good fortune to seize the helm of the Empain group during the surge of economic expansion known as the *trente glorieuses*, France's three decades of rapid growth following World War II. The oil shock of 1973 marked the beginning of a slowdown, but for the young baron, it was another stroke of luck: In 1975 his Framatome subsidiary won a monopoly to build sixteen new nuclear plants after the government decided to base its energy needs almost exclusively on atomic power as a hedge against oil dependency. As a result, Empain became one of France's most powerful figures, known to the press as "Monsieur Nucléaire"—respected, even feared, by the country's political leadership. The authoritative daily *Le Monde* dubbed him "the shining symbol of transnational capitalism."

Despite the rising inflation and unemployment triggered by the oil shock, it was a dynamic decade, a time of modernization, innovation, and dramatic technological advances. Under a thicket of cranes, the very face of Paris was changing. One of the biggest urban transformations of the '70s—the demolition of the historic Les Halles central food market—occasioned a massive excavation to build an underground shopping mall and a central hub joining the subway system with the suburban train network. To the west of the capital, work continued on the bristling clutch of Manhattan-style skyscrapers that loomed on the horizon at La Défense. On the Left Bank, the sleek fifty-eight-story Tour Montparnasse, the first (and so far only) skyscraper in the heart of Paris, was completed in 1973. At the Place

Beaubourg, the Pompidou art center, a controversial construction wrapped in multicolored, industrial-looking pipes, opened its doors in 1977.

French lifestyles were changing too. Innovative chefs were lightening the artery-clogging traditional French diet with their scaled-down *nouvelle cuisine*, while at the other end of the food chain, McDonald's opened its first French outlet. With the haute couture market declining, Yves Saint Laurent launched his first ready-to-wear collection. Though the cinematic "New Wave" had peaked in the late 1960s, France continued to boast a vibrant movie industry, with bankable stars like Alain Delon, Jean-Paul Belmondo, and Catherine Deneuve, who enjoyed international renown. Paris's younger generation, clad in bell-bottoms, hot pants, and wide-collared shirts, jammed the discothèques and danced to the pounding beat of the Bee Gees and the Village People—along with homegrown disco stars like Claude François (who wrote the music for Sinatra's "My Way" and later electrocuted himself in his bathtub). It was a time of sexual liberation, carefree exuberance, and a first coming-out of gay culture.

It was also a decade of dramatic political transition. The turbulence unleashed by the Paris-centered student upheaval of May 1968 had settled down, though it hastened Charles de Gaulle's departure from power the following year. His death in 1970 marked the end of an era. Valéry Giscard d'Estaing, elected president in 1974, ushered in a spate of modernizing reforms, with laws liberalizing divorce, legalizing abortion, and lowering the voting age to eighteen. A bald-domed patrician and technocrat, Giscard tried to soften his elitist image by playing the accordion and inviting garbage collectors to breakfast at the Élysée Palace—quite a change of presidential style after de Gaulle's austere gravitas.

Unlike Giscard, Baron Empain was not a reformer. Despite his relative youth, he considered himself an old-school capitalist who detested unions and had no qualms about laying off scores of workers at his companies. He had his share of detractors. Some saw him as a cocky rich boy, born with a silver spoon in his mouth and placed by mere birthright at the head of the powerful multinational founded by his grandfather. In a country that valued meritocracy, this titled Belgian had been handed his scepter without jumping through the requisite hoops. He held none of the advanced degrees that most of his peers had earned at France's highly competitive *grandes écoles*—in fact, his formal education went no further than secondary school.

Empain was hardly the only second- or third-generation scion to head a major French company. His close friend Michel Bolloré was running a major industrial group founded by his grandfather, for example, and Serge Dassault was being groomed to take over France's leading aviation firm from his long-lived father. But both men had paid their dues: Bolloré boasted a law diploma and a degree from the prestigious Institute of Political Studies, better known as Sciences Po; Dassault was a graduate of no fewer than three *grandes écoles*, including the elite Polytechnique military engineering academy. Empain had the equivalent of a high school diploma.

The tabloids published paparazzi photos of Empain with Brigitte Bardot and portrayed him as a jet-setting playboy. In reality, he was anything but. Inhabited by a natural timidity, he valued privacy and discretion over flashy displays of wealth. This was a man who bought his suits off the rack and cut his own hair. Though not given to introspection, he had moments of self-doubt rooted in a childhood deprived of affection from his parents—a former American exotic dancer and a hedonistic father who died young amid charges of Nazi collaboration. Empain was thereafter haunted by a secret sense of hurt and shame for which he compensated with an arrogance that the ancient Greeks would have called hubris.

He took pride in his title of nobility, though it did not descend from any ancient aristocracy. His namesake grandfather was a man of modest origins who had received his barony from Belgium's King Leopold II in recognition of his accomplishments as an industrialist. It was an honorific title, conferring on its holder no domains or privileges apart from a freshly minted coat of arms. Wado, who had inherited the barony, proudly wore the family crest on his signet ring and freely used his Belgian title in France. It looked good on a business card and sounded impressive when people addressed him as "Monsieur le Baron." In reality, though, it didn't mean that much. In Belgium, as in France, the feudal rights of the old aristocracy had long since been abolished, though their titles continued to command a certain prestige. The status of nobility was diluted by the new titles that Napoleon and Leopold II handed out by the bushelful as favors to friends and courtiers—not to mention the many fake ones that social-climbing parvenus conferred upon themselves. Still, Wado's title carried a measure of distinction and he savored it.

What he savored most of all, and wielded without any scruples, was power. He bragged that "everyone was on their knees" before him. "If a minister asked me for something and I said no, he didn't dare insist." Charles de Gaulle, whose orders he defied, called him an "annoying young man." The current president, Giscard d'Estaing, looked on this Belgian baron with suspicion—though he maintained friendly relations and was careful to invite him to his hunting parties at the Château de Rambouillet. Empain returned the compliment by letting on that Giscard was a "mediocre shot" and a "suitcase without a handle."

Empain's private life was well organized—ski vacations at the chic Alpine resort of Megève every Christmas, long sojourns in the South of France each summer, twice-a-week poker games with well-heeled friends. He had a weakness for fast cars, beautiful women, and gaming tables, but when he returned to his second-floor office on the Rue d'Anjou in central Paris, he was all business and as punctual as a Swiss chronometer. His life was carefully compartmentalized: He kept his family, his colleagues, his gambling partners, his mistresses, and his hunting buddies in separate, hermetically sealed boxes. That was how he managed his complicated existence.

But sometimes complications had a way of seeping through the cracks. Consider the scene at Juan-les-Pins, on the Mediterranean coast, where Wado and his family spent their annual summer vacations in a villa rented from the American railroad heiress Florence Gould. Like Dick and Nicole Diver in Fitzgerald's *Tender Is the Night*, the Empains would pass their days on the beach hobnobbing with their rich friends. When they were not swimming or waterskiing, the men would sit at card tables under the shade of beach umbrellas, sip pastis or chilled white wine, and play poker. The women in their designer sunglasses and swimsuits would gather on their beach chairs to gossip and trade beauty tips.

But there was one woman who preferred to play with the men. Her name was Shahnaz. She was a young Iranian widow from Lausanne who summered on the Mediterranean with her sisters and three kids. Shahnaz (the name means "pride of the king" in Persian) had a sultry Middle Eastern beauty—dark hair, dark eyes, olive-colored skin—and a warm-blooded temperament. One day she found herself sitting across the card table from Wado. She beat him at backgammon that day. He won the rematch. After that, they became frequent partners. When the summer was over, they continued to meet—but not to play backgammon. From those seemingly innocent seaside encounters, Shahnaz had slipped, like Alice through the looking glass, into the secret life that Wado carried on at his peril. She was not the only one.

. . .

ON THE THIRD weekend of January 1978, the baron joined friends for a hunting party in Sologne, a thickly forested region in the Loire valley. The snows were heavy, but the hunt was excellent: All told, the group bagged more than a hundred wild ducks. On Sunday afternoon, Wado took leave of his friends and headed back to Paris at the wheel of his midnight-blue Mercedes 450. At the risk of adding to his impressive collection of speeding tickets, he was rushing to make an important rendezvous. Not a mistress but his regular Sunday-night poker game, a ritual he wouldn't miss for anything in the world.

The players met that night at the apartment of one of the baron's friends near the Bois de Boulogne in the affluent sixteenth arrondissement. It was a group of regulars, about a dozen in all, who would gather twice a week to have dinner and play cards. Among them were actor-singer Yves Montand and film producer Bob Zagury, Brigitte Bardot's former boyfriend. The others were an assortment of businessmen and merchants who had little in common with Empain apart from deep pockets and a shared passion for the card table. The players would take turns hosting the gatherings but, strangely enough, they were never invited to the baron's apartment. "He didn't receive us at his home," said one, "because we weren't his personal friends, only acquaintances with whom he liked to unwind."

On this particular evening, the group sat down to dinner promptly at eight p.m., but they did not linger over coffee and digestifs. They were there to play cards. Before they gathered around the gaming table, there was an important ritual: Each man pulled out his checkbook and settled his debts from the previous game. The checks could reach the equivalent of $50,000 or more. The baron was known as a prompt payer.

The first hand was dealt at nine. Wado cradled a cheap plastic lighter in the palm of his hand. It was his lucky charm. As long as he was winning, he continued to clutch the lighter. When his luck changed, he would throw it away and replace it with one of a different color. He kept a jar full of them in his apartment, like Reagan with his jelly beans. His partners had their own fetishes and superstitions. One wore the same old shirt every time they met. Another took his shoes off on the bizarre theory that shoes were bad luck. Still another ripped off his brand-new shirt and threw it in the trash can after a losing streak. The men bet high stakes, but it was not all about the money. It was about winning. And Wado had the instincts of a conqueror. One fellow player described him as "a strong-willed fighter who hated to lose."

Though the men had drunk wine with dinner, everyone stuck to mineral water at the card table. In Wado's view, alcohol was the poker player's worst enemy. Poker was a sport: You had to be in top form to win. The same rule did not apply to tobacco, however, and the room was soon thick with cigarette and cigar smoke. Wado played with a rare intensity, scrutinizing every hand and placing each bet as if his life depended on it. Sitting across the table from him that night, Yves Montand noticed that one of Empain's eyes was bloodshot and wondered if he'd had an accident or a hemorrhage. Lately, he had seemed to be under pressure, worried, nervous. According to Montand, the baron was "a passionate player, lucid and cold in appearance, but all these traits disappeared when he had certain preoccupations."

His main preoccupation that night was that he was losing big-time—some 200,000 francs, according to one fellow player. At around two a.m., after a particularly disastrous hand, Empain folded his cards and got up to leave, though the game was far from over. Out in the street, hoarse and coughing after hours of chain-smoking, he chucked his lighter away. "You look tired," a friend told him as he parted. He was not just tired. He was exhausted, depressed, and dreading the dreary meetings that awaited him at the office the next morning.

On Monday, January 23, 1978, at precisely 10:20 a.m., the baron emerged from his nine-story apartment building at 33 Avenue Foch, a broad, tree-lined thoroughfare radiating out from the Arc de Triomphe. The modernistic concrete-and-glass structure—which some observers likened to a cruise ship—boasted a gym, a private cinema, a sauna, and an indoor swimming pool bordered by banana trees and hanging gardens. The baron's own 3,000-square-foot apartment on the ninth floor was no less luxurious, with its gray marble entry hall, atrium, and four large bedrooms.

Empain's chauffeur, Jean Denis, was waiting by the rear door of his metallic-gray Peugeot 604. The two men exchanged a few words, then the baron opened the door himself and slid into the backseat. There was no bodyguard with them—Empain had always refused close protection as an infringement on his privacy. He scanned the front page of the conservative daily *Le Figaro* as Denis pulled away from the curb and eased into the service road that paralleled the main avenue.

Normally the trip to Empain's Rue d'Anjou headquarters would take fifteen minutes, giving him plenty of time to prepare for his eleven o'clock meeting. But Denis advanced slowly, muttering under his breath. The baron glanced up from his newspaper and saw a man on a motor scooter zigzagging precariously in front of the Peugeot.

"He's completely crazy, this idiot," Denis growled, and honked the horn.

Suddenly the scooter toppled over and skidded on its side, causing the chauffeur to slam on the brakes. The rider got up and rushed toward Empain's car as a truck pulled up and blocked it from the rear. Four masked men armed with semiautomatic weapons leapt out of a blue van that had been pre-positioned on the left side of the road. One of them jerked Denis out of the driver's seat and shoved him into the van. Four other assailants emerged from the immobilized truck and jumped into Empain's car, two in front, two in back. One of the men grabbed the baron, slapped duct tape on his mouth, and pulled a black hood over his head. Empain felt the touch of cold steel on his skin and heard a metallic click as his assailant handcuffed his wrists. Someone shoved him violently onto the floor of the car and placed a gun barrel on his temple.

"Do what we tell you, or we'll blow your brains out," said a gruff voice.

The driver headed up Avenue Foch in the direction of the Arc de Triomphe. The car proceeded in silence for ten minutes, then descended into an underground parking garage at the Porte de Champerret on the northwestern edge of Paris. Empain was yanked out of the Peugeot and shoved into the trunk of another vehicle. This second car emerged from the garage and, after a series of turns, picked up speed.

Meanwhile, the stolen van containing chauffeur Jean Denis was abandoned by his captors near the Porte Maillot, the broad traffic circle west of the Arc de Triomphe that marks the boundary between Paris and the posh suburb of Neuilly. Roughed up and dazed, suffering from a broken rib, Denis was able to wriggle free from his bindings and tumble out of the van. A passing motorist drove him to a nearby police station to report the kidnapping. The desk sergeant called the police prefect, who immediately informed Interior Minister Christian Bonnet. The minister ordered police to hold back the news until roadblocks could be deployed around Paris. Checkpoints were set up throughout the capital, causing horrific traffic jams but failing to net the kidnappers. At 3:37 p.m., the popular RTL radio station broadcast a terse announcement: "Baron Édouard-Jean Empain was kidnapped in front of his domicile on Avenue Foch at eleven o'clock this morning."

In the Élysée Palace, President Giscard d'Estaing was furious. Empain could be a prickly character to deal with, but he was the head of one of France's flagship industrial groups, with a monopoly over nuclear-plant construction and tens of thousands of jobs under his command. Facing critical parliamentary elections in March, with a serious threat of a victory by the leftist opposition, Giscard could not afford for his government to look weak in the face of this challenge. In an unprecedented move, he immediately formed a crisis cell to ride herd on the case and give him daily briefings. It was a matter of national security.

Giscard's orders to the police were clear: Nab the kidnappers before any harm comes to Empain. For the moment, though, there were no clues as to who was responsible or what their motivations might be. Within hours, police recovered the baron's abandoned Peugeot and the two stolen vehicles that were used by the kidnappers, but there was not the slightest trace of a fingerprint. The men behind the kidnapping were obviously professionals.

AFTER A TWENTY-MINUTE drive, the car bearing the baron pulled into a private garage in eastern Paris that the kidnappers had rented for the occasion. One of them yanked Empain out of the trunk and shoved him onto the front passenger seat. Through the sleeve of his suit, he felt the sting of a hypodermic needle. They told him it was a sedative to make him sleep, but it merely produced a dreamy lethargy. There was no question of escape: His hands and feet were manacled; his two minders were armed and on the qui vive. All he could do was think. No more than an hour had passed since the motor scooter had tumbled in front of his car. But he sensed that his life would never be the same. In fact, he feared it might soon be over.

As a leading capitalist who had recently been blasted in the leftist press for laying off workers, Empain at first assumed that his captors were radicals who intended to assassinate him. When they removed the tape from his mouth, his first question was, "Are you a political group?" The man sitting next to him told him to shut the fuck up.

It was not an idle question. In September 1977, Hanns Martin Schleyer, head of two German employers' associations, had been kidnapped by the notorious Baader-Meinhof Gang. A month later, the radical left-wing group put a bullet in Schleyer's head and left his body in the trunk of a car. It was the same fate former Italian prime minister Aldo Moro would later meet at the hands of the leftist Red Brigades.

There were signs that Empain, a key member of the French employers' syndicate, might also have been targeted by left-wing terrorists. His chauffeur told police that one of his captors spoke German. That suggested the possible involvement of the Baader-Meinhof Gang, also known as the Red Army Faction. Shortly after the news of the baron's kidnapping was broadcast, several French press outlets received a communiqué signed by the so-called Armed Nucleus for Popular Autonomy (NAPAP in its French acronym), claiming responsibility for Empain's abduction and demanding the release from prison of three Red Army Faction members. Several hours later, the real NAPAP issued a statement saying, "It's not us!" Still, the French police and press initially focused on the thesis of a political kidnapping—and based on what had happened to Schleyer, that did not bode well for the baron.

EMPAIN AND HIS two minders sat for hours in the darkened garage. There was nothing to eat, but the three men passed around bottles of mineral water and, when the need struck them, took turns urinating in the same empty bottle—a form of egalitarianism that the aristocratic CEO was unaccustomed to. The baron could hear people coming and going just outside the garage doors, but he dared not call for help. "Keep your mouth shut," whispered the man next to him. "If you shout out, we'll kill you."

Around six p.m., one of the kidnappers announced, "We're taking you for a little drive in the country." Empain was stuffed back into the trunk, where he lay in the dark shivering and thinking this might be his last ride. Wrapped in a blanket with his mouth taped shut, he was afraid of smothering to death in that enclosed space. Or maybe they planned to shoot him, mafia-style, on some lonely road.

From his cramped position, he heard crackling voices pronouncing his name and relaying instructions about the blockades and checkpoints that were going up around the capital. He realized that the voices were coming from a radio tuned to the police frequency. Through a CB link, his captors were also in touch with another vehicle that was apparently piloting the way to their destination. The ride seemed endless, with frequent turns that jostled the baron like a sack of potatoes in the pitch-black trunk. Finally, after some forty-five minutes, the car came to a stop. Night had long since fallen. The air was frigid.

Empain's captors hoisted him out of the trunk and removed his shackles but left his mask in place. As they led him down a narrow path, he smelled the earthy odor of what, with his hunter's nose, he identified as a forest. It was a smell he associated with the exhilaration of the chase, the crack of shotguns, and the triumphal felling of wild animals. Now he was the prey.

The path snaked through the woods for more than a kilometer, captive and captors marching single file, stepping gingerly over the roots and stones that littered the ground. The blindfolded baron stumbled several times. At one point, the men made him turn around in circles, like a child playing blindman's bluff, to scramble his sense of direction. After what seemed like an interminable trek, they descended into what Empain thought was the basement of an abandoned house. It was actually a warren of underground tunnels some twenty miles north of Paris, abandoned stone quarries that the Germans had appropriated during World War II to store V-2 rockets. The entrance was now sealed off with a steel door, but the kidnappers had dug a hole underneath the barrier big enough for a man to pass through. Once the baron's jailers had entered with their prisoner, others on the outside concealed the opening with branches and earth.

The men—there were now five of them—advanced into the dark cavern lit only by flashlights and the beams of their miner's helmets. They finally reached an area they had prepared to house the captive. Several camp tents had been set up on the bare dirt floor, one for Empain, the others for the guards who were assigned to watch him day and night.

The kidnappers had stocked the tunnels for what they thought would be a short stay: bottled water, blankets, folding tables and chairs, canned food, a camp stove, a first-aid kit, a Polaroid camera, and a transistor radio. In 1978, there was no thought of cell phones or computers. Nor was there any electricity in this humid, tomblike bunker. To save their flashlight batteries, the men had placed candles and kerosene lamps around this holding space, giving it an eerie, trembling glow that cast their shadows on the walls like cave paintings of prehistoric hunters.

One of the men helped the baron take off the elegant suit, shirt, and tie he had donned that morning when he left for work. He was given a tracksuit and installed in his tent. The only amenities were a leaky inflatable mattress, a bottle of mineral water, and a yellow plastic bucket that served as a chamber pot. The temperature hovered just a few degrees above freezing.

As Empain sat cross-legged on the mattress, one of the kidnappers told him he must never try to see their faces. If he broke this rule, even once, he would be immediately executed.

"I understand," said Empain.

Then the apparent leader explained the situation to his titled guest, using the familiar "*tu*" form of address that, under the circumstances, was a sign of disrespect bordering on contempt. "You asked if this was a political action. The answer is no! It's a purely financial operation. But that doesn't mean your life is safe. It all depends on you. We're going to hand you a text. Read it and tell us what you think."

The man removed the baron's blindfold—the five kidnappers present were all masked at this point—and handed him a document. The typed text demanded a ransom of 80 million francs—equivalent to some $70 million today—payable in a mix of French, Swiss, and German currency. At the bottom of the page, the baron read this chilling coda: "We're going to cut off a finger to send to your people as proof that we are holding you."

Empain showed no emotion as he handed the paper back. He remained silent for a long moment. Then he exploded: "Eighty million? You're out of your minds. I don't have that kind of money!" And what money he did have, he insisted, could not be accessed while he was in captivity. About the finger, he said nothing at all, seeming to take that gruesome detail with a stoical acceptance that amazed his captors.

Hoping for a negotiated release, Empain gave them the names and direct numbers of René Engen, his number two, and Jean-Jacques Bierry, a lifelong friend and confidant who held a senior position with the Empain group.

"*Bon*," said one of the men, "now we're going to proceed with the operation."

They handed Empain a bowl of red liquid and ordered him to drink. It was a concoction of red wine, a muscle relaxant, and Valium 100, intended to plunge him into a deep sleep. While waiting for this elixir to take effect, the kidnappers drew lots to see who would amputate the finger. The loser—for none of the men relished the job—grudgingly gathered the materials they had prepared: a guillotine-style paper cutter, a heavy mallet, cotton, bandages, alcohol, and a small bottle. Then he crawled into the tent where Empain was lying on his side, his manacled ankles attached to a wall via a long chain. He was snoring like a hunting dog by the fireplace.

The operation lasted no more than five minutes, the time it took to put the baron's left hand on the paper cutter, place his little finger under the blade, and amputate the top joint with a swift blow of the mallet. The reluctant surgeon, wearing a miner's helmet to light his grisly work, recovered the tiny body part and plopped it into a bottle of formaldehyde. He doused the stump with alcohol—there was very little blood—and bandaged the wound. Then he passed the equipment to the others and backed out of the tent on his hands and knees. "I did it," he huffed as he stood up and ripped off his helmet, his sweaty forehead glistening in the light of the kerosene lamps.

IT WAS NEARLY dawn when Empain woke up. Still fuzzy from the potion he had drunk the night before, he at first thought he was in his own apartment on Avenue Foch. But the sensation of lying on a half-deflated air mattress and the sight of the bottle of alcohol at his side dispelled that idea. The excruciating pain from his mutilated and heavily bandaged finger confirmed the reality that it had indeed been amputated.

"Pour all the alcohol on your bandage," growled one of the guards who had spent the night watching over him. The man attempted to disguise his voice by pinching his nose when addressing the captive, creating an Alvin-the-chipmunk effect that would have been comical under other circumstances.

The contact of 90 percent alcohol on his raw wound unleashed a blinding jolt of pain, but the baron gritted his teeth and forced himself not to show it. To the astonishment of his kidnappers, he never voiced a word of complaint about the mutilation. In fact, he took the amputation as an encouraging sign: If these thugs were going to send the finger to his family, they were not planning to execute him. At least, not right away. They intended to negotiate. That would buy time.

As he sat in the pitch-black tent, he was momentarily blinded by the beam of a miner's helmet. One of the kidnappers, his face masked, handed him a pâté sandwich and an apple. He took them, one by one, with his uninjured hand. "Merci," he said, his voice no more than a hoarse whisper. Clutching the apple between his knees, he began to eat the sandwich. In the eerie silence of the tunnel, the crunch of the crusty baguette was clearly audible to his unseen guards, along with the sound of his chewing and swallowing and cautious sipping from his water bottle. He had not eaten since the previous day's breakfast, just before these men had snatched him in front of his home. Now, in spite of his fear, pain, and discomfort, he was almost thankful to them for the simple act of feeding him.

When the baron had finished eating, the group's leader asked him if he was up to writing. He said yes. Provided with a ballpoint pen, paper, and a flashlight, he copied down the words dictated by an anonymous voice. The text included the ransom demand—80 million francs—and threatened to kill the baron if that sum was not promptly paid.

. . .

ON TUESDAY, JANUARY 24, Jean-Jacques Bierry was lunching at the Cercle de l'Union Interalliée, a private club near the presidential palace. But his mind was not on food: Like his colleagues, he was preoccupied by the news of the kidnapping and worried about the baron's fate. His troubled thoughts were interrupted by a message from his office. An anonymous caller claiming to hold Empain had ordered him to pick up his "instructions" in locker number 595 at the Gare de Lyon train station.

Bierry was not just a professional colleague; he was one of the baron's oldest and closest friends. He had started out as an eighteen-year-old employee at the family's Château de Bouffémont, where he made himself indispensable and won the confidence of Wado's mother and stepfather to the point where he was given a job with the family firm. Over the years, he had risen through the ranks to a senior management position. Wado had adored him as a child. Now, in his time of need, Bierry was someone he could count on.

Bierry informed the police and rushed to the station, accompanied by a detective from the elite Criminal Brigade. In the locker, they found a military-style olive-drab canvas bag. It contained the ransom letter, signed by the "Red Liberation Army," along with the baron's identity card and handwritten notes addressed to Bierry, Engen, and his wife, Silvana. There was also a small bottle containing a severed finger joint floating in a yellowish liquid. The policeman suggested that the finger was not the baron's but one that had been sliced from a cadaver. Bierry shook his head. Empain had a nervous habit of chewing his fingernails. This one was gnawed down to the quick.

The locker's contents indicated that the kidnappers' central aim was money, though the "Red Liberation Army" reference suggested a political kidnapping that might result in an ideologically motivated execution. The mutilated finger made it clear that the baron's life was still in danger: The ransom letter warned that other body parts— hands, eyes, feet—would be sent to the family piece by piece until the ransom was paid or the captive was dead. These guys were serious. The only encouraging thing to emerge from locker 595 was Wado's handwritten note to his wife: "Dear Silvana, don't worry too much. This can all be worked out. I love you."

CHAPTER 2

Your Money or Your Life

Before the kidnapping, Empain had ruled over a vast multinational empire. Now his dominion was reduced to the interior of a red pup tent eight feet long, eight feet wide, and five feet high. His hands and feet were manacled and a heavy neck chain, bolted to the tunnel wall, prevented him from sitting upright. This metal collar choked him when he tried to move. Along with the mutilated finger, the collar and chain recalled the brutal treatment of Black conscript workers in the Congo, where Wado's grandfather had made a large part of his fortune—as if there were some kind of karmic taint on the money that the kidnappers were now trying to lay their hands on.

Dressed in a flimsy tracksuit, Empain shivered day and night in near-freezing temperatures. The only amenities in his tent were a leaky inflatable mattress, a bottle of mineral water, a vial of alcohol to sterilize his throbbing finger stump, and a yellow plastic bucket to accommodate his bodily functions. Not only did it reek—his captors only changed it when it was full—but its use presented a technical challenge to a prisoner whose hands and feet were bound. With practice, Empain managed to urinate without too much difficulty. But sitting on the rim of the bucket for more serious needs was a difficult and precarious proposition. Once, he fell over and emptied the contents inside the tent. Helpless to do anything about it, he lay there in his own mess for hours until one of his minders, apparently drawn by the smell, came to check on him. Empain was scolded like a baby who had wet his bed.

He didn't complain about this humiliation—no more than he complained about the pain of his amputated finger, or the cold, or the meager food. From the beginning, he decided that his best chance of survival was to maintain a quiet dignity and not attract the contempt or anger of his captors. If he was to die, he would do it with his boots on. Never once did he protest or denounce the kidnappers.

The main requirement for staying alive was to make sure he never saw his captors' faces, so as not to be able to identify them. As instructed, he put on his eyeless mask whenever he was in their presence. Which was not often, at least in the beginning. Apart from bringing him food and changing his bucket, they had little direct contact with him. He would have liked to talk to them, if only to break up the boredom of a timeless existence in which he could not tell day from night. Once in a while, one of them would ask, "How's your finger?" and order him to soak his bandage in alcohol. Other than that, silence. So the baron waited and wondered what was going on in the world outside. Was anyone working to free him? Would the ransom be paid? Would the police find the hideout and rout his captors? Or was death lurking at the end of the tunnel?

Before he was grabbed, Wado had considered the possibility of a kidnapping. He was particularly disturbed by the case of Hanns Martin Schleyer, the German industrialist who had been snatched off the streets of Cologne and murdered by leftist radicals. If he ever was captured, he instructed family and friends that there should be no question of making a ransom payment—"We must set an example," he told his wife. "We live in society and there are risks." Nor would he accept to be accompanied by a bodyguard, though he did seek a permit to carry a gun. He was unarmed on the day of his kidnapping—a pistol wouldn't have done much good in any case against the arsenal wielded by his captors. Even a bodyguard would have been outgunned. As he thought back on all this, one thing he regretted was his no-ransom rule. Now that he had lost one body part, with the threat of more mutilations to come—and facing the very real possibility of a Schleyer-like execution—he saw a negotiated payment as his only hope of salvation.

AT FIRST ALL parties involved seemed ready to pay for Empain's life. The family—his Italian wife, Silvana, his half-sister Diane, and his three children—were anxious to hand over a ransom, but they didn't have enough cash to meet the astronomical demand. The Empain-Schneider group, headed in Empain's absence by his number two, René Engen, was willing to advance funds—but only as a loan to the family. Concerned by the fate of a major industrialist and employer, President Giscard d'Estaing initially appeared to give a tacit green light to the idea of a payment: "The ransom is the family's problem," he told his staff. "The job of the police is to arrest the criminals."

Among the documents contained in the Gare de Lyon locker was a typed letter addressed to Jean-Jacques Bierry, the friend and colleague designated as a contact by the baron. It ordered him to be ready with the ransom money at one a.m. on Thursday, January 26. Instructions would be given him by telephone. "There must be no police involvement," the letter warned. "We will quickly observe their presence."

At noon on Wednesday, Bierry received a manila envelope that contained three gruesome photos of the baron with his bandaged hand, along with his driver's license and hunting license. Changing the earlier orders, the kidnappers now instructed Bierry to wait in his office at one a.m. on Friday, January 27, and be prepared to deliver the 80 million francs.

Since Empain's disappearance, his family had been frantically casting about in an effort to raise the funds. Until that moment, Silvana, age thirty-eight, had been content to play the role of *la baronne*, enjoying her life of wealth and privilege without troubling herself over the details. She was, as her husband put it, "a nice Italian girl who had absolutely no idea about my business affairs." Her two daughters, Patricia, nineteen, and Christine, eighteen, knew even less about the source of the wealth they enjoyed. Money had never been a problem for them—they went to posh private schools, took nice vacations, had maids and chauffeurs. They imagined it would be enough to sign a mortgage or sell off a couple of companies and pay the ransom. (Son Jean-François, fourteen, was off at boarding school and not directly involved in these discussions.) But the baron's American mother, Rozell, was better informed. She explained to the family what the group was and how it was organized. Wado was the titular head, but he was not sitting on a huge pile of cash. The family fortune consisted mainly of stock.

Rozell's response to her son's abduction was bizarre—and totally in keeping with her cold, self-centered personality. All her life, this former exotic dancer had considered herself a star, a diva, and since her marriage to Wado's father, a titled aristocrat. Empathy was not her strong suit—especially where her son was concerned. When Wado's secretary telephoned her with the news of his kidnapping, Rozell showed no emotion. Her first reaction was to say, histrionically, "My son has left for the battle front." Not only was she convinced that no real harm would come to Wado, she thought the experience might take him down a peg and teach him a lesson. He always expected people to "roll out the red carpet," she said. Now he could learn to crawl on it for a while.

The family soon realized that the baron's financial situation fell far short of the required sum. They phoned Wado's wealthy friends and colleagues seeking donations to help bail him out of captivity. The calls drew professions of support and sympathy, but no one actually opened a checkbook. In desperation, Silvana even offered to sell her jewelry. Rozell, for her part, said she wouldn't pay a cent out of her own funds. "If he comes back," she sniffed, "he'll have the money." Rozell had another suggestion: Ask Wado's wealthy mistress, the Iranian émigré Shahnaz Arieh, to come up with the funds. "If she loves Wado, and she has money, let's see what she can do."

Shahnaz, then thirty-six, was no stranger to Rozell. She had visited her at the Château de Bouffémont with Wado and called her every few months just to keep in touch. Rozell seemed to accept the Iranian as her son's quasi-official mistress, something that seemed normal in her milieu. She knew a lot about Shahnaz—that she came from an extremely wealthy Iranian family, had homes in Lausanne and Tehran, dressed in haute couture, and stayed at the posh and pricey Plaza Athénée during her frequent visits to Paris. Rozell also knew that Shahnaz and Wado had secretly spent a week together in Geneva just before the family's Christmas vacation in the Alps. Given their intimate relations, Wado's fate could hardly leave his lover indifferent.

In fact, Shahnaz had telephoned Rozell on the afternoon of the kidnapping, offering to help in any way she could. Rozell called her back three days later asking if she could do something about the ransom. Shahnaz then telephoned Raymond Vuilliez, a close friend of Empain's with high-level banking connections in France and Switzerland, and asked if he could put together the funds. Vuilliez first tried to calm the Iranian down, saying the ransom was a matter for the family and the police to deal with. Undeterred, Shahnaz called back repeatedly, insisting that Vuilliez do something. "I had the impression," he told the police, "that I was dealing with a woman who was completely distraught and preoccupied with winning the baron's liberation under the best conditions."

After receiving Shahnaz's passionate entreaties, Vuilliez contacted René Engen and said he could put together the 80 million francs. To his amazement, Engen said he didn't need his help. Even more perplexing, the unpredictable Rozell also rebuffed his proposal "in the most revolting manner." It seemed to Vuilliez that she was "not especially concerned about the baron's life."

Silvana Empain was furious, not only over Rozell's machinations but especially over her rival's brash attempt to insert herself into the family drama. She complained to one detective that Shahnaz Arieh had a long history of harassing her, threatening to commit suicide at one point and even claiming to be pregnant by Wado. The police called Shahnaz in for questioning, but she provided no useful information concerning the kidnapping. Asked if her affair with the baron had affected his family life, she snapped, "I don't want to answer that." It seemed that Shahnaz was doing everything she could to worm her way into the middle of the drama, hoping perhaps that it would destroy the marriage and that Wado would be hers once he was liberated. If so, the kidnapping was serving her interests.

JEAN-JACQUES BIERRY, MEANWHILE, made the rounds of the banks seeking to borrow the funds on behalf of the Empain-Schneider group. The most he could come up with was 30 million francs, just over one-third of the ransom demand, but hopefully enough to convince Empain's captors to liberate him. Interim chairman René

Engen drew up papers declaring this sum to be a loan to the family, with repayment plus interest due within two years. Clearly, he wasn't running a philanthropy. The family, including a reluctant Rozell, signed off on the deal. The Crédit Lyonnais, one of the country's leading banks, packed the cash into bundles (after microfilming each bill) and delivered it to the company headquarters via armored car on Thursday afternoon.

On the evening of Thursday, January 26, Engen and Bierry were summoned to a meeting with interior minister Christian Bonnet, the president's point man on what was now known as the "Empain affair." Bonnet, a bespectacled, cleft-chinned bantam rooster of a man, was livid over press reports about the baron's profligate gambling and his mistresses, implying that Empain had brought all this on himself through his irresponsible behavior. His interlocutors were shocked by the violence of the minister's diatribe, which perhaps reflected the government's complicated relationship with this headstrong Belgian baron who frequently defied their directives. Contradicting the president's tacit green light on the ransom, Bonnet now urged the group not to pay. Bierry told the minister that he expected a phone call from the kidnappers later that evening but refrained from mentioning the 30 million francs in cash that was already sitting in his office safe.

On Thursday night, Bierry sat by his phone and waited. As the hours ticked by, he became increasingly nervous, wondering how the kidnappers would react when he announced that he had only a fraction of what they expected. One a.m. passed with no call. He waited until eight a.m. and finally went home to catch a few hours' sleep.

The kidnappers called him at his office at 4:50 p.m. on Friday.

"You have the money?" said a voice on the other end.

"Eighty million is impossible. All we can give you is 30 million, not one cent more."

"You have one minute to decide," the caller growled. "If you don't come up with 80 million, we'll send you another piece of him."

"Thirty million, that's it."

"Tomorrow, you'll have a corpse!" the caller snapped, and hung up.

BACK IN THEIR tunnel, the kidnappers were seething over Bierry's lowball offer. What did Empain's people take them for? They had spent months preparing the operation, nailing down every detail, considering every scenario, every move and countermove. They had made sacrifices, cut themselves off from their families, spent thousands out of pocket on supplies, rent, and fake papers for their fleet of stolen vehicles. The leaders also had an ideological motivation: While their aim wasn't primarily political, they were left-leaning and anti-capitalist and believed they were justified in taking money from a rich captain of industry. Empain tried to explain that it was technically impossible to access his own accounts as long as he was detained. He'd have to sign in person to withdraw money. What about his conglomerate, with its 25 billion francs in annual sales? The baron protested that he didn't personally own all those companies. His interrogators weren't buying it.

"After all, Empain," one said, "it's called the Empain-Schneider group, right?"

"Yes, but you can't confuse annual sales with profits, personal fortune with business capital, minority with majority holdings, directorship with management."

"Cut the crap. We know your little shell game. You better find a solution, fast!"

On Tuesday, January 31, Empain penned an angry letter to Bierry, accusing him of indifference to his fate. "Perhaps you have slept badly for the past week," he wrote, "but I pity you when you'll have my death on your conscience. Have you all become so blind as to think that my kidnappers are joking? Chop off your own finger with a hatchet and tell me how it feels—but no, you won't tell me because you have practically thrown me in the garbage, the one who has always been friendly toward you." The letter went on to say (falsely) that the mutilated finger had become infected to the point of being life-threatening. "I know that all my assets are worth more than the 80-million-franc ransom demand, so pay up, dammit!" Empain claimed that the letter was "in no way written under constraint," yet it contained precise requests about the currencies and denominations of the banknotes, as well as instructions to Bierry about the logistics of the handoff, details that were obviously dictated by the kidnappers.

THERE WAS AT least one person who was not unhappy about Wado's predicament: René Engen. A bland and taciturn manager with heavy black-rimmed glasses and a face empty of all expression, Engen, then fifty-eight, had been working at Empain's side for more than a decade. Amiable and courteous on the surface, he kept his inner thoughts and motivations to himself. One detective who worked on the case described him as "inscrutable, the kind of personage you quickly forget. He didn't make a strong impression on me."

But he did make an impression on the young baron when he took over the family empire in 1968, determined to bring in a new management team. "I needed a man of my own," he said. "That man was René Engen." A native Belgian like Empain, Engen had first caught the baron's eye when he turned the group's ailing glass subsidiary, Verlica, into a strong profit-maker in the late 1960s. In 1972, Engen was named director general of the Empain group. At that time, Empain professed a "blind confidence" in his number two.

With his attention to organization and detail, Engen complemented the baron's more instinctive approach to business. He soon made himself indispensable, in effect running the vast industrial network day to day while Wado concentrated on long-term strategy and made the big decisions. While Engen relied on method and analytics, the baron tended to go with his gut.

As Empain described him, Engen was "slender, brown-haired, very attentive to his health, drinking nothing but water, a nonsmoker who subjected himself to a rigorous professional discipline." Lurking under the bland exterior of this faithful number two, however, was a burning ambition to become number one. For several years, Wado had noticed Engen's eagerness to assert his authority, making important decisions on his own and offering them up for the baron's approval almost as a formality. Engen had admitted as much in a 1975 interview with *Fortune*, saying, "All the problems are brought to me, and I decide which ones to pass on to the baron." Little by little, Wado got the impression that Engen was acting like "a king in my kingdom." With the kidnapping, Engen suddenly saw his chance to seize the crown.

CHAPTER 3

The Investigators

*P*resident Giscard d'Estaing was worried and angry. Worried about security leaks because Empain was central to the country's civilian nuclear program—his group had a monopoly over the building of France's atomic power plants. Angry because his party could take a hit in the upcoming parliamentary elections if the affair was not settled before then. And if that wasn't enough to give the president headaches, Belgium's King Baudouin kept phoning him to demand exceptional measures to ensure the baron's liberation. He also got a call from his friend Helmut Schmidt, the West German chancellor, who offered to share intelligence about radical groups on his side of the Rhine. On Giscard's orders, interior minister Christian Bonnet ratcheted up the pressure on the police to track down the kidnappers and free the captive.

The investigation was the responsibility of the Judiciary Police, the branch of French law enforcement that deals with all manner of criminal activity. It had its headquarters at 36 Quai des Orfèvres, located on the Île de la Cité a stone's throw from the Conciergerie, where Marie Antoinette was imprisoned before her beheading in 1793. The iconic four-story building—known familiarly as Trente-Six (36)—had provided the setting for countless French films and crime stories, including the seventy-five novels that Georges Simenon devoted to its most famous fictional resident, the low-key, pipe-smoking Commissaire Jules Maigret.

At the time of the Empain kidnapping, Maigret's real-life counterpart was Pierre Ottavioli. From his third-floor office, with its sweeping view of the Seine, he commanded the eighty-man team assigned to the Empain case. Ottavioli was the head of the Criminal Brigade, known familiarly as the "Crim," the arm of the Judiciary Police responsible for investigations, interrogations, and analysis. He could also call on the services of an elite action force: the Research and Intervention Brigade (BRI), aka the "Antigang" brigade, which carried out raids, arrests, and other on-the-ground missions—often with guns blazing. As Ottavioli liked to boast, the Criminal Brigade and the Antigang formed an almost unbeatable team: "No criminal band, however determined and organized, can rival them. It would take military commandos."

A tall, lean Corsican with unblinking steel-blue eyes and a beaky nose, Ottavioli—"Otta" to his colleagues—was the son of a cop and the grandson of a shepherd. Like a shepherd, he was a man of few words, a man with "the patience and tenacity of a crocodile," as one journalist put it. Ottavioli projected an air of command that won him the loyalty and admiration of his troops. At age fifty-six, he was athletic and physically fit, a committed nonsmoker in a profession of nicotine fiends. On quiet days, he would head over to the Racing Club at lunchtime to jog or play tennis. During his summer vacations, he would spend hours swimming and scuba diving in the Mediterranean off the coast of Ajaccio in Corsica. When things got tense, he was calm and unflappable. He decided quickly and gave his men terse orders that none dared to question. Ottavioli was no stranger to high-stakes cases—as a young man, he had investigated the attempted assassination of President Charles de Gaulle in 1962—but he knew that the Empain affair was a perilous challenge. The life of an important man was at stake, and he was responsible for saving him.

When the news of the kidnapping first broke, Ottavioli had been visiting friends in Los Angeles. His hosts expected him to hop on the next flight to Paris and take charge of the investigation. But the chief was in no hurry to trade California's sheltering palms for the cold January drizzle back home. He knew from long experience in these matters that the decisive phase of a kidnapping case did not arrive for several weeks. Seven days went by before he returned to his office on the Quai des Orfèvres and got a thorough briefing on the case. The bottle containing Empain's amputated finger was placed on Ottavioli's desk. He picked it up, held it to the light, and swirled it around like a sommelier judging the color of a vintage Sauternes. "We won't give in," he vowed.

Unlike the president, Ottavioli was adamantly opposed to any ransom payment. His personal experience with kidnappings in France, and his knowledge of numerous kidnap cases in Italy, convinced him that handing over the money was no guarantee that the victim's life would be spared. There were many instances of bodies being dumped in the road after a payment was made. His strategy was to play for time, to wear down the kidnappers and wait for them to commit an error. If a ransom was paid, he argued, the next day there would be a dozen new kidnappings. That was Ottavioli's inflexible position, but it would take time to bring the family and the business partners around to his point of view. And he knew he was taking a big personal risk: If the baron were killed, his own job was on the line.

Under Ottavioli's authority, the day-to-day investigation was headed up by Commissaire André Bizeul. It was a luck-of-the-draw assignment: Bizeul had been the rotating duty officer when word of the kidnapping first arrived at police headquarters on the morning of January 23. He was excited to work on such a high-profile case, though he initially had no idea who Baron Empain was and had to look up his address in the Who's Who. Then he and a colleague drove to Empain's apartment on Avenue Foch.

After inspecting the van and motor scooter that had been used in the attack—both stolen weeks earlier—they took the elevator up to the Empains' ninth-floor apartment. Bizeul was struck by the cold opulence of the place—the long marble entrance hall, the atrium, the sheer immensity of the spaces. Silvana Empain received them calmly, though she had clearly been crying. The detectives asked her a battery of initial questions: Had her husband received threats, anonymous phone calls? Did he have any enemies? Had there been any incidents? Nothing out of the ordinary, said the baroness. Along with photos of her husband, she provided a brief physical description—"five foot eleven, blond hair brushed straight back, light blue-gray eyes, broad shoulders, very athletic physique"—told them how he was dressed, said he smoked Marlboros and wore a gold ring bearing the family crest. And then she quoted something her husband had recently told her: "If ever I'm kidnapped, don't pay the ransom."

Bizeul, then thirty-two, was an ace detective who tracked criminals with the same determination he showed as a hunter—a passion he shared with Wado. Though short of stature, he stood out as the most elegant dresser on the Criminal Brigade, favoring chalk-striped double-breasted suits made to measure by his own father, a tailor by trade. Bizeul—"Dédé" to his colleagues—was also endowed with a resonant baritone that served him well, not only when he grilled suspects but also when he appeared onstage, microphone in hand, as a singer with an amateur dance band. His over-the-ear black hair and sideburns underscored the crooner image, paired with a thick mustache reminiscent of Peter Sellers's Inspector Clouseau. By his own admission, Bizeul was a man who worked hard and partied hard, sometimes going home at dawn after drinking with colleagues at the all-night bistros around Les Halles, formerly Paris's central food market and one of its hottest red-light districts (immortalized in Billy Wilder's 1963 film *Irma la Douce*).

Inspector Michel Desfarges, thirty-two, had just joined the Crim's investigative unit three weeks before the kidnapping. A ten-year veteran of the force, he had previously worked as a beat cop in the historic heart of Paris, a sector that included Notre-Dame, L'Hôtel de Ville, and Les Halles. Desfarges, endowed with a boyish grin and a thatch of dark-brown hair, had worn out a lot of shoe leather patrolling his quarter before being assigned to a special team that investigated all manner of forgeries, ranging from falsified papers and counterfeit money to fake paintings. At one point, his office looked like a cluttered art gallery, filled with confiscated canvases signed by the likes of Renoir and Picasso but actually painted in basement workshops on the Left Bank. He developed a passion for the meticulous work of sifting out the fakes from the true masterpieces. But when Ottavioli brought him to the Quai des Orfèvres in January 1978, Desfarges was suddenly thrust into the world of big-time criminal investigations—and the Empain kidnapping would turn out to be the biggest case of his career.

Working alongside the Criminal Brigade's elite detectives, the Antigang force stood ready to launch an armed assault when the time was right. Their chief was Marcel Leclerc, age forty-three, described by one crook he'd helped put away as "the kind of pitiless, icy cop you meet in the novels of James Ellroy." His deputy and sometime rival was Robert Broussard, forty-two, a beefy, bearded ex–rugby player who preferred leather jackets and jeans to Leclerc's business suits and cherished his reputation as a "supercop." Broussard's rugged good looks and natural charisma made him a media darling, which caused some grumbling among jealous colleagues who accused him of hogging the limelight. He would later make national headlines by leading the commando squad that gunned down France's Public Enemy Number One, the notorious Jacques Mesrine, on the outskirts of Paris in 1979. Still harnessed in his seat belt, Mesrine was sprayed with a barrage of machine-gun bullets fired through the windshield of his BMW.

SPECTACULAR AS IT was, the Empain case was only the latest in a wave of international kidnappings and assassinations that reached epic proportions during the 1970s—the so-called years of lead. Among the most sensational cases was the abduction of J. Paul Getty III, the seventeen-year-old grandson of the billionaire oil tycoon, who was snatched off a Rome street in July 1973. To back up their $17 million ransom demand, Getty's captors sliced off his ear and sent it to an Italian newspaper—a gruesome act that may have inspired Empain's kidnappers to chop off his finger. Getty's grandfather, then the world's richest man, initially refused to pay the ransom, claiming it would make all his other grandchildren kidnapping targets. The amount was eventually negotiated down to some $3.2 million. The notoriously stingy oilman—who had a phone booth installed in his mansion so his guests would have to pay for their own calls—agreed to shell out only $2.2 million, the maximum amount that was tax-deductible. He loaned the rest to his estranged son (the victim's drug-addicted father) at 4 percent interest. Freed by his captors in December 1973, young Getty was found shoeless and shivering at a bus shelter 250 miles south of Rome. Nine of the kidnappers—including two high-ranking members of the Calabrian mafia, the 'Ndrangheta—were later captured and tried.

No less sensational was the case of Patty Hearst, granddaughter of publishing magnate William Randolph Hearst (the model for Orson Welles's *Citizen Kane*). In February 1974, Hearst was dragged kicking and screaming out of her Berkeley, California, apartment by a ragtag band of leftist radicals styling themselves the Symbionese Liberation Army. Unlike the Getty case, there was no ransom demand, only an unsuccessful call to release two jailed SLA members. The main motivation was apparently to turn the daughter of a famously wealthy family into a poster girl for this bizarre urban guerrilla group.

Threatened with death, plied with revolutionary propaganda, and coerced into having sex with her captors, the nineteen-year-old eventually took part in an armed bank robbery, M1 carbine at the ready, and publicly swore allegiance to the SLA cause. She even adopted the nickname "Tania," after the nom de guerre of Che Guevara's comrade in arms Tamara Bunke. In September 1975, after most of her captors/comrades had been killed in a police shootout, Hearst was arrested as a fugitive and later tried for her role in the bank robbery. Despite the best efforts of celebrity lawyer F. Lee Bailey, who claimed that his client had been "brainwashed," Hearst was convicted and sentenced to seven years' imprisonment. (Jimmy Carter commuted her sentence in 1979, and Bill Clinton gave her a full pardon on his last day in office.)

The most chilling precedent for the Empain snatch was, as noted, the kidnapping in Cologne of Hanns Martin Schleyer, which had been such a focus for the baron himself. A high-profile industrialist like Empain, Schleyer, sixty-two, was the head of West Germany's two most powerful employers' associations. In addition to his reputation as an uncompromising strikebreaker—the *New York Times* once called him "a caricature of the 'ugly capitalist'"—the bull-necked, scar-faced Schleyer carried some unsavory political baggage as a former youth leader of the Nazi student movement and a junior SS officer during the war. All of which made him a logical target of Germany's Baader-Meinhof Gang, aka the Red Army Faction, an armed band of far-left terrorists founded in 1970. Over two decades the RAF, as it was known, carried out bombings, assassinations, kidnappings, and bank robberies that left thirty-four dead—a far bloodier record than similar U.S. groups like the Weather Underground.

On the morning of September 5, 1977, Schleyer's chauffeured car was forced to brake suddenly when a baby carriage rolled across its path, causing an accompanying police car to crash into the rear of Schleyer's Mercedes. Five masked commandos rushed from a parked van and sprayed both vehicles with bullets, killing the chauffeur and three police bodyguards. Schleyer was yanked from his car and thrown into the getaway van. Six weeks later, after the government rejected the kidnappers' demand to free eleven imprisoned comrades, they shot the industrialist in the head and left his body in the trunk of a car in Mulhouse, France. Haunted by the Schleyer case, French police were determined to prevent a similarly bloody denouement for Empain.

Ottavioli had considerable experience dealing with abductions on his own turf. In France, where money, not ideology, was generally the main motivation, a series of high-profile kidnappings detonated like a string of firecrackers during this turbulent decade: There were no fewer than fifteen cases between 1974 and 1977. One of the most dramatic episodes took place on December 31, 1975, when the CEO of Phonogram Records, Louis Hazan, age fifty-three, was grabbed in the middle of a board meeting at the company's Paris headquarters. The session was barely under way when six armed commandos burst into the conference room, gagged Hazan, and threw him in a wicker trunk. Taking the company's financial director along as a hostage, they disappeared through a private exit and drove off in a stolen van.

Next day, the kidnappers called in their ransom demand: 15 million francs. On their instructions, two undercover policemen posing as Hazan's colleagues drove to the Place de la Bastille in eastern Paris with a pair of sports bags supposedly containing the cash (but in fact stuffed with telephone books). When two men drove up to snatch the bags, they were set upon by Antigang forces and seriously roughed up on the way to police headquarters. One of them wound up in the hospital; the other coughed up information that led the police to an abandoned villa, where they discovered Hazan in a hidden closet, chained and blindfolded but otherwise unharmed.

The Hazan case was followed by other high-profile kidnappings. Among the targets were the directors of Saab France, Fiat France, and the Schlumberger-Mallet Bank. In all of these cases, the perpetrators had been captured and their victims liberated without the payment of a ransom. Ottavioli's success in foiling these plots earned him a reputation as "Monsieur Anti-Rapt"—Mr. Anti-Kidnapping. His method was simple: Don't play by the bad guys' rules, but use their own greed to trap them. That was how he approached the Empain case: While rejecting the idea of an actual payoff, he proposed to lure the kidnappers to a rendezvous with a fake ransom. At that point, hopefully, the Antigang boys could pounce and seize at least one of them as a counter-hostage. By putting pressure on their captive, or captives, the cops could extract the information they needed to locate and free the kidnap victim. That was the game plan. If it worked, Ottavioli was once again the hero. If it failed, it was the chief who would "pay the bill," as one colleague put it.

But it took several weeks for Ottavioli to win Empain's family and colleagues over to his point of view. Silvana and her daughters were initially intent on paying. Rozell, after reluctantly accepting the idea of a company loan, now considered any payment out of the question. Engen, ambivalent at first, seemed finally to accept the advice of the man he started calling "Otta." But Robert Badinter, the Empain family lawyer who had also been enlisted by the company, strongly advised against letting the police take all the initiatives and insisted on paying for Wado's life.

Badinter was a man whose weight and influence went far beyond the chambers of his prestigious law firm: He was an intimate friend and adviser to Socialist Party leader François Mitterrand, who would name Badinter justice minister after winning the 1981 presidential election. Badinter was determined to raise the cash by whatever means necessary—behind the backs of Ottavioli's troops. Accompanied by Jean-Jacques Bierry, he would later take a secret trip to Geneva, where they made the rounds of several Swiss banks. Tipped off to the plan, Ottavioli sent Commissaire Claude Cancès and another detective to tail them discreetly. The purpose of the trip, Bierry later admitted, was to explore the possibility of paying the ransom in Switzerland since French authorities had made that all but impossible on their turf. For whatever reason, their efforts did not succeed, and they returned to France empty-handed.

Seeking to head off precisely that kind of back-channel operation, Louis Chavanac, the magistrate in charge of the judicial investigation, sought an international warrant requiring Swiss banks to alert the French to any suspicious movements in accounts belonging to the Empain group. Upholding their tradition of bank secrecy, the Swiss authorities refused. As police later learned, one of the kidnappers had in fact opened a Swiss account, presumably to receive a ransom payment, but no transfer was ever made.

Meanwhile, Ottavioli's detectives worked day and night seeking clues that might lead them to the kidnappers. For two excruciatingly long months, their efforts were for naught. The criminals had left no fingerprints in their abandoned cars, nor were there any significant eyewitnesses to the kidnapping. The roadblocks of the first few days had produced nothing but massive traffic jams—more than 140,000 vehicles were stopped and searched in the first twenty-four hours—and were finally lifted on February 3. The detectives tapped their contacts in the French underworld and sifted through hundreds of unsolicited tips without unearthing a single solid lead as to the identity of the kidnappers or the location of their hideout. As the days and weeks went by, the French press became increasingly critical of the fruitless investigation into what the papers were calling "the kidnapping of the century."

In one area, however, Ottavioli's men hit on a promising lead. Following standard procedure in kidnap cases, they began digging into the details of Wado's private life to see if there was some link between the captive and his kidnappers. By interrogating his entourage, they soon learned about his gambling habit. Shortly after returning from California on January 30, Otta ordered all the baron's regular poker buddies hauled in for questioning. The detective assigned to oversee the grilling was Inspector Michel Desfarges, admired by his colleagues for his meticulous analyses and relentless interrogations. "Best not fall into his net," said one cop. "Big or little fish have no chance to escape."

Empain's fellow card players turned out to be little fish. Apart from Yves Montand and a couple of filmmakers, most of them were textile merchants based in Paris's garment district, known as le Sentier. None of them had a criminal record, but police operated on the assumption that anyone involved in high-stakes gambling with Wado was a potential suspect or might be linked to the case in some way. The dozen or so depositions they took on February 2 and 3 produced little useful information, apart from the fact that Empain seemed nervous the night before the kidnapping and left abruptly after losing some 200,000 francs. "They didn't know anything," says Desfarges. "They just got together to fleece the baron."

A far more significant lead was provided by a police investigative unit that specialized in horse racing and gaming: According to their information, Empain had lost some 11 million francs at the Palm Beach casino in Cannes in August 1977. Investigators speculated that this jaw-dropping sum—then equivalent to $2.2 million, worth some $9.7 million today and more than four times the baron's annual salary—was perhaps central to the case.

Summoned by Desfarges, the casino's director, Yves de Félix, hopped on a train to Paris. Under questioning, this rather pompous gaming executive said Empain had been a regular customer for twelve years, arriving in mid-July and departing at the end of August. During that long vacation season, he would arrive at the Palm Beach every evening around eleven p.m. and leave at two or three a.m., often accompanied by his wife. He played card games—chemin de fer or baccarat—and bet very high stakes. He was usually a net loser by the end of the season, said Félix, but considering his wealth, the losses were manageable. That is, until August 1977, when his debt to the casino soared to a staggering 11 million francs. The bulk of his losses had occurred in feverish sessions that pitted him against two Saudi princes and several oil-rich Iranians.

Félix told Desfarges that Baron Empain had been the biggest loser of the 1977 season. But as always, the client's losses are the casino's gains, and the Palm Beach had for years bent over backward to keep Wado hemorrhaging cash at their felt-covered tables. "When we entered the casino," said Empain's friend Pierre Salik, a Belgian textile mogul, "it was as if the President of the Republic had arrived. They made room for him, brought him to the best table in the restaurant, offered him caviar and champagne . . . When you watched him gamble, it was mind-boggling to see the amounts he would bet in several seconds."

Other friends who accompanied the baron to the casino told

similar stories. André Marcarof, one of Empain's regular poker partners, told investigators that "he risked enormous sums—fifty to a hundred thousand francs a hand. Baron Empain was convinced he could win at the casino. He could not admit that it's impossible to beat the house." Nor could he accept the image of a loser, telling his friends that he was up by as much as 600,000 francs for the 1977 season in spite of his crushing losses.

Empain eventually paid off most of his Palm Beach debt thanks to a Swiss bank loan discreetly negotiated by his friend Raymond Vuilliez, but who knew how much he owed to the other casinos he frequented? Investigators now had the picture of an addicted and indebted gambler, which provided them with a significant lead. As Desfarges and his fellow detectives well knew, gamblers could come into contact with disreputable characters, and slicing off a finger was a traditional punishment for a player who had been dishonest with his partners. Was there a link between the baron's gambling habit and his kidnapping?

The news of Empain's enormous gambling debts, splashed all over the press, shattered his image and fed speculation that he may have been snatched on the orders of enraged creditors—or perhaps even staged his own kidnapping in order to pay off his gambling debts. Some claimed, falsely, that he funded his gambling addiction with checks written on the Empain-Schneider group, or even robbed his workers by dipping into their pension fund. One theory was that criminal elements had seen him flashing his money in the casinos and marked him as a juicy kidnapping target. Indeed, some of Empain's friends told police they had been observed by shady characters while gambling in Cannes. "I immediately thought that this kidnapping was linked to his conspicuous presence at the casino," said his friend Marcarof. "He could have been noticed by the mafia types who also hung out at the Palm Beach."

Another revelation would prove especially devastating, not only to the baron's public image but also to his marriage. Seeing Empain's picture on the cover of *Paris Match* in early February, the concierge of a building near the Arc de Triomphe recognized him as the tenant of a third-floor apartment and informed the police. It was Wado's "secret garden," a discreet refuge where he kept a collection of books and personal mementos, but he also used it to tryst with his mistress Shahnaz Arieh. Taking along two of Empain's business colleagues as witnesses, police searched the two-room flat but found no evidence related to the kidnapping. When the story of Wado's secret apartment leaked, several articles falsely claimed police had taken Silvana Empain to the apartment and that she was shocked by photos of Wado with other women. Though she was never actually taken there, the press reports about Wado's secret "love nest" were a public humiliation to his wife and a further blow to his reputation.

At that point, in the eyes of a large swath of the public, Empain began to shift from victim to villain—a rich capitalist playboy who got what he deserved. President Giscard d'Estaing quietly sent an aide to make the rounds of media outlets and ask them to downplay talk of his friendship with the baron. Even the loyalty of Wado's family and colleagues was shaken. "We knew he gambled," said Jean-Jacques Bierry. "What we didn't know was the enormity of the sums involved. I nearly fell over when they cited the figures."

BIERRY WAS NOT the only one. Following the revelations about Wado's gambling and philandering, his own mother came to believe that his return to the presidency was not in the interest of the Empain group—or her personal interest as a shareholder. That was what she argued in the strategy meetings with the company's senior management at the Rue d'Anjou headquarters. The family was represented by Rozell, Silvana, and Diane, but, as usual, it was Rozell who took the lead.

Diane was appalled by her mother's coldness. "The question came up of what to do with Wado if he returned. Mother said, 'It is better that he not return. You know, you can make an omelet with the hair of the tiger'"—referring to an old superstition that whoever eats the hair of a tiger will die. In other words, even if Wado survived the kidnapping, he should be considered dead as president of the Empain-Schneider group. Behind his usual veil of discretion, interim president René Engen shared that view. But Diane was shocked. "In all this discussion, they forgot the hostage and the ordeal he was going through. My mother was diabolical, she had no affection. My only concern was Wado."

Unbeknownst to her mother and the company management, Diane was working secretly as an informant for the police investigators. At age twenty-eight, petite, blond, and athletic, she had been courted by detective André Bizeul and his colleague Claude Cancès and agreed to cooperate with them. Ottavioli, who had encouraged this "special relationship," quickly won Diane over to his view: no ransom payment—period. Through Diane, the police knew everything that was being said in the strategy meetings between the family and the group.

Engen had his own spy of sorts: Max Fernet, age sixty-seven, ex-chief of the Judiciary Police, who had been hired as a special adviser to the group. Ottavioli was not happy to learn of Fernet's involvement; the two men had been rivals since the 1950s. As Ottavioli described him, Fernet was a man "of average height who considered himself short and as a result developed a superiority complex toward everyone else" —a man so calculating that his colleagues nicknamed him "*Max le menteur*" (Max the liar). Through his intimate knowledge of how things worked at the Criminal Brigade and his personal contacts with former colleagues, Fernet was able to tell Engen and the others what the police were likely to think and do. Even as Ottavioli opposed the idea of a ransom payment, Fernet sought to keep the company's options open on that question. As for Robert Badinter, the family and company lawyer, he continued to insist on handing over the money. "Madame," he told Rozell, "you must pay if you ever want to see your son alive again."

The family's position held no secrets for the investigators. Starting from day one, police had tapped the phones at the Avenue Foch apartment, as well as the headquarters of the Empain-Schneider group. They also established close personal surveillance by assigning an agent to live at the Empain apartment twenty-four hours a day to filter phone calls and advise the family. The first officer to be "embedded" with the family did not stay long: Silvana complained to Ottavioli that the man had made crude advances and demanded that he be removed. He was replaced with Jean-Claude Murat, a good-looking young cop known to colleagues as "*le beau Jean-Claude*," who was much more to Silvana's liking. Diane Empain, who lived alone in a studio apartment near Avenue Foch, was accompanied day and night by two police guards.

Diane was soon led to play a direct role in the drama. On Saturday, January 28, at one thirty p.m., an anonymous caller gave instructions to fetch a message in an underground parking lot. It was a typed letter addressed to Wado's nineteen-year-old daughter, Patricia, who had just returned from the United States with her American husband. She was instructed to prepare 80 million francs for delivery the following Monday at two p.m. There was also a handwritten letter from Wado. "My dear Patricia," it began, "I am going to ask you for a proof of love and courage, the task of trying to save my life." The text, riddled with spelling mistakes, instructed her to take his Mercedes, fill the tank, put the ransom in the trunk, and await delivery instructions. The envelope also contained three photos of the baron's wounded finger stump without the bandage.

The letters were shared with the police. The spelling mistakes were puzzling but suggested a possible attempt by Wado to undermine the instructions dictated by his captors. In any case, there was no question of actually sending Patricia on this risky mission: She was six months pregnant. Diane, who bore some resemblance to her niece, volunteered to take her place.

Per the written instructions, the January 30 phone call from the kidnappers was to be placed to a bank branch around the corner from the company's headquarters. At the appointed hour, Diane, duly briefed, walked to the bank accompanied by Bierry and her two police guards. "If you hear gunshots, hit the ground," one of the cops told her. "The bullet's for me." She was not reassured.

The conversation was brief:

"Patricia?"

"Yes."

"You have the money?"

"Thirty million."

"That's not the whole sum."

"Thirty million and not a cent more."

"*Adieu*," said the voice on the other end, and the line went dead.

Five days later, the kidnappers photographed Wado holding the February 4 edition of *France-Soir* to prove he was still alive. They had loaded up his neck and shoulders with chains and padlocks to enhance the effect. More shocking than the chains was the pitiful demeanor of the once-elegant baron, now sporting a scraggly beard and long greasy hair, with a blank, despairing look in his eyes. Mailed to the company headquarters, the grainy Polaroid was turned over to police and placed in an evidence file under Ottavioli's control. It would later wind up on the cover of *Paris Match*, a popular magazine known to pay hefty sums for sensational photos—and the place where Ottavioli's own daughter worked as a journalist. However it got to *Match*—some of Ottavioli's former colleagues suspect he received a fat check for it—the photo was a graphic proof of Wado's ordeal and a further blow to his dignity. It was hard to believe that this soiled and broken figure wore a title of nobility.

HUDDLED IN HIS filthy tent, the captive baron could brave the hunger and the cold and even the prospect of a summary execution. But the news of the scandalous press leaks had the effect of stripping him naked in the public square. Already he was demoralized by the failure of his family and colleagues to come up with the ransom—a fact that the kidnappers hammered home with daily harangues claiming his people didn't care about him, that they had written him off. At first, he believed that his family and associates were doing everything they could to free him, but after two or three weeks he felt totally abandoned. Now that the police were funneling the details of his private life to the press, he came to regard them not as potential saviors but as the enemy.

In the depths of despair and humiliation, Wado had one luxury: time to think. Over and over, he reviewed the chain of events that had brought him here—the skidding motor scooter, the hooded men erupting from the parked van, the barked orders, the cold steel on his neck, the frigid walk in the woods to this dark hole. He tried to imagine what was happening on the outside. The other top executives on the Rue d'Anjou had doubtlessly adjusted the power structure and were doing just fine without him. Would he ever see his family again? If so, how would they receive the damaged goods he had become?

PART II

The Kidnappers

1942–1978

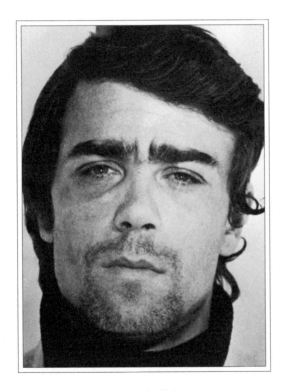

Alain Caillol

Houpline/Sipa

CHAPTER 4

The Making of a Gangster

Alain Caillol had a lot in common with Wado. Both men grew up in well-off families, both were sent away to boarding schools at an early age, both suffered from a lack of parental affection. And both men had what in contemporary-speak one might call Daddy issues. Wado's father, largely absent from his life, was a source of mystery and a vague sense of shame—a philandering playboy and accused Nazi collaborator who had died shortly after the war. Caillol's father, a successful businessman, was cold and distant, seemingly uninterested in his children even as he harassed them with strict lessons and rules. The young men's reactions could not have been more different. Wado fought for his rightful place at the head of the family enterprise; Caillol bolted from his family and became a hard-core criminal. Fate set them on a collision course.

Caillol was born in the southern city of Béziers in 1942, just four years after Wado. Before the war, his father, Pierre Caillol, had been wealthy. Not on the scale of the Empain clan, but rich enough to drive a Bugatti, keep a seaside apartment in Deauville and an apartment on the Boulevard Bineau in the affluent Paris suburb of Neuilly-sur-Seine. The bulk of the money came from his wife's manufacturing family, but Pierre also had a successful newspaper ad business. Then the war came, and his fortunes went south. His wife died of cancer and his business languished under the Nazi occupation. It didn't help that he had a gambling addiction and left bundles of money on the felt-topped tables of the Deauville casino. But probably the worst thing that happened to him at this time was his encounter with a woman from the eastern city of Nancy. She was not of his class, had no education and little to recommend her apart from a pretty face, long chestnut hair, and an attractive figure. Their unlikely encounter may have been limited to the coupling that conceived Alain's older brother, François, born in 1941. Pierre Caillol, rigorously old-school, did the "right thing" and married the woman. But the couple had nothing in common and no real relationship outside the bedroom. Alain came along a year later, followed by a sister, Catherine, in 1947.

By the end of the war, Pierre Caillol had lost most of his fortune and had to start all over again. He moved the family to the southern suburbs of Paris and reinvented himself as a bookseller. Business was slow, but he came up with a brilliant idea: Manufacture and sell affordable bookshelves to hold the cheap paperbacks that began to proliferate after the war. Within a few years, he had a whole chain of stores. Flush times returned: He purchased a new car, hired a chauffeur, bought expensive hunting rifles—and packed all his kids off to posh boarding schools.

Not that Alain missed being at home. His mother never talked to him, though she would occasionally give him a slap for an insolent word or look. She had no interests and no friends, didn't knit, never read a book or listened to music. Her only apparent pleasures were her unfiltered Balto cigarettes and the glass of wine she took with each meal. "She was hard, secretive, taciturn, and probably very unhappy," he would later write. When she died of pancreatic cancer in 1962, he didn't shed a tear.

Caillol's father, on the other hand, left an all-too-vivid impression on him and his siblings. He rarely spoke to them, but when he did, it was to criticize their manners and give them lessons—*don't put your elbows on the table, use your napkin, a gentleman uses a knife to eat an orange, don't they teach you anything in your boarding school?* He never struck his children, but he never showed any affection. Not a pat on the head, a hug, or even a handshake. His interests were limited to hunting, fishing, card-playing, and work. All he inspired in Alain was a sense of fear and loathing. As Caillol later explained to a friend, this was the genesis of his leap into criminality: "I was always afraid of my father. He terrified me by the enormous distance he imposed on his relations with us. I never remember him even touching my hand. He put an everlasting fear in me and I was horrified. I started to do incredible things, more and more risky, and that was not enough, so I finally threw myself into serious delinquency."

The my-parents-didn't-love-me argument is hardly a valid excuse for embracing a life of crime. But it does explain how a rudderless youth like Alain Caillol might look elsewhere for validation and fulfillment. Particularly when he had an older brother to show him the way. François, who had a talent for drawing, attended art courses in Paris. But he soon became fed up with the long commute between the family's suburban home and his classes in the city. So he began stealing Vespas to go back and forth. He soon graduated to break-ins and petty theft to pay for a cheap hotel room in the capital. Alain, meanwhile, got his first taste of thievery by shoplifting records, sweaters, and cheap souvenirs during school trips abroad, and found the game titillating. But François's luck suddenly ran out: Nabbed during a botched second-story job, he was sent to prison in 1961—the first of four convictions that would put him behind bars for a total of nearly ten years. Alain's periodic visits to his brother were his first experience of life behind prison walls—but not his last.

There was another side of Alain Caillol, one that sought the success and respectability expected of the sons of bourgeois families. In 1960, he received his *baccalauréat,* the French secondary-school diploma, with honors in philosophy. He took the competitive entrance exam for the elite Paris Institute of Political Studies but failed to make the cut. Instead, he entered the Assas law school, the breeding ground for France's leading jurists. It is an intriguing what-might-have-been scenario to imagine Alain Caillol in black robes administering the law instead of defying it. But Assas was highly politicized at the time and far too right-wing for Caillol's taste. So he dropped out after the first year, gave up his student deferment, and was drafted into the French Army in 1962.

Military life apparently suited him even less than his law studies. During his first leave, he went AWOL, hung out with wealthy friends on the Riviera, and in a moment of despondency, attempted suicide by cutting his wrists. The army tracked him down in the hospital, but instead of charging him as a deserter, they gave him a psychological discharge. François got out of prison at about the same time, so Alain joined up with him and his buddies and officially embarked on a life of crime.

Nothing very serious at first. They filched cameras and watches from stores, broke into apartments to rake up jewelry and cash, and, in one heist, carted off paintings by Maurice Utrillo. But the paintings were too well known and therefore unsellable. They did better with period furniture: The antique dealers worked mainly with cash in those days, and many of them were not too curious about the provenance of their wares.

In 1967, it was Alain's turn to sample life behind bars. Arrested for a series of thefts in Geneva, he was briefly imprisoned by Swiss authorities, then expelled to France. In 1969, he was caught during a break-in and sent to prison for eighteen months. Shortly after his release, he took another two years when police found falsified documents and counterfeiting equipment in the trunk of his car. Thrown in with real professionals—safecrackers, bank robbers, armored-car hijackers, arms experts—he was enthralled by the Robin Hood romance of their world and decided he wanted to be like them.

To all appearances, Caillol was a model of the successfully rehabilitated criminal after his release in March 1973. He moved to the Mediterranean port city of Montpellier to manage one of his father's furniture stores, bought a house in a rural suburb north of the city, and was ostensibly settled into a life of bourgeois respectability. In 1974, he married Pierrette Poye, ex-wife of a builder; their son Cyril was born the same year. Neighbors would see Caillol working in his garden, cutting the grass, or firing up the barbecue grill on weekends. In fact, though he was gainfully employed and not hurting for money—he earned the equivalent of $50,000 a year, a substantial sum in those days—Caillol continued sneaking off to Paris to rob banks with his friends. "It was a way of life," he explained. "It's the only thing I enjoyed doing."

Among Caillol's underworld relations was a hardened gangster named Michel Ardouin, known as "The Aircraft Carrier" because of his gargantuan size—6'6", 265 pounds—and the heavy-duty armaments he stuffed in his belt. One day Ardouin asked Caillol to help him spring a buddy from prison. The friend was scheduled to appear in court in the town of Compiègne, forty miles northeast of Paris, in June 1973. Caillol agreed. He and Ardouin procured a stolen car and parked it in front of the courthouse. On Ardouin's instructions, inspired perhaps by a famous scene in the 1972 film *The Godfather*,

Caillol hid 9mm Luger pistols in each of the building's two men's rooms. During the hearing, the prisoner faked a bout of diarrhea and persuaded his guards to let him use the toilet. He found a gun behind the pipes and concealed it in his pocket. As soon as he was escorted back to the courtroom, he stood up, drew his pistol, and shouted: "Let me go or I'll kill the judge!" Approaching the bench, he grabbed the terrified magistrate by the collar and planted the gun barrel in the back of his neck. "Everybody on the ground," he barked, and fired a warning round into the ceiling. Once outside, he shoved the judge aside and hopped into the waiting getaway car, exchanging gunfire with the gendarmes and wounding one as the car wheeled off. He was Jacques Mesrine, France's notorious Public Enemy Number One, the man who would later be gunned down by Robert Broussard's Antigang commandos.

When Caillol met him, Mesrine was already a legendary figure in the annals of French crime. A ruthless megalomaniac with a penchant for histrionic gestures and self-promotion, he had carried out a long string of heists, bank robberies, and murders across Europe and Canada. In his sensational memoir, *L' Instinct de mort* (death wish), Mesrine described himself as "one of these criminal beasts who can cold-bloodedly snuff out a life of flesh and blood without the least sense of guilt." He once boasted that he had killed as many as thirty-nine people, though the true number could never be confirmed.

Mesrine—nicknamed "Le Grand"—was a master of disguises and getaways, executing spectacular escapes from even the highest-security prisons. With the money he stole, he enjoyed the good life—beautiful women, Champagne, flashy cars—but what he loved more than anything was reading about himself in the papers. In order to remain on the front pages, he would bombard the newsrooms with boasting letters and give clandestine interviews—including one instance where he stripped a journalist naked, shot him three times, and left him for dead for writing articles that insulted his "honor." Mesrine was a psychopath and a sociopath, but his career was a subject of morbid fascination that was later packaged into a 2008 feature film starring Vincent Cassel.

Without intending it, Caillol found himself pulled into Mesrine's orbit. The day after his escape from the courthouse in Compiègne, Mesrine showed up at Caillol's Paris apartment with the severed handcuff chains still dangling from his wrists. He was broke and wanted to go out and rob a bank right away. That was the beginning of an uneasy collaboration in which Mesrine and Ardouin, hotheaded alpha-male rivals, were always at each other's throats. "It was a real Western between those two," Caillol later recalled. "Mesrine would gamble all night; the next morning he was broke and we had to start all over again. Sometimes we'd hit two or three banks in the same day. He was ungovernable."

He was also dangerous, with a hair-trigger temper that could get you killed if you looked at him the wrong way. Caillol learned that firsthand one day as they sat at the kitchen table of Mesrine's apartment counting the haul from a bank robbery. After the big bills had been divvied up, Caillol shoved a stack of fives and tens Mesrine's way. "Here, Grand, buy a dress for your girlfriend."

Mesrine froze him with a glare. "What? You're buying dresses for my girlfriend now? If I want to give my girl a dress, you think I need you?"

Caillol's apologies only fueled Mesrine's rage. He took out his .45 and placed it on the table. Caillol had seen this game before. It was Mesrine's idea of a duel. Both parties would empty their clips, and the first one to reload and shoot would win. The loser would die. Which was exactly what happened to the last man Mesrine had challenged.

"You have a .45?"

"No," Caillol answered, "and I don't want to play this game. I'm leaving."

He got up and walked out before Mesrine could reply. As he descended the stairs, Caillol's own .45—for he did have one in a back pocket—suddenly slipped out and tumbled into the void. It spiraled down four flights and bounced, without detonating, on the ground-floor parquet. Caillol continued down the stairs, expecting to be gunned down by Le Grand. But Mesrine did not pursue him. He had lost interest.

Though he specialized in bank robberies, Mesrine one day came up with the idea of a kidnapping. He would seize the billionaire banker Guy de Rothschild during the annual Grand Prix at the Chantilly racetrack, thirty miles north of Paris, and hide him in a barn. Once the ransom was paid, the plan called for an elaborate getaway via railroad tunnels, sewers, and canals leading to the Seine. But before they could put this scheme into execution, Commissaire Robert Broussard—Mesrine's perpetual nemesis—arrested him in an ambush in September 1973 and sent him back to prison. Much to Caillol's relief: He was sure that Mesrine's unpredictable antics would one day land them all in jail—or six feet underground. But Le Grand had planted an idea in his head that would later bear fruit.

FOLLOWING MESRINE'S ARREST, Caillol began to organize a gang of his own. His first recruit was Daniel Duchateau. Introduced by a mutual friend, Caillol and Duchateau were as unalike physically as two men could be. Duchateau, the son of a cop, was tall and muscular, with wire-rimmed glasses and a high forehead that gave him something of an intellectual look. Caillol was small-boned and short of stature—five foot seven in his stocking feet—with a boyish face.

But they shared a passion for the world of criminality that, in both cases, had begun as a revolt against an unhappy family life.

Duchateau had recently been released from prison after serving nine years for bank robbery. Taking a page from Ken Kesey's *One Flew Over the Cuckoo's Nest*, he had faked insanity in order to trade his prison cell for a mental hospital, a harrowing experience—including strait-jackets and electroshocks—that he would later describe in a book of his own. He was a neat dresser, favoring conservative suits and ties and sporting a gold Cartier wristwatch worth $10,000.

Behind his bland exterior, Duchateau was a complex character, bubbling over with anger and resentment, determined to grab what he considered his due in life. Despite Duchateau's intellectual preten-sions, a prison psychiatrist who examined him in 1973 judged him to be of only average intelligence and emotionally infantile: "Duchateau is a mystic living on dreams and illusions . . . This man has a pro-nounced taste for firearms. He's subject to fits of depression, during which he drowns himself in alcohol. My prognosis for his future is seriously reserved and his social readaptation is doubtful."

Readaptation was the last thing on Duchateau's mind when he was released from prison in 1974. As he made clear in his book, *Sainte Anne priez pour moi* (*Saint Anne, Pray for Me*), his only aim was to get his hands on money—lots of it, by any and all means. "Money for me," he wrote, "was independence, total freedom . . . I needed to drink champagne, eat my fill, buy whatever pleased me . . . Money gave me all that."

The reference to Champagne and good eating was not rhetorical: If Daniel Duchateau had a personal passion, apart from stealing other people's money, it was fine food and wine. He was, in fact, a talented chef who would invite his buddies over to dinner once a month and regale them with gourmet dishes and rare vintages. When he was not "working"—that is, planning or carrying out a bank robbery—he liked to whisk his girlfriend off to some luxurious venue he'd read about in *Relais & Châteaux* for a weekend of wining and dining. It was an expensive hobby—far more than Caillol's private passion for the opera—and one that required a steady flow of cash.

One day at the Marché aux Puces, the sprawling flea market on the northern rim of Paris, Caillol and Duchateau were approached by a younger man—Caillol calls him "Mathieu" to conceal his real identity. A charming and rakish youth who dabbled in petty crime and prostitution, Mathieu offered to sell them two pistols he had stolen. The son of a French Communist Party militant and a former Resistance fighter, he was far more politicized than Caillol and Duchateau. His embrace of crime was linked in his mind to a visceral hatred of capitalism and bourgeois society in general. Caillol liked the cut of his jib. He invited him to lunch the next day, ostensibly to buy the pistols, but his real aim was to recruit this so-called Mathieu as a member of the gang. The younger man immediately accepted and recommended a childhood friend of his, an Algerian immigrant who had grown up with him in a tough, working-class suburb. Caillol knew him as Idir, his true first name, but never learned his family name.

Idir and Mathieu had played soccer together as kids and regularly sparred with each other at a local boxing gym. Idir's father, an assembly-line worker, had been killed at a Paris march for Algerian independence in 1961. Since then, Idir had been responsible for his mother and two sisters, a poor family held together by their Muslim faith and largely financed by Idir's petty thievery. Behind the wheel, Idir proved to be what Caillol called "an exceptional urban pilot." He became the band's regular driver.

The foursome soon formed a well-oiled team that specialized in bank robberies, shopping-center holdups, and payroll heists. Thanks to meticulous preparation—staking out the targets, choosing the right moment, keeping a low profile, and rapid execution—they hauled in more than a million dollars over four years without ever being caught by the police or identified by witnesses. But it was a grueling full-time job. "To plan a bank robbery correctly, you have to work," Caillol explains. "You have to wake up at five a.m., relay each other in eight-hour shifts, consider all the angles. While you're looking at one possibility, you see another, and another. You always have to have several irons on the fire."

During the planning stages, says Caillol, he and Duchateau were the "thinking heads." The two others were there to help with the execution. "Daniel was serious in his work. He was discreet, not at all the hoodlum type, didn't hang out in bars and nightclubs. You couldn't really say he was an intellectual, even though he wrote that book. His way of thinking was first-degree. But for most people, that's enough."

One day, after the gang had split up the money from a big bank job, Duchateau told the others, "That's it, it's all over. I'm going to start my own business." His decision confirmed what they all were feeling at that time. It was hard, dangerous work, and they knew that sooner or later their luck would run out. So, like the Beatles, the foursome broke up and went their separate ways. Caillol went back to his furniture store in Montpellier. Idir bought a bar-restaurant. The man Caillol calls Mathieu took off on a long road trip. But unlike the Beatles, this band was slated for a dramatic reunion.

CHAPTER 5

"Make the Money Come to Us!"

Considering Duchateau's passion for fine cuisine, he might have opened a restaurant. But for some bizarre reason, he decided to go into the pottery business—not making pottery but selling it. Caillol was skeptical. "He must have read in some magazine that pottery sold well. When he told me that's what he wanted to do, I said, okay, see you in a year." But Duchateau forged ahead. With money from the last heist, he rented a shop on the Rue Vavin, near the Luxembourg Gardens, one of Paris's most upscale neighborhoods. He ordered a large stock of expensive merchandise from Vallauris, the village in the South of France where Picasso once spent time working among the local potters. Then he sat behind the counter and waited for customers.

Meanwhile, he and his girlfriend lived the high life—Michelin three-star restaurants, luxury hotels, rare vintages bought by the case. The money poured out, but only trickled in. Caillol's timeline turned out to be optimistic: Within six months, Duchateau's business had gone belly-up and he was reduced to burning his landlord's furniture in the fireplace of his rented house in order to keep warm. One day, he called Caillol and told him he was so hard up that he was ready to rob the ticket booth of his local cinema. "Watch the film first," Caillol advised. "At least you'll have something to tell us about."

With Duchateau's desperation acting as a catalyst, the gang decided to get back together. Caillol was more than ready. He was bored selling bookshelves in Montpellier and, by his own admission, was not cut out to run a business. Besides, he was having domestic difficulties with a wife devoured by jealousy and paranoia and a three-year-old son who was developing serious behavioral problems. "My life was rotten," he recalls. "The only time I felt good was when I was with my brothers-in-crime." Mathieu and Idir, both in need of cash, also returned to the fold.

But when the four comrades gathered together in November 1976 to map out their future, there were disagreements over how to proceed. Duchateau and Idir wanted to return to bank robbing; Mathieu, ever the radical, ruled out armed action unless it had a political aim. Caillol was undecided. Then one of them came up with an intriguing idea: "Instead of going after the money, why don't we make the money come to us?"

"It was brilliant," Caillol recounts. "We would revive the good old days of the knights-errant, capture versus ransom. That's what we needed to do: create the danger ourselves in order to reignite a sense of fraternity that was on the verge of crumbling. We all found the idea excellent and began to think about how we would theorize a kidnapping."

Working methodically, pencil and paper in hand, they concentrated on three points: Devise a way to collect the ransom without coming into contact with the police; find the perfect hideout, isolated and undiscoverable; choose the right target. On the last point, they briefly considered seizing a child as a way of putting maximum pressure on the family. Caillol ruled that out on humanitarian grounds. He had a better idea: Why not choose the head of some big company? That way his band could satisfy their left-leaning political views while extracting a few million from a capitalist exploiter who surely deserved it. "Our main goal was the money," he explains. "But at the same time, if you can give a slap in the face to a big boss, throw him in a cave and show him what it's like to eat canned beans, why not?" They left the final choice for later while they focused on the logistics.

It promised to be an expensive operation. The gang would have to rent safe houses, acquire a fleet of stolen cars, procure fake IDs and forged papers for the vehicles, and buy equipment and provisions for the hideout. Caillol was advancing money out of pocket, but he was running low on funds. So the foursome decided to carry out one last holdup to finance what they all expected to be the multimillion-dollar payout that would allow them to retire in style. But the July 1977 bank job they planned nearly ended in disaster.

Over the years, they had closely observed the routines of the armored-car drivers who hauled bags of cash to and from the banks. The gang generally refrained from attacking them, as the guards were heavily armed and trained to neutralize would-be thieves. Caillol came up with the idea of impersonating transporters and receiving the cash directly from the bank. He and Duchateau armed themselves with the same regulation .38 pistols and black leather holsters as the guards. To look the part, Duchateau wore a pair of reflecting aviator-style Ray-Bans and Caillol donned a fake mustache. Both wore regulation black boots and rolled up their shirtsleeves like the real transporters did.

Shortly before the appointed hour for the actual transfer, they knocked on the side door of a Paris bank. The door opened electronically. When Duchateau and Caillol entered, hands on their hol-sters, the bank employees spontaneously handed them a canvas sack stuffed with bills. As Duchateau calmly sauntered out with the goods, the bank manager handed Caillol a clipboard and a pen. "You forgot to sign the register," he said. Caillol hesitated, wary of leaving prints on the pen though his fingertips were covered with glue. When finally he took the pen in his sweaty hand, his mustache suddenly fell off. The game was up. He pulled out his .38 and aimed it at the manager's chest. The manager froze and Caillol dashed out the door. Within seconds, the bank alarms went off. As they sped off in their stolen armored car with Idir at the wheel, they heard the shriek of approaching police sirens. Moments later, they ditched the vehicle and disappeared with the money into the Métro. That close call sealed the gang's decision to abandon the bank-robbing business and focus on the big jackpot they were all expecting.

EVEN BEFORE THEY had worked out all the details, it was obvious that the gang would need reinforcements for what promised to be a complicated operation: A kidnapping would require coordinated action, the use of multiple vehicles, several men to guard the prisoner round the clock, others to negotiate and collect the ransom. The first recruit was Jean Brunet, a battle-hardened veteran of the war in In-dochina with a fascination for guns and a penchant for using them. He owed his nickname, "Willie the Crutch," to a war wound that had left him with a limp. Considered something of an underworld "star," even by the cops, Brunet was a professional criminal who spe-cialized in bank robberies and break-ins. Among other things, he liked to relieve posh vacation homes in Normandy of their furniture. Police also suspected him of involvement in several previous kidnap plots. One fellow conspirator described Brunet as "a key player in shock operations." Caillol had helped him out on a bank job a few years earlier, and Brunet was more than willing to return the favor—especially in view of the promised payout.

Brunet suggested they bring in a longtime partner of his. René Rigault, nicknamed "La Grise" because of his gray hair, was an old-school gangster with links to the French mafia. In his seventies at the time, he had started robbing banks in the 1950s and was considered something of an elder statesman in the crime world—a "consigliere" in the words of one French detective. La Grise was a fastidious dresser who would show up to work in a coat and tie, with knife-edge creases on his trousers, his hair parted with laserlike precision. He was a seasoned professional who knew all the tricks, but he was getting up in age and Caillol wondered if the old boy still had the stamina for this kind of work. With his silver hair and drawn features, he seemed tired, perhaps even sick.

It was La Grise who recommended a guy to work on logistics: a car thief and pimp named Georges Bertoncini—nicknamed "Jo le Marseillais" for his singsong Marseilles accent. Jovial, round-faced and pudgy, with an unkempt mop of brown hair, Bertoncini was a hot-blooded, back-slapping type who seemingly knew everyone in the business. "Bertoncini was not like us," says Caillol. "He lived in the world of whores, bars, and nightclubs. Jo had all the street vices. He wasn't my cup of tea, but he could get things done." That much was true: In addition to rounding up vehicles and renting apartments, Bertoncini could also be depended on to arrange forged papers, license plates, and IDs. His facility at obtaining documents was surprising for a man who could hardly read or write, a man of "limited intelligence" in the words of his own lawyer.

To help manage the fleet of a dozen cars, trucks, and vans, Bertoncini hired one of the coterie of younger guys who hung around him and jumped when he snapped his fingers. He called him Fredo. Nobody seemed to know or care about his last name. With his thin mustache and shifty eyes, Fredo was what the French call a *petite frappe*—a petty delinquent. Caillol thought he was useless. His first week on the job, Fredo managed to crumple the fender of a stolen car while exiting a parking lot. He was the kind of low-rent bungler who could make a fatal mistake and botch the whole job.

Another recruit was Bernard Guillon, age thirty, a stocky auto mechanic from a rough Parisian suburb. Though he had no police record, Guillon had trafficked in stolen cars with Bertoncini and was a close friend of both Caillol brothers. After a difficult childhood—apparently a common trait among the kidnappers—he had bounced around from job to job and at one point started an auto-repair business that went belly-up. Caillol describes him as "a nice young guy who wouldn't hurt a fly." A cop who later encountered him tells a different story: "Guillon was a big fish. The worst kind of reprobate. When he looks you in the eye, you're not at ease."

Caillol also called on his brother François. Tall, bald, and stone-faced, François Caillol then lived with his wife near Grenoble, where he ran the local branch of his father's furniture chain. After serving a total of ten years in prison for multiple offenses, he had promised his wife that his former life of crime was finished, and to all appearances that was true. Quiet and discreet in his private life, he bore no outward resemblance to a dangerous gangster. On the contrary, he was a nature enthusiast who loved painting, music, and quiet walks in the great outdoors. His father, whom he detested, described him as "odorless, colorless, and tasteless." Alain Caillol has never specified his brother's exact role in the plot—but it's probable that François took part in the commando operation that grabbed the baron. Police later concluded that François was actually one of the organizers if not the mastermind of the operation. The "mastermind" claim seems highly doubtful, but it's unlikely that Alain would have relegated his older brother, his first mentor in crime, to a mere secondary role.

IN THE SUMMER of 1977, Caillol, Duchateau, Guillon, La Grise, and Bertoncini flew to Palma on the Spanish island of Mallorca to work out the logistics of their kidnap plan. Bertoncini kept a speedboat in the marina and knew a ton of people—with his infectious laugh and chatty conviviality, he seemed to make friends everywhere he went. That could be a problem in a case where discretion was needed, Caillol thought, but they were far from the French cops and their informers, and Le Marseillais was the perfect party companion. And party they did: dancing in the bustling nightclubs, sipping daiquiris in the bars, enjoying seafood in the beachfront restaurants.

On the Air France flight back to Paris, Caillol did not notice the woman in the brown wig who was eyeing him intently. It was his pathologically jealous wife, Pierrette, who was sure he had planned the trip to tryst with another woman. She had flown to Palma ahead of time and was waiting in the airport when Caillol arrived, hoping to catch him with a girlfriend at his side. She was mistaken—Caillol generally preferred the camaraderie of his male buddies to cruising for women—but his wife's spying mission would have consequences.

CHAPTER 6

Planning the Caper

*I*t was supposed to be Hitler's "miracle weapon." The sleek forty-seven-foot-long missile traveled at supersonic speeds, carried a two-thousand-pound high-explosive warhead, and boasted a range of two hundred and twenty miles. Originally designated the A4, it later acquired the name by which it is best known: V-2, for *Vergeltungs-waffe 2*—"vengeance weapon number two."

Starting in 1936, the A4/V2 was developed at Germany's Peenemünde base on the Baltic island of Usedom by Wernher von Braun and his team. Though this formidable missile was not yet operational at the start of the war, the invading German armies began almost immediately to scout out and prepare V-2 storage depots in the occupied territories. Of the six sites that the Wehrmacht planned to build in France, the one closest to Paris was situated on the outskirts of Méry-sur-Oise, a sleepy little town of 2,500 souls nestled in a loop of the Oise River some twenty miles north of the capital. Among its advantages, the town was located far from the front and next to a railroad line. But the main thing Méry had to offer the occupiers was its eighty-five acres of underground limestone quarries on the edge of the thickly wooded Garennes forest. The Wehrmacht designated Méry as *Nachschublager* (storage site) 1401.

In 1942, after expropriating the quarry owners, the Germans launched a vast construction project aimed at enlarging the existing tunnels and blasting new ones into the rock. The passages were wired for electricity and reinforced with hundreds of tons of steel-armed concrete. To allow train cars and vehicles to access the base, new entrances were built, along with blockhouses for the machine gunners assigned to defend it. Once completed, the Germans expected to stock as many as six hundred missiles in the tunnels. From there, they could be transported by rail to launch sites in the Netherlands.

In fact, not a single V-2 was ever stored in the Méry tunnels. Von Braun's missiles did not become operational until September 8, 1944, when the first V-2 was fired against newly liberated Paris and exploded near the Place d'Italie. Two days later, the first of 1,300 rockets was launched against London. In all, some four thousand V-2s rained down on Britain and Belgium between September 1944 and March 1945, killing an estimated nine thousand people. Though they caused horrific devastation, the rockets were not the game-changer Hitler had counted on. But they later provided a prototype for both U.S. and Soviet missile development and thus paved the way to the Space Age.

The Germans abandoned the Méry base following three massive bombardments by RAF and U.S. Army Air Corps units in July and August 1944. After the war, American troops de-mined the site and returned it to its original owners, who continued to quarry limestone there until the late 1960s. The tunnels were subsequently used as a subterranean mushroom farm, then quietly abandoned, leaving the trees and vines from the surrounding forest to invade and obscure the entrances and blockhouses.

As Caillol's gang cogitated over the crucial question of choosing a hideout, Mathieu and Idir remembered stumbling upon the Méry tunnels while playing in the Garennes as kids. The band went together to check it out. It was perfect, Caillol thought. Hidden, isolated, dark, with walls so thick that no one outside—not even the squirrels in the forest—would hear the screams of their captive. The entrances had long since been sealed off with steel doors, but the team managed to dig an opening under one of the barriers. Entering the dank cavern with flashlights, they followed the tunnel to a place, about eight hundred yards from the entrance, where several other corridors branched off. That's where they decided to pitch camp. Inhospitable surroundings, to be sure, but they only expected to be there four or five days—one week maximum—before collecting the ransom and releasing their prisoner.

THE A6 AUTOROUTE heads south from Paris, slices through the Burgundy wine country and the Rhône River valley, and winds up in Lyons. From there a branch highway leads to the Mediterranean port of Marseilles. The A6 is nicknamed Autoroute du Soleil—the highway of the sun—because it's the road that millions of French vacationers take to the beaches of the Riviera each summer. Alain Caillol drove the A6 regularly, but he was not on vacation. He used it to commute between his home in Montpellier, where he half-heartedly ran his father's furniture outlet, and Paris, where he would meet up with his fellow gangsters and rob banks.

Alone behind the wheel of his Renault 16, Caillol had a lot of time to think during the seven-hour drive. One day, as he was heading back to Montpellier, he noticed a metal door in the concrete soundproofing wall that ran parallel to the highway. It was situated next to an emergency telephone stand. Curious to find out where the door led, he took the next exit and looped back through the suburb of L'Haÿ-les-Roses, located some twenty miles south of Paris. Cruising slowly along the outside of the wall, Caillol spotted another metal door. He parked his car and went to investigate. It was apparently an access door for highway maintenance crews. When he forced it open, he saw that the interior of the wall was hollow, like a tunnel. The door on the highway side was some thirty yards away.

Caillol couldn't believe his good luck. He had stumbled upon the solution to the knottiest problem the gang faced: how to take possession of the ransom and make their getaway without coming into direct contact with the police. They could arrange a rendezvous at the emergency telephone stand—B12 was its number—grab the money, and disappear through the door. If the cops tried to follow them, they could hold them off with gunfire and defensive grenades long enough to scoot through the tunnel to the other door and jump into a waiting getaway car. The police, blocked on the highway side of the wall, would have no way to pursue them. Brilliant!

With two problems solved, they now faced their final, most momentous decision: choosing their victim. They considered the banker Guy de Rothschild (the man Mesrine had planned to grab some years earlier) and the aviation magnate Marcel Dassault. They had the money and the high profile that would maximize pressure and media attention. But Caillol didn't like the idea. Both men were Jews who had suffered during the war: Rothschild had to flee France in 1940, and Dassault had been deported to Buchenwald. Despite his anti-capitalist sentiments, he recoiled at the idea of targeting two elderly men who had been persecuted by the Nazis.

Another possible target was Liliane Bettencourt, France's richest woman and the heiress to the L'Oréal cosmetics fortune. They even staked out her mansion in the Paris suburb of Neuilly to learn the routines of her comings and goings in a chauffeur-driven car, usually accompanied by her beloved dachshund, Tomas. But there was a problem: Liliane Bettencourt was a woman. Some of the gang members were uncomfortable with the idea of cutting off a woman's finger. The ever-fastidious La Grise, assigned to be one of the guards, objected that he would have trouble managing the problems of "feminine hygiene." So Liliane was off the hook.

Empain was not an immediate backup choice. For all his megalomania, he managed to maintain a low profile during these years. He kept his private life largely out of sight and rarely appeared on TV or granted interviews. Thanks to his discretion, and what he himself described as his natural timidity, he could go to a restaurant, a movie theater, or a nightclub without being recognized. Though the specialized business press reported on the activities of his group, he himself was largely unknown to the general public.

That would change in 1976, when the left-leaning satirical weekly *Le Canard Enchaîné* ran an investigative piece on Baron Empain, criticizing him for mass layoffs and revealing his use of private vigilantes to intimidate unions at companies under his control. The paper's tongue-in-cheek conclusion: "Baron Empain has a weakness for tough guys." It so happened that Alain Caillol was an attentive reader of the *Canard Enchaîné*. Poring over some back issues, he came across this article and showed it to his comrades. "Here's our man!" he said. "He likes tough guys? He'll see what it's like."

There were several reasons for the kidnappers to target the baron. "Empain was the rising star of French capitalism," Caillol explains. "He was also young and athletic, so he was physically suited to endure the harsh conditions we would subject him to in the tunnel. We observed the group's headquarters on the Rue d'Anjou. Within days, we knew what car he used, we knew where he lived, we knew what time he left home in the morning, always about ten thirty. We watched him at least ten times. Once we knew he lived on Avenue Foch, we decided we would take him there in the morning by blocking his car in the service road. He'd be trapped like a rat."

MOST OF THE original planning had been done by Caillol and Duchateau. Once the essential questions were settled—the hideout, the location of the ransom pickup, the victim—the gang concentrated on the final preparations. It was only at that point that the others were brought in to help with logistics. Bertoncini took charge of the motor pool, renting two private garages and corralling ten stolen vehicles, ranging from sedans and trucks to a driving-school car and a postal van, all with fake plates and papers. But the resourceful Bertoncini also posed a problem: He knew everyone in the Parisian underworld, and he talked too much. The others were afraid someone would suspect his involvement in what would soon be known as the Empain affair. To keep him out of circulation, they rented a two-story house in the Paris suburb of Savigny-sur-Orge and told him to lie low there with his girlfriend, Marie-Annick, their infant son, Bruce, and their German mastiff until the operation was over. The gang also lined up an apartment in eastern Paris as a safe house.

The other big logistical task was preparing the Méry tunnel for what they expected to be a short stay. It was a complicated job because the tunnel entrance was located in a dense forest a long distance from the road, so they had to carry everything by hand and only at night to avoid being seen. Since back-and-forth trips were problematic, there was no provision for resupplying the tunnel.

Finally, the holding space was ready. Caillol compared it to "the mortuary room of a pyramid," furnished not with gold, incense, and myrrh but with more practical objects: "The tent intended for our prisoner, with an inflatable mattress and a bucket for his bodily needs, five other mattresses, bottles of water, small folding tables, more tents, blankets, canned food, a gas burner, a Polaroid camera, battery-powered electric lamps, candles, a long chain bolted into a wall and running into the tent, writing materials, a first-aid kit, a portable radio." Not to mention the paper cutter and mallet that would be used to amputate Wado's finger. (A clean chop, they reasoned, would do less damage than hacking the finger off with a knife.)

Most of the supplies had been prepared by Mathieu and Idir at the direction of Caillol and Duchateau. When the others visited the hideout for the first time, there was some initial grumbling about the living conditions. The fastidious La Grise complained about the lack of hygiene and the impossibility of washing or changing clothes. Despite the discomfort, the old man fell sound asleep on one of the air mattresses while the others toured the site. Fredo, the youngest of the bunch, was afraid of the dark. Brunet, the gun-loving Indochina veteran, took note and decided to have some fun with him once the operation was under way.

Each member of the team had his assigned role. All eight men would take part in the actual kidnapping; afterward, Brunet, La Grise, and Fredo would guard the hostage, spelled by Mathieu, Idir, and Bertoncini. Caillol and Duchateau would handle the negotiations and pick up the ransom. Regardless of their individual tasks, the gang decided to share the money equally. That is how they calculated the ransom demand: 10 million francs per man times eight added up to 80 million. A nice round figure, democratically distributed, that promised each man a future life of ease. But this was the first of several major miscalculations: It would have made more sense to investigate Wado's finances to estimate how much he could actually pay.

In mid-December 1977, six of the conspirators returned to Palma, accompanied by their wives or girlfriends. This was not a time for discussing the kidnap plan; it was a chance for the band to relax and enjoy a little R & R before leaping into action. They made the most of their vacation, even renting a yacht and heading out to sea on a cruise. Caillol couldn't join them this time: His jealous wife was throwing fits and he had to mind the furniture store during the busy Christmas season. But he expected to get back to Palma soon enough. Once the ransom was paid, the gang planned to retreat to this sunny Spanish island and cool their heels, far from the reach of the French police.

At that same moment, Empain was schussing down the mountains in the Alpine ski resort of Megève on his annual Christmas vacation. A champion skier in his youth, he could still tackle the most formidable slopes, hardly stopping for lunch before heading back to the lifts. In the evenings, he would sit by the fireplace and nurse a glass of vintage brandy in the cozy bar of his hotel. And of course he would play a few hands of poker with his friends. Wado was living the good life.

THE MANEUVER UNFOLDED with military precision. On Sunday, January 22, 1978, the team parked two cars on the service road near the entrance to 33 Avenue Foch. These cars would play no direct role in the action. They were intended to reserve parking spaces for the operational vehicles that would be brought there the next day. On Monday, January 23, all eight members of the gang arrived at eight a.m. and began their preparations. The cars were removed and replaced by a beige-colored van, parked just beyond the building's entrance, and a blue truck, parked just before it.

Once the vehicles were in place, the eight members of the commando took up positions in the general vicinity, taking care to remain inconspicuous. Duchateau and La Grise sat on a park bench on the wide grassy median of Avenue Foch, one in a Burberry trench coat, the other in a green loden coat, looking for all the world like bourgeois denizens of the sixteenth arrondissement. Bertoncini and Idir, dressed in workers' blue overalls, swept the sidewalk. Caillol and the man he called Mathieu stood at a distance on the other side of the avenue, smoking cigarettes and patiently awaiting the moment to spring into action.

At ten fifteen they saw Empain's gray Peugeot 604 approaching along Avenue Foch with chauffeur Jean Denis at the wheel. Fredo positioned his motor scooter fifty yards before the building's entrance. The others all joined their assigned vehicles and prepared the materiel they would need for the job: weapons, handcuffs, ski masks, duct tape, even a sledgehammer to break into Empain's car in case the chauffeur tried to lock it from the inside.

The Peugeot came to a stop in front of the building. Idir, at the wheel of the van, turned on the engine. Bertoncini, in the driver's seat of the truck, did the same.

Shortly before ten thirty, the baron emerged, exchanged a few words with his chauffeur, and slid into the backseat. As the Peugeot pulled away from the curb, Fredo passed it on his scooter, then skidded and tumbled. Within seconds, Wado was a prisoner.

PART III

The First Baron

1852–1929

Mover and Shaker: Édouard Louis Joseph Empain

Apic/Getty Images

CHAPTER 7

The Founder

*H*e was not an impressive man to look at. Standing only five foot three, he was somewhat paunchy, with a Vandyke and a droopy mustache that gave a mournful cast to his otherwise bland face. When posing for photos, he would puff out his chest to give an impression of manly vigor. He held a general's rank, though he never fought a battle. Born a commoner, he was befriended by a king and proudly wore a noble title. Historians and biographers have dubbed him a "great man"—and there was indeed greatness in the sheer energy, drive, and vision that propelled this brilliant autodidact to the front rank of European industrialists. Like Carnegie, Vanderbilt, and Rockefeller across the sea, he was an insatiable builder who left a profound mark on his era. What's more, he founded a dynasty that, through three generations, ruled over one of Europe's most powerful business empires, the fabulous multinational that Wado would one day inherit.

When Édouard Louis Joseph Empain was born at the midpoint of the nineteenth century, his native Belgium was rapidly evolving from an agricultural and rural country into one of the world's leading industrial powers. The nation had won its independence from Holland only in 1830, and its population of 3.8 million was divided uneasily between Dutch-speaking Flanders in the North and French-speaking Wallonia in the South. National unity was embodied in a brand-new constitutional monarchy. The first king, Leopold I, was in fact not a Belgian at all but a prince from the small German duchy of Saxe-Coburg-Gotha, who had been invited to the throne by the new parliament in 1831 after a son of French king Louis Philippe turned down the job.

Despite the linguistic and religious frictions, it was a country with enormous economic potential, thanks to its rich coal mines and steelworks, and to a rising capitalist class dedicated to free trade, hard work, and the feverish accumulation of wealth. By the latter part of the nineteenth century, Belgium boasted some of western Europe's most important industrial enterprises. But none was more powerful than the one Édouard Empain would found.

Nothing predestined this man to become a captain of industry. Least of all his humble origins. His father, François-Julien Empain, the son and grandson of tailors, was a village schoolteacher who supplemented his meager income by playing the organ in church and the fiddle at local dances and weddings. His mother, Catherine Lolivier, descended from a family of brewers and barrel makers. The future baron was born on September 20, 1852, exactly nine months and two days after his devoutly Catholic parents exchanged vows. This fecund couple produced nine more children—eight girls and one additional boy—over the next nineteen years.

In the early 1860s, the Empain family moved from Belœil to the nearby village of Blicquy, where François was appointed schoolmaster under the patronage of the local mayor, a highborn notable named Alexis du Roy de Blicquy. For some reason, the mayor took a particular interest in the education of the family's eldest son, offering to pay for his studies at the Collège Épiscopal Saint-Augustin, a prestigious Catholic secondary school in the city of Enghien.

If young Édouard had in him the makings of a world-class mover and shaker, he gave no hint of that at Saint-Augustin. He was a mediocre student, bored and easily distracted—not exactly *le cancre*, the class dunce, but far from the top of the heap. Much to his chagrin, and that of his patron, his grades did not qualify him to pursue higher education. When he left the school in 1870 at age eighteen, Édouard Empain had no diploma, no practical training, and no clear career path. Though he would later have the title "engineer" printed on his business cards, there is no evidence that he ever undertook any formal studies in that demanding discipline. For the time being, he appeared to be a rudderless young man with few prospects for advancement.

That would change in 1873, when Blicquy got him an apprenticeship as a draftsman in a Brussels-based company, La Métallurgique, which specialized in the construction of rolling stock and bridges for the Belgian and French railroad networks. Empain had no more training in industrial drawing than he had as an engineer, but he rose through the ranks at a vertiginous pace, named successively to the posts of office manager, engineer in chief, and finally a member of the board of directors at age twenty-nine.

How does one account for his rocketlike trajectory? The benevolent patronage of Blicquy is only part of the explanation. In a company with a fluid hierarchy, where meritocracy trumped formal diplomas, Empain had a combination of charm, ambition, audacity, and a keen intelligence that belied his lackluster performance as a bored schoolboy. He could also be shrewd and calculating, unrestrained by excessive scruples when he saw a chance to seize an advantage. In sum, Empain had the same instincts—and the same fire in his belly—as America's famous robber barons. In addition, perhaps, to a Napoleon complex by which a man of modest stature is driven to prove that he can outsmart, outproduce, and outearn the ordinary giants who surround him.

Not the least of Empain's endowments was a keen eye for opportunity. While still working at La Métallurgique, he began acquiring shares in several stone quarries. It was a propitious moment to be selling marble: The Belgian king Leopold II, who would later become Empain's personal friend and patron, had recently launched a vast construction project aimed at modernizing and beautifying the capital with monumental public buildings made of the noble stone.

Windfall profits from the marble business provided the capital Empain used to fund a succession of more ambitious projects. First he created his own bank, La Banque E.L.J. Empain, then used it to finance new ventures in the fields of transportation and energy. His initial focus was on local transport—tramways and short-haul train lines to complement the trunk rail networks that were crisscrossing Europe. To help him run his nascent empire, he relied on his brother, François, six years his junior, and the husbands of four of his sisters. Though he also recruited professional managers, he always considered the Empain group a family affair—and it would remain that way through three generations, all the way down to Wado's time.

Empain was a visionary among a rising breed of capitalists who imagined new ways of harnessing technology and finance to industry through the creation of vast holding companies—Russian-doll structures comprising numerous interlocked entities. He was also one of the first to think in multinational terms, making investments and launching projects far beyond his national borders. His group would eventually create nearly a hundred companies in more than a dozen countries and territories, including Belgium, France, the Congo, Egypt, China, Russia, South America, Spain, Turkey, and Syria.

Central to Empain's method was the mounting of vertical structures by which his group controlled each level of activity from the generation of electric power to the laying of rails to the manufacture of locomotives and rolling stock. Wherever possible, he also sought long-term concessions to operate the lines he had financed and built. He advanced all the pieces of this fast-growing empire with the genius and foresight of a chess master.

The first nucleus of his industrial network was the Compagnie Générale des Railways à Voie Étroite (general company of narrow-gauge railways), founded in 1881. With Empain as the majority shareholder, it drew funding from a web of smaller investors and spawned a dozen new companies dealing with various aspects of the transport industry. The group built numerous tramway networks in Belgium, Holland, and France. Moving far afield from its western European base, the Compagnie Générale and its offshoots next pursued tramway projects in Russia, Tashkent, Uzbekistan, China, and Cairo, the beginning of a fascination with Egypt that would later loom large in Empain's fortunes and affections. Meanwhile, inspired by the recent development of electrified trolley lines in the United States, Empain created a network of electric power plants to provide the energy for his own trains and tramways and sold excess capacity to other Belgian industries.

As the end of the nineteenth century approached, the Empain group was a major player in the fields of transport, energy, finance, and civil engineering. But Empain was not a man to rest on his laurels. Ever eager for new worlds to conquer, like Alexander the Great, this irrepressible tycoon seized upon an affair that would multiply his already considerable fortune and cement his place in history: the building of the Paris Métro.

CHAPTER 8

The Birth of the Métro

They call it the Belle Époque. The years from 1890 until the outbreak of the First World War were marked by an exuberant faith in progress, an eager embrace of modernity, and a belief that science and technology would lead to a new era of universal prosperity and well-being. That optimistic worldview accompanied advances in the arts, industry, fashion, and architecture that would come to define the period. The Belle Époque zeitgeist touched other European capitals—Vienna and Berlin among them—but in the popular mind, its epicenter was Paris. Perhaps its most enduring symbol was the Eiffel Tower, that thousand-foot assemblage of bolts and steel beams that was built for the 1889 World's Fair and, though widely contested at the time, seemed to proclaim the credo of this new age: upward, ever upward!

In the last decade of the nineteenth century, Paris was a bubbling cauldron. France was coming out of a twenty-year depression that had begun with its humiliating defeat in the 1870–1871 Franco-Prussian War. The Paris stock market, La Bourse, was booming once again. Investments were flowing into new forms of machinery, energy, industry, and colonial development. Parisians thrilled to new inventions and innovations—the automobile, the telephone, the phonograph, and, not least, the cinema: the Lumière brothers held audiences spellbound with the first public showing of their moving pictures in 1895. In the arts, the Impressionists' delicate explorations of light and shadow gave rise to more modern styles, as Gauguin and Vlaminck celebrated the boldness of color and form and Cézanne's distortions paved the way for the cubists who would soon follow. In architecture, formal neoclassicism was challenged by the curves and vegetal intertwining of the Art Nouveau school. In music, Debussy, Satie, and Saint-Saëns were rewriting the rules of harmony and composition.

Social life, at least for the affluent bourgeoisie, was scintillating. Top-hatted swells with waxed mustaches dined at Maxim's, sipped aperitifs at the Café de la Paix, or attended racy reviews at the Folies Bergère and the Moulin Rouge with their plumed and perfumed mistresses at their sides. This was the city of Marcel Proust and Gustave Caillebotte, the painter whose depictions of rain-slick avenues and elegant bourgeois interiors stand as intimate portraits of late-nineteenth-century Paris.

But there was also the Paris of Émile Zola, whose popular novels portrayed a darker image of the era: the social injustice and political unrest that often threatened to erupt into insurrection—as it had in fact done with the bloody revolt of the Paris Commune of 1871. The 1890s were marked by repeated strikes and terrorist attacks, including the 1894 assassination of President Sadi Carnot, stabbed to death by an Italian anarchist after attending a banquet in Lyons. The notorious Dreyfus affair, in which a Jewish army officer was wrongly convicted of treason in 1894, unleashed a wave of anti-Semitism combined with a truculent nationalism that set the stage for the Great War.

There was another area where the Belle Époque's celebration of progress clashed with reality: Paris was saddled with a primitive transport system that was not up to the growing demands of the local population of 2.5 million and the increasing influx of visitors. Apart from walking, getting from place to place could be complicated. For hardy souls willing to brave the traffic and the cobblestones, there were bicycles, then called *vélocipèdes*, which France had been producing since the late 1860s. According to one estimate, there were some 165,000 bikes on the streets of Paris by 1900. Armand Peugeot and the Renault brothers started making gasoline-powered automobiles in the 1890s, but they remained a rarity on the streets of Paris and their speed was limited to a snail's pace of seven miles per hour. The fastest means of conveyance was the *bateaux-mouches* that plied the waters of the Seine, though their itinerary was limited to the contours of the river. There was an urban railroad, *la petite ceinture*, that circled the periphery of the city starting in 1854, but it was mainly utilized for freight and was of limited use to the majority of Parisians. The main type of urban transport was, literally, horse-power: horse-drawn omnibuses, tramways, wagons, cabs, and private carriages. (In 1900 there were some eighty thousand horses in the capital.) The prevalence of vehicles of all sorts on the city streets created monstrous traffic jams. Walled in by a ring of fortifications that cut it off from the surrounding suburbs, *les banlieues*, Paris was literally choking.

The problem was not new. Starting in the 1850s, Baron Georges-Eugène Haussmann, prefect of the Seine Department that comprised the French capital, had launched a radical program of urban development at the direction of Emperor Napoleon III. Haussmann totally redrew the map of Paris, ripping up the tortuous alleys and dark warrens of the medieval city, razing thousands of ancient buildings, and laying down a network of broad, straight avenues intended to provide light and air and, especially, to relieve the congestion of the Parisian streets. He also designed the handsome multistory stone apartment buildings that even today define the look of the capital's elegant thoroughfares. Though he created some thirty miles of new roadways, it was obvious by the 1890s that Haussmann's bold transformations were not enough to unclog a city whose population had quadrupled since the beginning of the century.

The problem had reached near-crisis proportions in 1889, when some 32 million visitors invaded the city during the Exposition Universelle, the world's fair that celebrated the centennial of the French Revolution. With an even bigger exposition scheduled for 1900, the city fathers began to debate the need for an underground transport network. Paris was in fact far behind other major cities in building a subway system. London's was inaugurated in 1863, followed by New York, 1868; Berlin, 1877; Chicago, 1892; and Budapest, 1896. Previous projects, going back to the 1850s, had been studied and aborted as Paris's municipal authorities clashed with the central government over the control and financing of an urban transport system. What finally broke the logjam was the imminence of the new Exposition Universelle, set to open on April 15, 1900. Faced with the prospect of paralyzing congestion, the central government finally relented and, in November 1895, accorded Paris the right to plan and build its own transport network on condition that the city finance the operation.

Over the years, there had been numerous proposals—some serious, others frankly wacky. One called for a roller-coaster approach that would use gravity to propel trains through the tunnels on inclined tracks. Another imagined pneumatic train cars propelled through underground tubes by compressed air. Still another suggested a fleet of gondolas suspended from cables attached to metal pylons. A certain J. Chrétien proposed to crisscross the city with an elevated electric railway whose hub would have destroyed the Place de l'Opéra. Yet another idea would have run an elevated rail line through passages carved out of existing buildings.

Once the municipal council got its green light from the central government, there were heated internal debates over what a Parisian subway system should look like, focusing on far less fanciful ideas. Some of the council members wanted a network that would accommodate mainline trains, allowing for freight shipments and troop movements through the capital in case of war. Others called for narrow-gauge tracks and cars, effectively isolating the subway from the national railroad network. Then there were those who were fiercely opposed to any kind of underground system. They argued, for example, that the excavations would disrupt and disfigure the city; that digging into the Parisian substratum would stir up sewage and microbes, unleashing murderous epidemics; that thousands would die of pneumonia after descending into the cold, humid tunnels. One particularly hostile council member told his colleagues that "the Métro is anti-national, anti-municipal, anti-patriotic and damaging to the glory of Paris!"

The council's pro-Métro majority was led by André Berthelot, head of the commission appointed to study the question. The son of a brilliant chemist, Berthelot was one of the most impressive men of his generation, with doctorates in history and geography and a solid grounding in urbanism. Unfortunately for the Métro's detractors, Berthelot was also a persuasive orator. On April 17, 1896, he stood before the council and issued an eloquent appeal, refuting the arguments of the Métro-skeptics and stressing the urgent need to combat "the dramatic choking of urban life"—especially with a world's fair looming on the horizon. In this and subsequent debates, he argued forcefully for a narrow-gauge system, lighter and cheaper to build and operate, that would guarantee the city's autonomy in the face of the state and the big railroad interests. Not least important, Berthelot maintained that the system should be operated by a private concessionaire, since French law forbade municipalities to engage in commercial activities.

Waiting in the wings was Édouard Empain, well experienced in the building of tramway and train networks, who had long seen the Paris Métro project as a juicy affair for his industrial group. The plucky little Belgian had already zeroed in on Berthelot as the key man on the municipal council and had managed to make his acquaintance. Though Empain was a conservative Catholic and Berthelot a left-leaning freethinker, the two men immediately hit it off. Whatever their philosophical differences, they could agree on the faith in progress, technology, and industry that infused the end-of-century spirit—and the Paris Métro was one of its most exciting manifestations. Not to mention a phenomenally lucrative operation for the company that would win the concession.

But first, the council had to develop a specific plan for the future network. For that they turned to Fulgence Bienvenüe, an engineer who specialized in railroad and urban transport matters. Born in Brittany in 1852, the same year as Empain, Bienvenüe had been a brilliant student with a passion for philosophy and classical literature and a penchant for quoting Latin and Greek verse. No less fascinated by science and technology, he was admitted in 1870 into the École Polytechnique, France's elite military engineering academy, and went on to the prestigious École Nationale des Ponts et Chaussées to study civil engineering.

Bienvenüe had started his career building railroad lines in his native Brittany. In 1881, a rail accident cost him his left arm, amputated at the shoulder after being crushed by a train car. He thereafter wore suits with an empty sleeve hanging at his side, remarking stoically that his arm had been "expropriated." Moving to Paris in 1884, he joined the municipal department of public works, overseeing the construction of the Avenue de la République, a major traffic axis in northeast Paris, as well as building an ingenious funicular tramway and designing the layout of the famous Buttes-Chaumont Park. In 1896, the municipal council created a Service du Métropolitain—the name was borrowed from London's Metropolitan Railway—and put Bienvenüe in charge. His task was to draw up a preliminary plan for the subway network and, once it was approved, oversee its construction.

Bienvenüe was forty-four years old when he embarked on what would turn out to be a lifelong mission. In accordance with the council's specifications, he laid out six initial lines covering forty miles of track. The first line, literally the backbone of the system, was the 6.4-mile stretch between the Porte de Vincennes in the east and the Porte Maillot in the west, following a more or less straight line running under the Rue Saint-Antoine, the Rue de Rivoli, and the Champs-Élysées. Line 2, a semicircular northern route, would go from the Porte Dauphine to the Place de la Nation, paralleling the fortifications that surrounded the city. It would be mirrored by a semicircle passing to the south (currently Line 6) that would link the Place de l'Étoile with the Place d'Italie. The future Line 4 traced a north–south trajectory from the Porte de Clignancourt to the Porte d'Orléans. These main axes were later to be linked by supplemental lines so as to meet the requirement that no point within the city's boundaries would be more than five hundred meters distant from a Métro station. In order to limit the expropriations of private property, the network would run largely under the broad avenues traced by Baron Haussmann nearly a half century earlier. Most of the system would be underground, including a technically challenging passage beneath the Seine, though the plan also called for elevated sections and two rail bridges over the river. As for the engines, since steam trains posed the problem of evacuating smoke and fumes from the tunnels, Bienvenüe opted for an innovative electrical power system using a third rail, a technique borrowed from the Americans.

Under Bienvenüe's supervision, the city would be responsible for building and financing the infrastructure: digging the tunnels, constructing the bridges and elevated spans, and restoring the streets torn up by excavations. The future concessionaire would have the responsibility of laying down the rails and electrical grid, providing the rolling stock, and building the stations—including the entrances that would be the visible manifestation of the Métro at street level. Financing this part of the work, estimated at one-third of the system's total cost, was up to the concessionaire, who would then operate the Métro for an initial period of thirty-five years. Despite the substantial investment, the operating company stood to rake in handsome profits from ticket sales minus a commission to the city of 5 centimes per passenger, or one-third of the cost of a second-class ticket.

In March 1897, a technical commission headed by Bienvenüe began to examine six candidates for the concession. Two received serious consideration, but Empain's Compagnie Générale was the overwhelming choice when the council voted on January 27, 1898. A law of March 30, 1898, formally approved Bienvenüe's plan for a six-line Métro network and granted the concession to Empain's company. There was one hitch, however: The council required that all board members and employees of the concessionaire must be French nationals. Empain got around that by launching a new company, La Compagnie du Chemin de Fer Métropolitain de Paris (CMP), and appointing a board of French straw men, although as the majority shareholder, controlling some 80 percent of the stock, Empain remained the company's de facto head. Founded in April 1898, the

CMP set up its offices on the Avenue de l'Opéra, one of Paris's most elegant thoroughfares.

Once the Métro project won final legal approval, its builders were engaged in a formidable race against time: Only two years remained before the world's fair was scheduled to open its doors on April 15, 1900. That was the target date for the completion of Line 1. It was a tiny window for such a prodigious undertaking, but Bienvenüe and Empain eagerly embraced the challenge.

CHAPTER 9

The Big Dig

*E*arly on the morning of August 4, 1898, work began at four different locations along the main east–west line that would be the first to open. More than two thousand workers armed with shovels, pickaxes, and wheelbarrows began the job of ripping up streets and removing some 1,000 cubic meters of earth each day. The digging went on round the clock with the teams working in shifts.

Wherever possible, Bienvenüe had opted for the "cut-and-cover" method of excavation, digging trenches along the major avenues, building the tunnel framework in the open air, then covering it with a metal ceiling and restoring the roadbed. This was the quickest and cheapest method, the one with the best chance of getting the job done in time for the world's fair. Where cut-and-cover was not feasible, tunnels had to be bored starting with a vertical shaft and proceeding horizontally using shovels, pickaxes, and specialized digging machines known as *boucliers*. The interior of each tunnel section was consolidated with wooden formworks and covered with concrete.

On paper these techniques looked straightforward, but there were complications. The Parisian substratum, unlike London's, was not homogeneous but an unstable mix of sand, clay, and crumbly sedimentary rock. Seepage from the water table was a major problem, as was the presence of abandoned underground quarries and the need to reroute major sewerage, water, and electric lines. Occasionally, work was slowed when the tunnel men stumbled upon fossils and artifacts—mammoth tusks, rhinoceros vertebrae, funerary statuary—that had to be carefully removed and preserved.

Some parts of the network presented special challenges. To facilitate the tunneling under the Place de la Bastille, where three lines were destined to meet, the Saint-Martin Canal was drained for fifty days and its bed covered with concrete to prevent leakage. Though the passage under the Seine would not begin until a later phase of the work, it was an especially complicated problem for which Bienvenüe devised an ingenious solution: the tunnel frameworks were built on land, then loaded onto barges and sunk into the riverbed. The earth under the Place Saint-Michel, located near the river's edge, was so waterlogged that it had to be frozen chemically and dug out with pickaxes. Then there were the special cases: The eminent members of the Académie Française, fearing that vibrations would disturb their important work on the national dictionary, prevailed upon the authorities to forbid tunneling beneath their building. As a result, Bienvenüe had to redraw the route, adding considerably to the time and cost of the project. Not least among the complications were the inevitable accidents, including a cave-in under the Place de l'Étoile that injured two workers and a separate incident that left five tunnelers dead and sparked a protest strike.

As the digging progressed, scores of Parisians gathered around the yawning excavations and, being Parisians, loudly voiced their opinions. Not since the days of Baron Haussmann had the city seen such a massive and disruptive undertaking. Traffic had to be rerouted through narrow side streets as main axes—including the colonnaded Rue de Rivoli and the broad expanse of the Champs-Élysées—were turned into muddy trenches filled with workmen in loose vests and baggy trousers, cigarettes dangling from their lips, wallowing through the mire, filling the air with Gallic shouts and the sound of clanging metal. As poet Jules Romains described the scene: "The Métro worksites, which appeared like fortresses of clay and wooden planks, armed with an artillery of cranes, finished by choking the streets and blocking the intersections. Meanwhile, the boring of the tunnels that crisscrossed the earth in every direction threatened Paris with collapse."

Among the worksite observers, of course, was Édouard Empain. Though the Belgian's part of the project had to wait until the tunnel work advanced, he went everywhere, saw everything, and did not hesitate to give his advice on every aspect of the construction. Bienvenüe, superbly trained engineer that he was, listened patiently to the opinions of this autodidact industrialist whose experience in the transport business was well worth a diploma.

Empain's keen interest is understandable: Not only was he a cocreator of this magnificent underground railroad, but he would also run it—virtually own it—once it was open for business. In addition to sating his own curiosity, Empain's frequent worksite visits enabled him to keep his friend Leopold II informed about every stage of the Métro's progress. The Belgian king had long dreamed of building a subway in Brussels and hoped Empain's experience in Paris could serve as a model. Leopold also had a more direct interest in the project: Empain had given him a large number of shares in his company. (His generosity would later be reciprocated when the king offered him lucrative interests in the Congo.)

. . .

ONE OF THE CMP's most important decisions concerned the design of the station entrances, destined to be the public showcase for the whole Métro network. In June 1899, the company invited architects to submit proposals to a competition before a specially appointed jury. The winners had designed an ensemble of metallic structures that an irreverent press compared to news kiosks, tombs, or even Paris's famous *pissotières*, the semi-enclosed men's urinals placed on many of the city's sidewalks. The CMP, judging the approach too conventional, rejected the projects and instead appointed one of its own architects to come up with a synthesis of the best designs. Empain's company was stunned when the Paris prefecture rejected its proposal and called for something "more satisfactory from an aesthetic point of view." The situation was becoming desperate, as the clock was ticking and the CMP feared that the entrances might not be completed in time for the world's fair opening.

It was at that point that the company turned to a rising star among French architects, Hector Guimard, age thirty-one, a leading exponent of the Art Nouveau style that was much in vogue in the early years of the Belle Époque. It is said that Empain, enamored of the Art Nouveau school, which had its origins in Brussels, personally pushed for this choice, which the municipal council and the prefecture hastily approved on January 12, 1900. It was a consequential decision, for Hector Guimard's graceful designs would become iconic emblems not only of the Métro but also of the French capital itself. And Guimard, who had not even thought to enter the competition, would owe his place in architectural history largely to his work on the Paris Métro.

Pressed for time, Guimard came up with a method that allowed him to quickly mass-produce the main elements of his entrances in cast iron. Since the same set of molds could be used over and over again by the foundry, there was theoretically no limit to the number of pieces that could be made. They could then be assembled in modular form according to the same basic designs.

The most common type of entrance featured a cast-iron balustrade linking a series of escutcheons bearing a stylized letter *M*. Two tall tuliplike lampposts tipped by red light globes framed the opening to the stairwell. Their tendrils came together to hold a plaque bearing the word "Métropolitain" using a fanciful calligraphy designed by Guimard himself. These entrances, called *entourages*, or barriers, were intentionally made light and airy, so as not to intrude on the Parisian landscape. Other designs, known as *édicules*, were more substantial, featuring lava-stone side panels and translucent glass roofs with fanlike marquees to protect voyagers from the rain. Two entrances planned for Line 1 were even more imposing: a large pagodalike pavilion at the Place de la Bastille and a similar structure at the Place de l'Étoile.

But the public would have to wait to see Guimard's entrances. At the time he was recruited, the tunnel construction and station-building still continued at a breakneck pace. While Bienvenüe and Empain exhorted their respective teams to work harder and faster, Guimard's founders were pouring the cast-iron bits and pieces that he would assemble around the completed stations. Both artistically and professionally, the stakes could not have been higher for the young architect. He knew that his idiosyncratic creations would be the first thing people would see when the Métro finally opened. Would they be embraced or vilified by the fickle Parisian public? Only time would tell.

CHAPTER 10

Opening Day

On April 14, 1900, Fulgence Bienvenüe awoke, as usual, at six a.m.—a habit since his boarding-school days. Through his bedroom window, he could see a light drizzle falling on the street outside. His housekeeper brought him his modest breakfast and a selection of newspapers whose headlines touted the big event that would take place later that morning: the official opening of the Paris Exposition. The papers also announced a strike by the coachmen who drove the city's horse-drawn cabs. That was sure to complicate things for the several thousand dignitaries who had been invited to attend the ceremony at the foot of the Eiffel Tower—but would also underscore the utility of the future Métro, which was not quite ready to open its doors. Fortunately for Bienvenüe, he had a private carriage at his disposal.

Neither did Édouard Empain have any worries about his personal transportation: The Belgian millionaire enjoyed the use of a chauffeur-driven motorcar. Like Bienvenüe, he worried that the drizzle might turn into a harder rain and drench the outdoor ceremony. Inveterate optimist that he was, he swept his doubts aside and proceeded to don the silk top hat and black cutaway coat that were de rigueur at an event that would be attended by distinguished guests from around the world. Empain's friend Leopold II was among those invited, but the king chose to visit the fair incognito at a later date under his usual alias, Comte de Ravenstein.

Arriving separately at the fairgrounds, Empain and Bienvenüe joined the large crowd that converged on the Champ de Mars and gathered around the large flag-draped stage that had been set up on that immense grassy field. The ground was muddy, but the drizzle had stopped and a glimmer of sunlight was poking through the low-hanging cloud cover. At precisely 11:00 a.m., French president Émile Loubet mounted the steps, flanked by a double row of Garde Républicaine troops in their gleaming brass helmets topped with red plumes. At the end of a largely unmemorable speech hailing the event as "an important step in the evolution of labor towards happiness and man towards humanity," Loubet proclaimed the official opening of the Exposition Universelle de Paris. The crowd cheered as a military band struck up "La Marseillaise."

The long-awaited event had been eight years in the making, covered 267 acres of land, cost 119 million francs (equivalent to nearly $580 million today), and hosted some eighty thousand exhibitors from forty different countries. By the time it closed seven months later, more than 51 million visitors would pass through its grand entrance, La Porte Monumentale, a 115-foot-high domed structure flanked by minarets and topped by a gigantic female figure representing the city of Paris.

In fact, everything about this manifestation was gigantic. It was the biggest and most spectacular of the series of world's fairs that had begun at London's Crystal Palace in 1851. More than a half dozen other cities—including Vienna, Brussels, Milan, Philadelphia, New York, and Chicago—had since held similar events. But none had done them as often or as grandly as Paris, which was on its fifth exposition since 1855. The previous one, in 1889, had given the capital its most visible and enduring symbol, the Eiffel Tower. The 1900 gathering was even more ambitious: Its aim was to celebrate the technological, scientific, industrial, and artistic advances of the nineteenth century and usher in a new era of progress and well-being. Most of all, in the midst of the bitterly divisive Dreyfus affair, anarchist bombings, and a wave of crippling strikes, the Paris Exposition was intended to unify the country around a symbol of national prestige and provide a dazzling international showcase for the values of the Republic.

As Loubet led a group of dignitaries on a tour of the fair, which would not open to the public until the following day, he was somewhat embarrassed by the fact that a number of the exhibits were not quite finished. The air reverberated with the sounds of hammering and sawing as workers raced to put the final touches on some of the pavilions that lined both banks of the Seine. When the delegation trooped through the glass-domed Grand Palais, the neoclassical museum and exhibit hall that was built for the exposition, they were greeted by exposed plaster, paint buckets, and canvas tarps that hid unfinished sections.

No matter. The eight-hundred-thousand-square-foot Grand Palais and its smaller neighbor, the Petit Palais, were impressive edifices that had been constructed in an astounding thirty-six months and would remain major showcases of French art and culture. They are still standing today, along with the ornate Pont Alexandre III, built to celebrate the Franco–Russian alliance and inaugurated as part of the exposition. Spanning the Seine with a single 360-foot arch, adorned with four columns topped with gilded statues of winged horses, it was hailed by *Scientific American* as one of the most beautiful bridges in the world.

These structures were part of the permanent architectural legacy inherited from the 1900 exposition. But to the millions of visitors who flocked to the Paris fair, the ephemeral exhibits were no less impressive. Among the most popular was the Grande Roue, inspired by the famous Ferris wheel unveiled at the 1893 World's Columbian Exposition in Chicago. With its 328-foot diameter and forty cars, it could accommodate 1,600 riders at a time. From its summit, visitors could survey the fair's entire perimeter, stretching three-quarters of a mile along both banks of the Seine from the foot of the Eiffel Tower to the Pont Alexandre III.

The event offered a stunning array of innovations and amusements. To speed visitors from place to place, an electric-powered moving sidewalk made a two-mile circuit through the fairgrounds in tandem with an elevated electric train moving in the opposite direction. There were no fewer than seventeen cinema sites, where the Lumière brothers delighted spectators with their collection of short films. Among them: *The Sea*, *The Gardener*, and their most famous early work, *Train Arriving at La Ciotat Station*, which gave viewers the chilling impression that they were about to be run over by a locomotive.

Alongside the exotic pavilions of the participating countries, there was a pseudohistorical re-creation of medieval Paris, complete with costumed extras, that foreshadowed the pop nostalgia of modern theme parks. Of course there was no shortage of taverns, cafés, and restaurants, not to mention theaters, cabarets, and concert halls. One of the most popular attractions was the American dancer and choreographer Loïe Fuller, a star of the Folies Bergère, who performed her famous silk-winged "serpentine dance" to packed houses and would later teach it to her fellow American Isadora Duncan.

Without a doubt, the most spectacular venue was the Palais de l'Électricité. Seen from the outside, it was a temple-like metal-and-glass structure, 1,400 feet long and 230 feet high, with elaborate arches and colonnades that one journalist compared to the Arabian Nights. Over the summit reigned a twenty-foot-tall statue of the "Fée électricité"—the electric fairy—a goddesslike figure flanked by mythical creatures, her head surrounded by a scintillating glass halo representing rays of light. A 130-foot-high cascade gushed from the building's façade, feeding a fountain that sent jets of colored water towering into the sky. The whole structure was illuminated at night by thousands of electric lamps.

The interior featured an assortment of electric devices—wireless telegraphs, telephones, X-ray machines—but the real nerve center was the ground-floor power station: thirty-five steam-driven dynamos working day and night to produce electricity for the entire exposition—including the Ferris wheel, the electric train and sidewalk, the machines on display in the various pavilions, and, of course, the nighttime illumination that bathed the whole ensemble with a magical glow and gave Paris its enduring nickname, the "City of Light." Among the admirers of the Fée électricité was Édouard Empain. Though there is no precise record of his visit, it is unthinkable that the future-oriented industrialist did not make a pilgrimage to this shrine of electric energy, which would soon become one of his group's central activities—not to mention the power source of the Paris Métro.

EMPAIN, LIKE BIENVENÜE, was impatient to see their new subway open its doors to the public. Though the event was supposed to coincide with the inauguration of the exposition, the builders missed that mark by three months due to various technical complications—including cave-ins, accidents, and strikes. Strange as it seems, given all the attention the Métro had attracted during its three years of highly visible construction, there was no formal ceremony to mark its opening on July 19. President Loubet was attending a naval review in Cherbourg that day, and apparently no city officials saw fit to stand for him—perhaps choosing to treat the occasion with discretion because it was three months behind schedule. Nor were any large crowds of Parisians huddled around the entrances eagerly awaiting the one p.m. opening of the gates. The weather that day, a sweltering 96 degrees Fahrenheit, hardly encouraged a large outdoor celebration.

The first hardy souls to venture down the steps of the Porte Maillot terminal on the western end of Paris must have been surprised by what they discovered. For years, critics had warned that a descent into the murky subterranean depths would expose voyagers to microbes, disease, muggers, and all manner of danger. But far from menacing, the stations turned out to be reasonably well lit, their walls covered by hygienic-looking white tiles, their gray-uniformed personnel welcoming and reassuring. At the bottom of the stairs, voyagers were greeted by wooden ticket booths, where they were offered a choice of first-class passage for 25 centimes or second-class for 15 centimes. A few stations also boasted well-stocked newsstands.

Tickets in hand, voyagers descended another set of stairs to the concrete platforms that lined the tracks. At that level, the air was agreeably cool, despite the strong odor of creosote and fresh paint—to be joined in time by the acrid smell of tobacco smoke and unwashed bodies. On that first day, at least, the platforms were spic and span, the walls gleaming white, even though the lighting from the overhead 15-watt bulbs left something to be desired. In the beginning, there were no seats or benches on the platforms. Nor were there any publicity posters, though the frames had been prepared and colorful ads would soon be touting the merits of everything from aperitifs and chocolates to cabarets and department stores—another source of income for Empain's CMP.

The three-car trains clattered into the stations every ten minutes, each pulled by a motorized cabin, or *motrice*, powered by a 600-volt third rail. The narrow cars were made of wood with elegant interiors. First-class seats were cushioned and covered in red leather. Second-class seats were made of varnished oak slats comfortably contoured to the body. A uniformed employee was stationed in each car to open and close the doors.

Only eight of the line's eighteen stations opened on July 19; the others would open progressively over the following two months. But even on that first day, Métro riders could go from one end of Paris to the other in a mere thirty minutes—compared with an hour or more by carriage or omnibus. From their windows, they could read the names of the stations telling them what piece of Paris real estate they were rolling under: Vincennes, Nation, Gare de Lyon, Bastille, Hôtel de Ville, Palais-Royal, Champs-Élysées, Porte Maillot.

The speed, convenience, and technical prowess of it all must have been breathtaking for those first customers. "Along with the extraordinary coolness that greeted the curious voyagers as they entered the platform," reported the daily *Le Figaro*, "there was a veritable sense of admiration for the colossal work of Bienvenüe and Maréchal." Empain didn't get the credit, of course: Though he was the principal shareholder, financier, and éminence grise behind the CMP, it was the company's director and chief engineer, Henri Maréchal, who was best known to the public—in part because he had also built the electric train and moving sidewalk that delighted visitors to the Paris Exposition.

What about Hector Guimard's Art Nouveau entrances that were supposed to give the Métro its cachet? When Line 1 opened, only the balustrades had been completed on most of the stations—not surprising, since his commission had only come through five months earlier. The public would have to wait another year to see the fully finished versions, but opinions were mixed from the start. The initial articles in the press were generally favorable—one magazine praised Guimard's creations as "a brilliant departure by a true artist with a superior sense of the harmonious line." Later, when the final touches had been added, they started to meet with scathing criticism. Some patriotic souls claimed that the dark-green color of the cast iron was reminiscent of German military uniforms. Other naysayers complained that the unconventional calligraphy of the signs—blasted by *Le Temps* as "disordered hieroglyphics"—would make it hard for children to learn to read. One disgruntled journalist compared the vegetal lamp posts to "fragments of an ichthyosaur skeleton." Another denounced the "contorted ramps, and hunchbacked candelabra [with their] enormous frog eyes." Still another found the entrances "tortuous, with unhealthy lines and colors dredged up from the depths of the Apocalypse!" In the eyes of at least a part of the press, it seems that Guimard was a prophet without honor. Over time, though, the brilliance of his creations transcended the barbs of these contemporary critics. Of Guimard's 167 original Métro entrances, 86 are still standing. They are classified as national historic monuments and considered, as one urban historian has put it, "works of art and symbols of Paris."

ONCE THE MÉTRO was up and running, it proved to be a stunning success. Between July and December 1900, some 17 million people climbed on board. In 1901, the first full year of operation, the number swelled to 48 million and would continue to rise vertiginously. Public enthusiasm was momentarily chilled by a deadly fire that left eighty-four dead on the platform of the Couronnes station in August 1903, but fears about underground transit dissipated relatively soon. Parisians of all stripes, particularly the working population, had become dependent on the Métro in their daily lives. Within a short time, they were flocking back to the ticket booths in record numbers: 117 million in 1904, 149 million in 1905, 254 million in 1909. Meanwhile, the network continued to expand, undeterred even by the outbreak of World War I. By July 1916, all of the original six lines were up and running, comprising some fifty miles of track serving seventy-one stations. By the end of the Great War, the annual number of voyagers had reached 485 million.

For Édouard Empain and his company, the Métro was an excellent business: For every ticket sold at the outset, the CMP pocketed between 10 and 20 centimes. As the annual frequentation soared into the hundreds of millions, Empain's cash registers were smoking. By 1906, the company's annual profits were topping 50 million francs, the equivalent of $242 million today. The CMP was by far the biggest moneymaker in his constellation. Indeed, it was the profits from the Paris Métro that provided the main financing for all his future endeavors and formed the bedrock of the vast industrial dynasty that his grandson would one day inherit. No Métro, no Wado—and no kidnapping.

CHAPTER 11

In Leopold's Heart of Darkness

The first Baron Empain was ennobled by his friend Leopold II on April 18, 1907. The letter of patent calls the act "a public testimony of Our high esteem for Édouard-Louis-Joseph Empain" and makes the title transmissible from male heir to male heir by order of primogeniture. The monarch also granted the freshly minted baron a resplendent coat of arms consisting of a green shield topped by a jewel-studded crown, flanked by a golden lion and griffin, and bearing the motto "Labore"—"by labor" in Latin. A disembodied hand hovering over the crest clutches three lightning bolts, symbolizing the electric force that Empain had so successfully harnessed through the generating plants he had built in Belgium and France—including the one that powered the Métro. It was a grand piece of heraldry for the son of a humble schoolteacher, but it symbolized the high value Leopold placed on industry and wealth-building in this golden age of Belgian capitalism. Granting a title of nobility, which in fact cost the king nothing, was also a way to secure Empain's continuing support and thank him for services rendered.

Empain played his new role to the hilt. Shortly after obtaining his title, he purchased a magnificent home on Paris's Rue de Lisbonne, overlooking the Parc Monceau, and installed the group's headquarters in an adjoining building. Yielding nothing to modesty, he had his initials and coat of arms engraved on the façade and the sculpted oak door of his new residence. He even designed his own furniture, massive wooden hulks emblazoned with the family crest that his grandson would later deem "rather ugly." Three years earlier he had purchased the Château de Bouffémont, a mid-nineteenth-century edifice surrounded by 620 acres of forests and farmland some ten miles north of Paris. Apparently finding the brick and stone architecture too plain, he adorned the northern front with a grand double staircase and applied multiple bas-reliefs of his coat of arms to the exterior. The Bouffémont estate would remain a family fiefdom through three generations.

EMPAIN OWED HIS title in no small measure to the support he gave to Leopold's adventures in the Congo Free State, a 90-million-square-mile swath of central Africa that was neither free nor a state, nor even a Belgian colony, but rather the personal property of the king. Leopold had secured control over that vast territory, its inhabitants, and its natural resources in one of history's boldest and most cynical land grabs.

Even before ascending to the throne in 1865, young Prince Leopold had been fascinated by geography and exploration. As king, he chafed at the smallness of his country and the limited ambitions of its inhabitants. *"Petit pays, petites gens"* was the way he put it—little country, little people. Casting a jealous eye at the overseas dominions of his neighbors France and Holland, not to mention the globe-spanning British Empire ruled over by his first cousin Queen Victoria, he decided early on that his officially neutral country had to expand its power and wealth by acquiring a colony. He sought opportunities in Southeast Asia and South America, tried unsuccessfully to buy Fiji and the Philippines, and finally looked to the vast, uncharted expanse of central Africa as his promised land.

In September 1876, he invited a handpicked assembly of forty academics, diplomats, and explorers to a geographical conference in Brussels to discuss ways to "pierce the darkness" and develop the African interior. His stated aims were altruistic and philanthropic—civilize and Christianize the natives, establish scientific missions, explore the Congo River basin, and especially end the Arab slave trade in the region. Portraying himself as the disinterested monarch of a small neutral power, he denied any territorial designs for Belgium. At the end of the weeklong conference, the attendees voted to form a vaguely defined International African Association with Leopold as its president.

In November 1877, the king's eye fell on a newspaper article in Britain's *Daily Telegraph* recounting Henry Morton Stanley's dramatic seven-thousand-mile east–west trek across equatorial Africa. Stanley, a swashbuckling Welsh-born American, had already won fame by tracking down the Scottish missionary-explorer David Livingstone on the shores of Lake Tanganyika in 1871 and writing breathless articles about his exploit for the *New York Herald* (later turned into a bestselling book). Seeing Stanley as the ideal agent for his interests in Africa, Leopold offered him a job with his renamed International Association of the Congo. After initial hesitations, Stanley finally agreed to meet the king in Brussels in November 1878 to discuss his proposal. Leopold hid his real design, describing it vaguely as a "job of exploration." But Stanley quickly realized the king's real aim. "So now," he wrote in his diary, "I am engaged by a foreign people to try to obtain the Congo for them. So be it!"

Stanley's assignment was to build roads and stations along the Congo River and, more important, to seize control of the land through a series of treaties with local tribes. In exchange for bolts of cloth, trinkets, and bottles of gin, more than 450 illiterate chieftains granted Leopold's cutout association absolute sovereignty over their territories. The legally questionable documents, most of them signed with an "X," also required the tribes to provide manpower in support of the association's development projects. In effect, Stanley's treaties stripped the local populations of their land and converted them into conscript laborers. The treaties also established what was, on paper, a confederation of fictitious mini-states under the benevolent protection of a charitable society.

It now remained to obtain diplomatic recognition for this strange entity. Circumventing Europe's rival colonial powers, Leopold set his sights first on the United States. The king shrewdly enlisted the lobbying efforts of Gen. Henry Shelton Sanford, a personal friend and a former U.S. ambassador to Belgium. Well connected in Washington, Sanford played on the antislavery sentiments of the Republican administration to win support for Leopold's supposedly humanitarian enterprise. In April 1884, Congress officially recognized Leopold's association and its newly concocted banner, a single yellow star on a blue field, as "the flag of a friendly government." France and Germany soon followed suit in exchange for guarantees that the Congo would be open to free trade. In February 1885, an international conference in Berlin recognized Leopold as the sovereign and proprietor of what would soon be named the Congo Free State. With that, the Belgian king became the owner of a territory bigger than England, France,

Germany, Italy, and Spain combined. The Belgian government had no stake or say in the matter.

Now that he was the undisputed master of the Congo, Leopold continued to claim that philanthropy and science were at the heart of his project. "Only scientific explorations are intended," he assured one journalist. In fact, his true interest in the Congo was to extract as much money from it as possible. His first profit source was ivory, collected by the thousands of tons and hauled overland to trading posts along the Congo River. But the river was navigable only as far as Stanley Pool, near the settlement that Stanley called Léopoldville (now Kinshasa). The main method of transport, on the backs of native porters, was painstakingly slow. As Stanley pointed out to his employer, "Without railroads, the Congo is not worth a penny."

The king agreed and launched the construction of a 250-mile link from the western port of Matadi to Léopoldville, paid for largely out of his personal funds. But the project wound up costing three times the budgeted amount and the king was reduced to begging his own parliament for a 25-million-franc loan. By the time the Matadi–Léopoldville railroad was finished in 1898, Leopold had no money left to build the much longer line to the territory's eastern frontier in the Great Lakes region. That's when he called on his friend Édouard Empain, whose vast wealth and expertise in railroad building cast him in the guise of a potential savior.

In December 1901, Empain launched the Compagnie des Chemins de Fer du Congo Supérieur aux Grands Lacs Africains (CFL), raising an initial 25 million francs in capital on the Brussels and Paris stock markets. In reality, most of the shares were bought up by Empain and his family or companies controlled by the Empain group. The titular presidency of the CFL was held by a figurehead representative of the king. But Édouard Empain, as vice president, actually ran the company and called the shots.

The January 1902 agreement with the Congo Free State was exceptionally generous to Empain's company. The CFL was contracted to build two railroad lines, one going from Stanleyville (currently Kisangani) to Lake Albert in the east, the other running farther south to Lake Tanganyika. In exchange, the company received a concession to operate the railroad for ninety-nine years, plus nearly 10 million acres of land. The grant included not only the terrain needed for the railroad tracks and installations but also forestry and mineral rights across a vast expanse of territory. It turned out that the company's lands contained deposits of gold, copper, silver, platinum, tin, and sapphires. Over the years, Empain created several mining subsidiaries from which he reaped extraordinary profits—not to mention the substantial revenues from his plantations, factories, and real estate interests in the so-called Free State. According to one estimate, his activities in the Congo multiplied his fortune by a factor of ten. Like the Paris Métro, the Congo was a perennial cash cow—though one fraught with the moral complexities of colonial exploitation.

EMPAIN'S FRIENDSHIP WITH Leopold actually began long before his Métro adventure. It is not clear how and when the two men first met, but it appeared to be love at first sight. Leopold, seventeen years the elder and a monarch to boot, was something of a father figure to Empain—"my old master" he called him. Empain, a phenomenally successful industrialist and deep-pocketed enough to finance Leopold's projects, became a favorite adviser to the king.

Seen together, they were a Mutt-and-Jeff odd couple: The gangling six-foot-three monarch, with his unruly thatch of a beard and his enormous hatchet-blade nose, towered over the diminutive tycoon like a buzzard over a lark. One had inherited a kingdom and a fortune, the other had pulled himself up by the bootstraps. But the two men shared a reverence for wealth and a single-minded ruthlessness in pursuit of it. As Empain put it, "Whoever doesn't know how to kill doesn't know how to live." The baron's words were metaphorical, but they turned all too literal during Leopold's rule over the Congo.

From the outset, but particularly after the beginning of the fabulously lucrative rubber trade in the early 1890s, Leopold's agents—backed by his brutal Force Publique security service—imposed a reign of terror on the Congolese. Forced to labor as porters, ivory gatherers, rubber tappers, and railroad builders, the natives were reduced to the level of virtual slaves under the pretext of working off their "taxes." Village women and children were taken hostage to force the men to join the labor corps. Recalcitrant natives were whipped, shot, and mutilated—the accounts of severed hands and even heads were legendary. "To gather rubber in the district," wrote one Congo agent, "one must cut off hands, noses, and ears."

Through his fictional Captain Marlow, Joseph Conrad described a group of Congolese conscripted to work on the initial railroad project: "I could see every rib, the joints of their limbs were like knots in a rope, each had an iron collar on his neck and all were connected together with a chain whose bights swung between them, rhythmically clinking." The atrocities recounted in Conrad's *Heart of Darkness*, based on his own experience as a Congo steamboat captain, were rooted in reality. His fictional Kurtz's dying words famously summed up the situation: "The horror! The horror!"

The horrors that reigned in Leopold's Congo were eventually denounced by missionaries and other travelers and found their way into the European press. The complaints reached such a crescendo that in 1903 the British Foreign Office ordered its longtime consul in the Congo, Roger Casement, to investigate the allegations. Published the following year, Casement's shockingly graphic report called Leopold's regime in the Congo "one of the more infamous international scandals of the turn of the century." It was followed by a blistering book from another Briton, Edmund Morel, who launched the Congo Reform Society to campaign against the abuses. Leopold responded to his mostly British accusers with indignant denial and chalked up the criticisms to jealousy on the part of a perfidious colonial rival. To be fair, the king had never set foot in the Congo and did not personally order the atrocities to which he apparently turned a blind eye. In an attempt to refute his critics, he finally appointed his own commission of inquiry. He was stunned when their 150-page report essentially confirmed the criticisms of Casement and Morel.

That was the last straw. Faced with a torrent of international criticism, Leopold agreed in 1908 to turn over his Congo Free State to the Belgian government. It was quite a prize: By that time the Congo had become the most profitable colony in all Africa, largely thanks to the rubber revenues. In exchange, the aged king demanded payments totaling more than 205 million francs. He died the following year at the age of seventy-three, his image forever tarnished by his rapacious African venture. By one measure it was one of history's most horrendous mass exterminations: During Leopold's twenty-three-year rule over the Congo, it is estimated that the native population dropped by half, with between 8 million and 13 million lives lost to starvation, disease, exhaustion, murder, and execution.

What about Empain's role in all this? There is no record that the baron himself ever visited the Congo. As with most of his foreign ventures, he left the on-site management in the hands of local agents. Did Empain's people deal with the natives in the same brutal way as Leopold's henchmen? His companies apparently relied on the same forced labor system that prevailed elsewhere in the Congo. One of the reasons the Free State's government retained a direct role in Empain's railroad project was to be able to "requisition" native laborers, something a private company had no authority to do. The work of cutting railroads through the jungles was the same for Empain's lines as for the original Matadi–Léopoldville link—an undertaking that involved some sixty thousand workers and took untold thousands of lives due to accidents, disease, overwork, relentless floggings, and summary shootings.

There is little documentary evidence about the treatment of Empain's railway workers apart from a cryptic comment by Leopold's successor, his nephew Albert I, that they appeared "prosperous" when he toured the area in 1909. A missionary quoted the new king as saying that Empain's company treated its laborers "as humanely as possible, with a minimum of disease." Assuming these vague reports are accurate, Empain's agents would appear to have dealt with the natives somewhat more kindly than Leopold's—though a cynic might attribute that approach to a concern for maintaining productivity among these unpaid forced laborers. In any case, one cannot escape the fact that a substantial part of the Empain fortune was based on colonial exploitation and that many Black lives were lost in the process. That put a certain moral taint on the money that Wado would later inherit—and that his kidnappers sought to grab a piece of.

THOUGH ALBERT DID not share his uncle's close personal friendship with Empain, the new king respected the baron's talents and relied on his support. When World War I broke out, Albert named Empain a major general in the Belgian Army and assigned him the task of organizing the country's armaments industry and food provisions. Empain, who contributed heavily to the war effort out of his own funds, handled the job with his usual energy and efficiency and was grandly decorated by the monarch. Thereafter, Empain used the title of general-baron and proudly wore his military uniform and medals on public occasions.

Neither the war nor the transfer of the Congo to the Belgian state impeded Empain's activities in the colony. On the contrary, his affairs there continued to prosper. Shortly after the Brussels government took over, Empain's company received an additional land grant of 10 million acres under the terms of the original agreement and doubled down on its mining and other operations. Meanwhile, his railroad lines were a continuing source of revenues. Long after the baron's death in 1929, the Empain name was revered in the Congo—at least among the Belgians who ran it.

IN 1953, AT the age of sixteen, Wado was given a VIP tour of the colony. He went rather reluctantly at the behest of his mother and stepfather, who considered it an "educational vacation." Though still an awkward and timid adolescent, he was treated like royalty by the obsequious managers of the Empain mines, factories, and forestries he visited. He traveled across the country in a special "presidential" train car complete with bedroom, dining room, and bathroom—the whole convoy had to stop when he took his bath. Every two hours, he would step out and throw cartons of cigarettes to the locals who lined the tracks to get a look at the "young white chief." He was ill at ease with all the special attention. "I knew that I didn't deserve all this deference. I didn't like that way of being the son of my father and the grandson of my grandfather."

He liked it better when he went back seven years later with Silvana at his side. As heir apparent to the Empain dynasty, the young baron took an active interest in the activities of this tentacular group that at its peak employed eight hundred European agents and fifty thousand local workers in the colony. As it turned out, Wado's second tour marked the last hurrah of the Empain dynasty in the Congo. During the decade after the country won its independence in 1960, most of the Empain holdings were nationalized by the new Republic of the Congo government—and along with them went the profits that for seven decades had flowed into the group's coffers.

CHAPTER 12

A Place in the Sun

In the last week of January 1904, Édouard Empain embarked on a passenger liner in the port of Marseilles and settled into his first-class cabin en route to Alexandria, Egypt. Though he had business interests in the four corners of the world, he hated to travel. It is not even clear whether he ever set foot in the Congo, despite his major railroad and mining interests there. An inveterate hypochondriac and germophobe, he regarded foreign countries—particularly those in the less developed parts of the world—as potential sources of dirt and disease.

Many of his fellow travelers were headed to Egypt as tourists, but for Empain this was strictly a business trip. Since 1894, his group had railroad and tramway operations in and around Cairo. Though he himself was the majority shareholder in these ventures, he had always left his agents to negotiate with the government of the Ottoman viceroy—and, more important, with the British officials who had administered Egypt as a protectorate since 1882. But now his presence was required in order to arrange an extension of his tramway lines.

Upon arrival, the baron took up residence at Shepheard's, Cairo's most elegant and best-known hotel. As it turned out, it did not take him long to settle the tramway business. After brief discussions, he was able to sign a contract with a British administrator to extend the existing lines under the aegis of a new company. But in fact, Empain had bigger projects in mind. His friend Leopold II, still very much alive at the time, had long encouraged Belgian entrepreneurs—and Empain in particular—to invest there. It was part of the king's obsession with extending the international reach of his little country. Empain was already active in Egypt's transport sector, but now he was looking for something more ambitious.

To examine the possibilities, he counted on the advice of Boghos Nubar Pasha, a Paris-trained engineer and businessman. A consummate charmer and wire puller, Boghos (who was known by his first name) was also plugged in to the British establishment that actually ran the country under the authority of the consul-general, Lord Cromer. Scion of one of Egypt's wealthiest families—his father was a former Egyptian prime minister—Boghos had made a considerable personal fortune through shrewd speculations in real estate, agriculture, and farm equipment. (Among other exploits, he had invented a tractor that won a gold medal at the 1900 Paris Exposition.) It is not clear exactly how Boghos and Empain first met, but they were well acquainted before the Belgian's first visit to Cairo. A former administrator of Egypt's national railroad, Boghos had been recruited to sit on the board of one of Empain's local rail companies four years earlier.

Shortly after his arrival, Empain invited his friend to join him for lunch at Santi's, one of the city's finest restaurants, located in the public gardens across from his hotel. Fellow diners could see at a glance that the two men came from different worlds. Empain, in his white linen suit, buttoned-up vest, and bow tie, was the very picture of the dapper European traveler. Boghos, who usually sported a fez, had an air of world-weariness about him. His face bore a trace of his Armenian origins, with sad, deep-set black eyes under thick brows, a prominent nose, and a mustache as stiff as a badger's quills. Yet the Belgian and the Egyptian actually had much in common. They were exactly the same age—fifty-two years old. Both men were short and paunchy, both were involved in transportation and engineering—and both were endowed with a relentless drive to make money.

Empain talked vaguely of possible projects he had in mind—further extensions of his railroad lines, a luxury steamer service between Marseilles and Alexandria, real estate developments in the capital. The problem, he confessed, was that he really knew very little about Egypt. The first thing Boghos could do for him was show him around. For the next few days, Boghos led his friend through the narrow alleys and bazaars filled with spices, perfume, carpets, and jewelry—perhaps helping him negotiate a purchase or two. The two men also toured the newer residential neighborhoods, with their broad avenues and European-style buildings, and visited museums filled with Egyptian antiquities.

What impressed Empain most, however, were the great pyramids at Giza, south of Cairo. A photo shows him riding on the back of a camel at the foot of the Great Sphinx, dressed incongruously in a white three-piece suit and a high-topped hat; Boghos, sporting a dark suit and fez, rides a camel at his side. Here was an embodiment of the kind of pharaonic glory that the Belgian entrepreneur could aspire to. Call it megalomania, call it vision, call it passion—what is clear is that at this moment, in the shadow of the pyramids, Édouard Empain fell in love with Egypt, its history, its culture, its architecture.

Another photo from this period, apparently a studio portrait, depicts Empain in Bedouin robes with a kaffiyeh on his head and a medal pinned on his left breast. It was a telling juxtaposition: The medal, possibly a decoration from the hand of Leopold II, spoke of European honor and rank; the robes and headdress evoked the nomadic culture of the desert. Empain wanted it all. And now he had found his project: He would build a magnificent Egyptian city to stand as his own monument.

Boghos liked the idea, not so much for the glory of it all but for the profits that might flow from what was in fact an ambitious real estate development. But where would they find the land? Cairo itself was congested and densely populated, not to mention the fact that speculators had driven real estate prices through the roof. It was probably Boghos who came up with the idea of looking at the vast tract of desert some six miles northeast of Cairo around the oasis of Abbassia. Used occasionally for military maneuvers, this was once the site of the legendary city of Heliopolis—City of the Sun. Until the Persians sacked it in 522 BC, Heliopolis had been a religious center populated by astrologers and theologians dedicated to the cult of Ra, the Egyptian sun god. Christian legend has it that the Holy Family sojourned near there during their flight to Egypt. Over the ensuing centuries, the ruins of Heliopolis were looted for building stones, its temples dismantled, its magnificent obelisks destroyed or shipped to such far-flung places as Rome, Florence, New York, and London. Only one remained of the hundreds that once stood on the site: the obelisk of Sésostris I. All the rest was sand. Yet when Empain visited the area with Boghos, he did not hesitate: This was the spot where he would build the modern city of Heliopolis.

Boghos and Empain agreed to buy the land together. Thanks to the Egyptian's privileged contacts, they convinced the government to sell them nearly ten square miles of desert—an area roughly the size of Cairo—for the modest price of 5,000 Egyptian pounds, equivalent to just under $800,000 in today's money. (The territory was later increased to twenty-nine square miles.) In addition, they procured a seventy-year concession to build and operate a rail line and two tramways linking the new city to the capital. The sale was formalized on May 27, 1905. Eight months later, Empain and Boghos launched the Cairo Electric Railways and Heliopolis Oases Company to develop the project. Empain was the majority shareholder and president of the new company, known familiarly as Cairo Electric, with Boghos as his vice president.

At that point, Heliopolis existed only on paper. Empain had a grand vision, but neither he nor Boghos was an urbanist or architect. Yet Empain had proven over the years to have an uncanny knack for finding the right people to advance his plans, and it happened that a young Belgian architect named Ernest Jaspar had recently checked into Shepheard's after an extended tour of Greece and the Orient. Empain ran into him in the hotel and was intrigued by the young man's passion for Arab and oriental architecture. According to a memoir by Jaspar's son, Empain accompanied the architect on horseback to the site of his desert tract. Waving at the barren sand, he told Jaspar, "I want to build a city here. It will be called Heliopolis, the city of the sun. First of all, I will build a palace. I want it to be magnificent! I want the architecture to reflect the traditions of this country. I need a specialist in Arab art, but I haven't yet found one. You like mosques, you're an architect, would you like to draft a project?"

Jaspar came back a week later with some preliminary plans. Empain was enchanted. "Go back to Europe, fetch your family, and come back here as soon as you can." It was an unhoped-for chance for an untested thirty-year-old architect, and Jaspar leapt at it. For the next ten years, Heliopolis would be the center of his life and the source of his renown.

Empain's vision for Heliopolis was indeed pharaonic. He wanted to create palatial villas, apartment buildings, churches and mosques, public gardens, concert halls, a racetrack, a golf course, an amusement park, cricket and polo grounds, and even an aerodrome. Like Moses calling forth a spring with a tap of his rod, he would turn the desert into a verdant paradise, with palms and jacaranda trees lining the broad avenues; jasmine, bougainvillea, and honeysuckle spilling from balconies; fountains gurgling in public gardens.

For all its grandiosity, Heliopolis was at bottom a vast real estate speculation intended to sell or rent properties for profit. Empain hoped to attract a wealthy and leisured class of clients by posing as a competitor of Europe's better-known spas. Lacking a seashore or salubrious mineral springs, he could boast a dry, sunny climate, cultural and sports facilities, and exotic décor. Though the façades of his buildings were mostly done in traditional Arab styles, he insisted that the interiors conform to European standards of comfort. A company report grandly described the development as "an oasis rising over the ancient city to become the Champs-Élysées of modern Cairo."

Ernest Jaspar's daunting assignment was to build one of the world's biggest and most luxurious hotels. He succeeded on both counts. With its 650-foot-long façade, the four-story Heliopolis Palace Hotel boasted three hundred guest rooms, a monumental entrance hall topped by a 115-foot-high cupola, and a circular dining room with a spectacular view of Cairo and the distant pyramids through its picture windows. Featuring ornate balustrades, pointed arches, and bas-reliefs, the palace was a mix of traditional Arab, Moorish, and Indo-Islamic styles done with modern construction methods and pitched to European tastes. Like most of the Heliopolis structures, it was built of steel-reinforced concrete with molded cement ornamentation and covered with a pale-yellow stucco. The interior was replete with gilded friezes, frescoes, and trompe l'oeils. The hotel, which had cost some 5 million francs to build and furnish, opened for business in December 1910.

Without a doubt, the most spectacular Heliopolis structure was the bizarre Hindu Villa that Empain ordered up as his personal residence. The idea for it probably went back to the 1900 Paris Exposition, for which the well-known French architect Alexandre Marcel had built several exotic pavilions. Like his friend Leopold II, who had visited the fair incognito, Empain was enchanted by Marcel's work. The king, who always tended to appropriate what he liked (the Congo, for example), commissioned Marcel to rebuild the Japanese Tower and the Chinese Pavilion in the park of his château in Brussels. Empain, for his part, was enamored of Marcel's Cambodian Pavilion, a mix of Asian and northern-Indian styles based on Hindu and Buddhist temples. When the time came to build a temple to himself, he called on Marcel.

The architect basically produced a copy of his Cambodian Pavilion, enlarged and enhanced to suit the baron's penchant for grandiosity. The 100-foot-high tower is virtually identical to the Paris version. Like much of the elaborate exterior ornamentation, it was cast from Marcel's original molds. The façade, pillars, and columns were covered with a phantasmagoric menagerie of sculpted elephants, dragons, Shivas, Vishnus, and Buddhas—a rather odd jumble of Eastern religious symbols for a devout Catholic like Empain.

The interior décor echoed the oriental motifs, but the layout was conventionally European: reception rooms and dining room on the ground floor; bedrooms, bathrooms, and a library on the upper floors, which were reached by an immense helicoidal stairway. An elevator led to the rooftop terrace, offering guests splendid views across the desert to Cairo. Breaking with the pale-yellow façades of the other Heliopolis buildings, Empain had his palace covered with a burnt-sienna coating, giving it a look of old stone. Built on an elevated plot at the end of Heliopolis's main avenue, Empain's showplace was one of the most visible of all the city's structures. It was completed in 1911, just in time for the baron to receive his first guests of honor: Belgium's King Albert I and his wife, Queen Elizabeth. It was one of the thirty-six-year-old monarch's first foreign trips since ascending to the throne on the death of his uncle Leopold II two years earlier.

Empain's other personal monument was the Roman Catholic cathedral built at the opposite end of the central axis. On his instructions, architect Alexandre Marcel literally copied the monumental cathedral of Saint Sophia in Constantinople, reduced to one-fourth scale. Marcel's version, completed in 1910, faithfully reproduced the Byzantine arches and domes of the original, though the downsizing left it looking a bit dumpy—one critic compared it to "a fat Belgian lady." The baron grandly dubbed it a basilica and named it Notre Dame de Tongre, after the Belgian church where he had once served as an altar boy. Though he made it available to the Catholic Church as a permanent loan, the building remained the baron's personal property throughout his lifetime. He chose its crypt as his final resting place—a sign not only of his devotion to the church but also of his attachment to Egypt and to this fantastic city he had built on its sands.

Despite Empain's hopes of reaping a big profit from his development, he faced financial problems from the beginning. The 1907 crash of the Cairo stock market depressed real estate prices, forcing Empain to sell many Heliopolis properties at a loss. The baron continued to pump his personal funds into the project, and the situation finally stabilized, though it never produced the kinds of profits he drew from the Congo and the Paris Métro. During World War I, the Palace Hotel was requisitioned as a British Army hospital. It reopened in 1922 but never regained its former luster and in fact became a serious money loser.

Heliopolis was gradually absorbed into Greater Cairo and stands today as one more neighborhood in the urban sprawl. Empain's company, Cairo Electric, which continued to manage Heliopolis after his death in 1929, was nationalized by Nasser in 1960, along with his railroad and tramway companies. The magnificent Palace Hotel was also taken over by Nasser's government and turned into a government headquarters. Hosni Mubarak adopted it as his presidential palace in 1985.

EMPAIN FELL ILL and left Heliopolis in 1913. He only returned briefly in 1927, two years before his death. Though his tomb lies in the crypt of the basilica, his most visible monument is the dreamlike Hindu Villa, later renamed the Empain Palace—*Qasr al Baron* to the locals. After the general's death, his playboy son Jean Empain used it as his Egyptian pied-à-terre, lavishly entertaining friends he would bring by the boatload on his yacht. Wado spent time there as a child. A touching set of photos shows him at age two or three cuddling with a smiling Rozell on the steps of the palace—scenes whose tenderness contrasts with his memory of a cold and distant mother. In another photo from that period, baby Wado, wearing a kaffiyeh, sits atop a camel, nestled in his father's arms. As an adult, he had only the vaguest recollection of the Hindu Villa as a magical place shrouded in the veil of time.

PART IV

The Showdown

FEBRUARY–MARCH 1978

The kidnappers' bullet-ridden getaway car, March 24, 1978

Houpline/Sipa

CHAPTER 13

Operation Snowplow

February 1978. Two weeks after Wado was snatched, the snows started to fall. Just a light powdering at first, then a heavy, persistent snowfall that covered the floor of the Garennes forest with a thick white carpet. That was a problem for the kidnappers. They had made no plan for resupplying the tunnel, expecting the operation to be over in a few days. But now that the negotiations were cut off, with no end in sight, they were running short of food and water. If they attempted to replace the provisions, their back-and-forth movements would leave telltale footprints in the snow leading to the tunnel.

To make matters worse, the men assigned to guard the prisoner were growing restive. La Grise complained about the sanitary conditions and the execrable quality of the canned food. Jean Brunet, the Indochina war veteran who sported combat fatigues and kept his AK-47 at the ready, tormented the feckless Fredo by playing on his claustrophobia and fear of the dark. Claiming to hear strange noises, he would send Fredo off, rifle in hand, to patrol the pitch-black labyrinth. When he was not goading Fredo, Brunet was gripped by his own paranoia, fearing an imminent irruption by police. "Make sure you're not tailed when you come here," he would tell Caillol and Duchateau. "Something doesn't feel right about this thing."

From inside his tent, Wado would hear snatches of conversation among his jailers, but he wasn't aware of the mounting tensions among them. On the contrary, he was impressed by their discipline and their quasi-military hierarchy. Based on the voices and movements he heard, he estimated that about a dozen men were involved in the operation, including the leaders who visited only occasionally. Though they sometimes threatened and insulted him verbally, Wado's jailers never roughed him up—apart from the amputation, of course. His suffering came not from physical abuse but from the harsh conditions of his incarceration. In addition to the numbing cold, the filthy clothing, and the discomfort of being chained by the neck and manacled, the guards kept him destabilized by serving his food—such as it was—at erratic intervals. He had plenty of hot coffee, but never a hot meal. They would give him an apple, some canned beans, or a piece of sardine. Four or five hours later, maybe he would get a cold bouillon. He never knew whether these tidbits were supposed to be lunch or dinner, because he had no notion of time.

As for the kidnappers, time was not on their side. The longer the situation dragged on, the more time the police had to pursue leads, prepare their countermoves, and perhaps, aided by the tracks in the snow, even locate the kidnappers' lair. By mid-February, they were ready to reestablish contact with Empain's entourage in an effort to close the deal.

. . .

MEGÈVE IS NOT a town for everyone. Nestled in the French Alps, it is a favorite ski resort of Europe's jet-setters, a place where people go not just for the winter sports but also to be seen in their furs, jewelry, and designer outfits after their last schuss down the mountainsides. The cobblestone roads in the town's medieval center are lined with chic boutiques and Swiss-style wooden chalets. The slopes offer superb skiing—the highest peak rises to eight thousand feet—while the trendy bars, nightclubs, and casino cater to the beautiful people well into the wee hours. That's where Baron Empain and his family spent their Christmas holidays each year. Wado tried to avoid the flash-and-bling crowd, staying at one of the more modest hotels before finally renting a private chalet. After hearing from Empain about his attachment to the place, Caillol and his band chose to stage the next act of their sordid drama at Megève.

On Friday, February 17, 1978, Robert Badinter, the Empain company lawyer, received an anonymous call in the middle of the night instructing him to pick up an envelope at an underground parking lot on Paris's Left Bank. The package contained six letters handwritten by Wado pleading for his family and colleagues to do everything possible to pay the ransom and spare his life. One of the letters relayed precise instructions from the kidnappers: Send an employee of the Empain-Schneider group to Megève on February 22 with two sports bags containing 17 million Swiss francs in used banknotes. That was equivalent to 40 million French francs (worth nearly $9 million at the time, or $37 million today), meaning the kidnappers had cut their original ransom demand in half. The envoy was to wait at the four-star Hôtel du Mont d'Arbois starting at eleven thirty a.m. He would receive a call around noon from "Félix Le Chat" and answer to the code name "Jacques Dupont." Once the contact was made, the emissary was to drive to a designated spot and hand over the cash. If the instructions were not followed precisely, the note said, "The baron will be executed the same day and we will not hand over his body." Defying the kidnappers' orders not to contact police, Engen immediately turned the documents over to the investigators.

By this time, both the group and the family had come around to Ottavioli's point of view and ruled out the payment of an actual ransom. Instead, technicians at the Criminal Brigade prepared a fake ransom consisting of telephone-book pages cut to the dimensions of Swiss 1,000-franc notes. The pages were assembled into bundles with real Swiss banknotes on the top and bottom and shrink-wrapped in plastic. They filled two identical sports bags, unlocked as per instructions, that weighed a total of about 50 kilograms, or 110 pounds.

To deliver the fake ransom, Ottavioli had the perfect candidate: Inspector Jean Marc Mazzieri, age thirty-eight, who normally worked a paper-pushing desk job at the Crim headquarters. Mazzieri was not part of the action squad, but he had a special talent that made him the ideal choice for the job: He was a martial-arts black belt. The Eurasian son of a French colonial army officer and an Indo-Chinese mother, he was born in the province of Tonkin, grew up in Corsica, and fought in the Algerian War. He started studying judo and jujitsu when he was eighteen, later adding aikido and karate to his skill set. At the time of the kidnapping, he had been teaching martial arts for more than five years and would later publish a book on self-defense. When Ottavioli tapped him for this risky job, he readily accepted the challenge, considering himself a "designated volunteer."

With his almond eyes and dark-brown hair, Mazzieri—nicknamed "Le Chinois" by his colleagues—cut an unassuming figure: five foot nine, 132 pounds, and skinny as an alley cat. But his supple body was all muscle and his hands were potentially lethal weapons. His assignment in Megève, though, was not to kill anyone but to capture at least one of the criminals alive to serve as a counter-hostage. Until the moment of the handoff, he was to pose as a midlevel employee of the Empain-Schneider group using the alias "Monsieur Mazeaud" (pronounced *Mazo*).

Mazzieri was not alone in Megève. Under the code name "Operation Snowplow," more than forty agents converged on the resort in advance of the February 22 rendezvous. Marcel Leclerc, head of the Antigang squad, and André Bizeul, liaison for the Criminal Brigade, arrived on the evening of Sunday, February 19, and set up their operational headquarters in a rented chalet. Shortly after his arrival, Bizeul went up on the roof with a technical team and set up an antenna to relay radio communications in those pre-cellphone times. For the next two days, the team carried out reconnaissance missions in Megève and its surroundings, with particular attention to access routes. Two helicopters and ten unmarked vehicles with fake plates stood ready to pursue the kidnappers in any possible direction.

Meanwhile, Robert Broussard and Mazzieri headed from Paris to Geneva in Broussard's Citroën DS. The fake ransom was in the trunk, but the kidnappers had instructed them to get the money from a Swiss bank. To simulate compliance, they rented a Swiss-registered Mercedes in Geneva, transferred the fake ransom, and drove to Megève. Mazzieri spent much of the drive in the backseat with his eyes closed. The Antigang agent at the wheel thought he was asleep. In reality he was preparing mentally for the challenge ahead, like a samurai before a battle. For hours he reviewed his martial-arts technique and tried to map out his encounter with the kidnappers. Mazzieri knew they would be armed, but he was serene: He knew he could neutralize two or even three of them with his bare hands.

Broussard and his commando squad settled into a small hotel in the nearby village of Sallanches, located on one of the likely escape routes leading to the Swiss border. There, they assembled a veritable assault arsenal: bulletproof vests, helmets, long-range rifles with infrared scopes, assorted pistols and automatic weapons, even James Bond–style fountain pens that fired .22 bullets. The rifles, tucked away in long cases, aroused the curiosity of other hotel guests. Broussard told them that he was heading a team of inspectors from the Environment Ministry, sent to measure the snowpack and evaluate the risk of avalanches in the region. The cases, he said, contained state-of-the-art sounding poles. Rather than placate the curious vacationers, Broussard's cover story set off an alarm: A number of guests, fearing the possibility of real avalanches, packed up and left the hotel.

Mazzieri checked into the luxury Mont d'Arbois under the name of Mazeaud. A radio technician shared his room to handle the communications. An adjoining room was occupied by a male and female agent posing as a vacationing couple, ready to intervene in case of trouble. Mazzieri didn't think their help would be necessary. Waving off Broussard's offer of a tiny one-shot derringer—"a boudoir weapon for ladies" he called it—the judoka chose to remain unarmed.

On February 22, Mazzieri waited in his hotel room for the phone call from "Félix Le Chat." It was expected between eleven a.m. and one p.m., but there was no call. After lunching in his room, Mazzieri stretched out for a nap and was soon sound asleep. Suddenly the phone rang. The communications specialist handed Mazzieri the receiver. It was not the kidnappers but Leclerc seeking news. "Nothing yet," said Mazzieri. "You just woke me from my nap." Leclerc couldn't believe his man was calm enough to sleep at a time like that.

The team remained in place until the afternoon of the twenty-third, but no one ever called. Operation Snowplow evacuated Megève that evening, without having encountered the kidnappers. Nor had they made any "useful observations," as the official mission report put it. Someone, however, had observed them: A French radio station reported that police units from Paris had converged on Megève in connection with the Empain kidnapping. No one ever knew whether that announcement was the result of a leak or astute reporting, but the police assumed that the news flash had scared off the kidnappers.

In fact, the radio report had nothing to do with it. Caillol's band never intended to go to Megève; they just wanted to yank the cops' chain and see what they would do. Now, thanks to the news bulletin, they knew for sure that the Empain group and family were working hand-in-glove with the police. The kidnappers were furious. From inside his tent, Empain heard one of them growl, "Fucking cops, fucking Engen, they thought we'd fall for that?" Out of his earshot, his jailers launched a heated discussion about how to proceed in the wake of the Megève episode. For the baron it was literally a matter of life and death.

Meeting in a parallel tunnel gallery, the kidnappers paced back and forth and argued, the beams from their miner's helmets slicing through clouds of cigarette smoke. La Grise complained about the discomfort of the seemingly endless vigil. Brunet, limping from his old war injury, fingered his AK-47 and angrily demanded to know when they would get their money. Bertoncini, the Marseilles pimp and car thief, tried to lighten the mood with some X-rated jokes. Slightly apart from the others, Caillol and Duchateau, the "thinking heads" of the operation, exchanged their thoughts on what to do in the wake of the Megève episode.

Finally, a grim-faced Caillol raised his reedy voice and delivered his conclusion: It was time to consider executing the prisoner. With the police involved, it now seemed doubtful that they would ever get their hands on the ransom. In that case, Empain's incarceration served no further purpose, but his execution might stand as an example for future operations. "Shoot him in the head, take his picture, and leave him in the trunk of a car," Caillol told his confederates. "The next time we kidnap someone, we show the picture, and they pay up immediately." Not everyone agreed with Caillol's brutal recommendation. Some of the jailers who watched over Empain had developed a human relationship with him. Shooting him like a dog was not to their taste.

Caillol proposed to decide the matter democratically by taking a vote. The method was simple. Idir rolled a piece of cardboard into a cone in which the eight kidnappers were instructed to drop a coin. A one-franc coin was a vote to kill the hostage; a larger five-franc piece was a vote to spare him. An almost comic scene followed as the men fished in their pockets, the light from their helmets crisscrossing in the pitch-black cavern. La Grise, ever the dapper dresser, said he had no coins because they deformed his pockets. Duchateau loaned him two coins. Bertoncini, dressed in a pocketless tracksuit, disappeared momentarily then returned shaking his head. "I went to borrow a coin from our friend under the tent," he explained in his twangy Marseilles accent, "but Wado is like La Grise; he never has any money on him." He had filched a coin from a table near the tent. They were about to throw their coins in the cone when Bertoncini, smirking, held up his hand. "And Wado, doesn't he vote?" "No," Caillol snapped back, "he's Belgian, he doesn't get a vote."

The eight men lined up single file and dropped their coins in the cone one by one. When they were done, Idir knelt down and poured the coins on the dirt floor. There were four one-franc coins and four fivers. Though the vote was supposedly secret, Caillol was sure that the original four members of his band, including himself and Duchateau, had voted to execute the prisoner. The later recruits had voted to spare him. They voted again. This time, it was five to three in favor of letting Empain live. Caillol assumed that it was Duchateau who had changed his vote, because he immediately began to talk about lowering the ransom demand and trying again to collect it. Caillol said no—keep radio silence until further notice. Let the baron's people stew in their own juices for a while.

Empain was unaware of the vote that took place, but he had been told by one of the men that his execution might become necessary at some point. His life apparently meant nothing to his family and entourage, because they weren't willing to pay, but his death could serve as an example. There was nothing personal about it, of course. Hearing this, the baron asked only that it be done cleanly. One of the jailers assured him that, if it came to that, he would do the job himself and make sure the end came painlessly. Wado had been spared this time, but that was no guarantee for the future. His life still hung by a thread.

CHAPTER 14

On the Move

*A*fter the vote to spare Empain's life, Caillol ordered a total blackout on communications. During the hiatus, he returned to Montpellier to check on the furniture store, which he had left in the hands of an employee. Finding the business in reasonable shape, he decided to take his wife and three-year-old son on a ski vacation in the French Alps, stopping to visit his brother, François, in Grenoble on the way. Caillol, like Empain an accomplished skier, hoped to decompress while dashing down the slopes.

During Caillol's absence, Daniel Duchateau was left in charge of the operation—perhaps not the wisest move. Suddenly, without informing Caillol, Duchateau decided to abandon the tunnel and move the hostage to a different hideout. One reason was the continuing snowfall and the telltale footprints leading to the entrance. Another was the insistent carping of the men who were assigned to watch over their captive, mainly La Grise, Brunet, and Fredo, because they found conditions in the tunnel "too uncomfortable."

Empain was blindfolded and led down a snow-covered forest path. Confined to his tent, he had not walked or even stood up for a month and had trouble negotiating the long trek. When they arrived at the roadside, his captors grabbed him by the shoulders and legs and stuffed him in the trunk of a car. After an hour's drive, the car stopped and Wado was transferred into a coffinlike wooden box that had been built to measure by one of the kidnappers. When they nailed the lid shut, he was gripped by panic. He feared they might be planning to kill him, maybe bury him alive or throw him in the Seine, like gangsters in a mafia movie.

His fears were stoked by a violent argument that had broken out among the kidnappers before they abandoned the tunnel. He didn't hear the precise words, but there were threats and insults, perhaps even an exchange of blows. He thought that one of the men might have been killed by the others. No one was killed, but there was indeed an altercation. Bertoncini, assigned to drive the car, had adamantly refused, claiming that he had "something else to do." Brunet, wielding his assault rifle, exploded. "I'm fed up with this bullshit. You're going to drive the fucking car, or I'll pop you." The others weighed in, and finally Bertoncini relented. It was a dangerous job because of the risk of being stopped by police with Empain in the trunk. To limit the potential damage, Bertoncini was alone at the wheel, though he was trailed by an escort vehicle.

When the car finally came to a stop, Empain heard footsteps and muffled voices as other men joined Bertoncini. They opened the trunk and removed the cargo. Empain had the impression that his box was being hoisted into the air by a machine. He imagined that he was being lifted up to some kind of grain-storage facility located on a farm and even thought he heard the cry of a peacock. According to Caillol, it was in fact an apartment located in the nineteenth arrondissement of Paris, in the northeastern part of the capital. The building had an underground garage with an elevator that allowed the kidnappers, posing as movers, to transfer Wado's box discreetly to an upper floor. Arrived at their destination, the men lugged the box into the apartment, extracted the blindfolded hostage, and installed him in the tent that they had brought from the tunnel—along with the hated yellow bucket.

It had never been part of the plan to bring the hostage here. But in fact, the original plan had been virtually abandoned when the negotiations broke down. Instead of closing the deal in three or four days, more than a month had gone by and they were now drifting into an open-ended cycle whose end no one could predict or control. Moving Wado to Paris, says Caillol, was a "total improvisation."

For Wado, it was an unhoped-for improvement over the miserable conditions of the tunnel. He was still handcuffed and chained by the neck, but his captors had removed the painful manacles from his ankles. What's more, they had installed a small electric lamp in the tent, along with a real mattress and a television. (The TV in fact brought him little comfort, as it constantly reminded him of what he did not have: the freedom of the world outside.) They brought him hot food—chicken, steak—and newspapers, including his favorite, the conservative daily *Le Figaro*. Best of all, the space was heated—it was so warm, in fact, that the baron spent most of his time in his underwear even though it was late February. And for the first time in a month, he was able to wash himself using a plastic basin of warm water and soap provided by his minders.

A week after his arrival, he received a special treat on his food tray—a piece of cake from a local pastry shop. He was not hungry after finishing his meal, so he shoved the cake aside without removing it from its wrapper. When a guard collected his tray, he asked why Wado had not eaten the cake. "I don't like cake, and I wasn't hungry," the baron replied. The guard suddenly realized that someone had committed a grave error: The name and address of the pastry shop were printed on the wrapper, which might permit the hostage later to identify the neighborhood of the safe house and perhaps put police on the trail of the kidnappers. Wado swore that he hadn't looked at the address, but his captors suddenly decided to break camp.

The gang was running out of places to hide their captive. One possibility left to them was the house in the suburb of Savigny-sur-Orge, just south of Paris, where Bertoncini and his girlfriend had hunkered down for the duration. Sedated and nailed back in his wooden box, Wado was driven there in the dead of night (this time with Daniel Duchateau at the wheel) and delivered to the basement of the modest two-story house.

Once again, Wado was installed in his all-too-familiar tent with a neck chain bolted to the wall. All the back-and-forth movement suggested to the hostage that the standoff might be moving toward some conclusion—for better or worse. But Bertoncini told Empain that everything was on hold until the end of the parliamentary elections two weeks hence. For now, the government was unlikely to make any concessions. If Giscard d'Estaing's conservatives retained their majority, the powers that be might be more amenable to a deal. If the Socialist-Communist opposition took over, saving a capitalist millionaire would be the least of their worries.

Bertoncini, with his southern sense of conviviality, treated the baron as his guest. "Édouard, you are at home here," he told him. "You have everything you need? I know it's not an agreeable situation, but if I can do anything for you . . ." Bertoncini did what he could to make Wado's stay more bearable, serving him delectable meals prepared by his girlfriend—including poached trout, roast duck, and rabbit stew—washed down with strong Algerian wine. He also provided him with reading material—at least what the semi-literate Bertoncini considered reading material: porno magazines, erotic novels, and crime stories. When he found out that Wado smoked Marlboros, he bought him a pack. He also offered to bring over a prostitute, but Wado drew the line there.

Something like a friendship developed between Empain and Bertoncini, though the baron never saw the other man's face and recognized him only by his distinctive Marseilles accent. Wado's relationship with Bertoncini was part of a curious psychological inversion. Over time, he began to see those on the outside as the bad guys. The kidnappers, though they had mutilated his finger and subjected him to harsh treatment, were the good guys, those on whom his life depended, those with the godlike power to liberate him or kill him. After the first few weeks, a bond formed between captors and captive. They got to know him, called him Wado, asked him about the famous people he'd rubbed shoulders with, about his women, his sports cars, and his hunting rifles. They even took pride in showing him their own guns—Lugers, Kalashnikovs, Colt Magnums.

Wado took comfort in hearing their voices and appreciated the cigarettes and other simple favors they sometimes offered. And they came to admire the uncomplaining courage with which he endured his ordeal. In a bizarre confluence of interests, it seemed they were in this together. After all, both parties desired the same thing: the payout that would free the baron and make his jailers rich. Caillol observed the change in Empain's attitude and rejoiced: "Empain joined our team to play the match against the others, because he had understood that he could not expect any real help from the outside. He was now with us, against them!"

Though Empain had never heard the term, he was experiencing a common reaction known as Stockholm syndrome. It was a phenomenon that French cops like Robert Broussard knew all too well: "When a hostage feels abandoned by the outside world, he convinces himself that no one cares about his fate, and winds up seeing good qualities in his jailer. If the jailer knows how to manipulate his victim psychologically, he can cultivate a sort of understanding, or even solidarity."

ON THE MORNING of Wednesday, March 9, police in Lyons received a strange phone call from an unidentified woman. She claimed to have witnessed a struggle in the street during which three men threw a hood over the head of a fourth man, whisked him into a green Mercedes, and sped off. She told police that one of the men had dropped a card on the sidewalk. Wanting no involvement in the affair, this informant said she had thrown the card in a mailbox. When the police retrieved it, it turned out to be a membership card for an exclusive hunting club in the name of Baron Empain. The discovery set off a massive operation involving more than two hundred police and gendarmes who scoured the surrounding neighborhood and surveilled the zone around the Swiss border on the assumption that the incident and the card were related to a ransom payoff.

In the middle of this probe, who should call the Lyons Judiciary Police but Shahnaz Arieh, Wado's not-so-secret lover. She had read about the hunting card in the papers and offered to verify its authenticity, saying she knew the baron quite well. Informed by his colleagues in Lyons, Ottavioli sent a detective to question her in Geneva. It turned out she knew nothing about the card but merely wanted information about the state of the investigation. In the end, this lead went nowhere, and for good reason: One of Caillol's confederates had taken the train down to Lyons and thrown Wado's card in the mailbox just to mess with the cops. Another episode in the cat-and-mouse game that had started in Megève. It was far from over.

CHAPTER 15

The Fatal Rendezvous

 After the Megève episode, as we have seen, Alain Caillol had ordered his comrades to maintain radio silence then left for an extended ski vacation with his wife and son. Around March 20, Daniel Duchateau called him at his hotel in the Alpine resort of Montgenèvre, near the Italian border.

"Everything's okay," said Duchateau. "I worked it out with Engen. We're going to get paid."

"Are you sure?"

"Absolutely, it's good. We're going to get the money in a couple of days. The big jackpot!"

Caillol was not happy that Duchateau had taken it upon himself to relaunch the negotiations. As usual, he thought, Daniel was so desperate for money that he didn't think things through. But his comrade assured him that it was a done deal: "You have my word for it."

Caillol left Montgenèvre immediately, driving all night through a snowstorm, his wife at his side and his son asleep in the back of the car. He dropped them off at Montpellier, then drove on to Paris alone.

Duchateau briefed him on what had happened in his absence. There had been a big fight. Jean Brunet and La Grise, fed up with the endless wait, had slammed the door on the project, leaving Duchateau to pick up the pieces of the shattered plan. In desperation, Duchateau had contacted Engen at the Brussels Hilton on March 17 and proposed a deal: Empain's release for 17 million Swiss francs in cash—equivalent to some $37 million in today's money—the same amount that had been agreed on for the aborted Megève rendezvous. Engen signaled his accord. Duchateau told him to await further instructions.

On March 22, following a now-familiar pattern, an anonymous phone call to one of Engen's collaborators said an envelope had been left in an underground parking lot. It contained a handwritten letter from the baron. Composed under dictation, the document relayed the kidnappers' requirements for the handoff:

"The payer must know Paris well and know how to drive, be prepared to take notes, carry a little pocket money and a watch set to standard time . . . The [ransom] money must be placed in two sports bags, closed but not locked . . . If the police are informed of this operation in any way, [the kidnappers] will be without pity for me. I will be irreparably mutilated . . . If the police intervene before my liberation, they will dig a large hole and throw me in it."

The letter instructed the payer to wait in the bar of Fouquet's, a well-known restaurant on the Champs-Élysées, at three p.m. on Thursday, March 23, 1978. There he would receive a phone call from "Charlotte Corday," and answer to the name of "Monsieur Marat." (The kidnappers were having a little fun with the names: During the French Revolution, Charlotte Corday stabbed the radical journalist Jean-Paul Marat in his bathtub on July 13, 1793.) Despite the warnings, Engen immediately shared the letter with the police.

Jean Marc Mazzieri, the martial-arts expert, was again tapped for the job of delivering the fake ransom and trying to apprehend at least one of the kidnappers. Once again playing the role of "Monsieur Mazeaud," an employee of Empain's company, he was fitted out with an elegant business suit and a camel-hair coat. To complete the effect, André Bizeul loaned him a leather briefcase. In his coat pocket, he carried a fake grenade and a Motorola two-way radio. Under Ottavioli's orders, Robert Broussard mobilized a team of thirty-two Antigang agents who were assigned to follow Mazzieri at a discreet distance in an assortment of sixteen vehicles ranging from unmarked cars and taxis to delivery trucks, postal vans, and two motorcycles.

Ottavioli prepared to follow the action from his office, accompanied by Claude Cancès and other senior staffers of the Criminal Brigade. The Crim's André Bizeul joined Broussard in the command car, a powerful Citroën DS 21. The evening before the fateful rendezvous, Ottavioli had called all the agents involved in the operation to his office for a final briefing. One of the Antigang agents asked, "Chief, what if we have to shoot?" Otta's answer was clear: "Then you shoot." He gave his authorization to fire without warning if the kidnappers attempted to seize Mazzieri, or if they opened fire on the police or attempted to flee the scene. But he hoped to avoid gunfire, he said, because the aim of the mission was "to put our hands on a counter-hostage and not to wind up with a pile of cadavers."

On Thursday, March 23, Mazzieri drove to Fouquet's at the wheel of a rented Peugeot 504 with the fake ransom in the trunk. He took a seat at the bar and ordered a bottle of Vittel mineral water (he abstained from alcohol as part of his martial-arts regimen). The day before, he had been handed a thick folder containing hundreds of names and titles of all the group's executives in case the kidnappers interrogated him to verify his identity. He had flipped through it and decided it was impossible to memorize all those names. He would just have to wing it.

At the appointed hour, the barman announced a call from Charlotte for Monsieur Marat. Mazzieri took the phone.

"This is Charlotte Corday," said an anonymous voice.

"This is Marat."

"You have the money?"

"I have what you demanded."

"Are you alone?"

"Yes."

"Your name, your position within the group?"

"Jean Mazeaud, secretary to Monsieur Bierry."

"We'll verify that. What kind of car are you driving?"

"A white Peugeot 504."

"Go to the café Le Murat, at the Porte d'Auteuil."

Le Murat (no relation to Marat) was located near the Bois de Boulogne park in southwest Paris, a twenty-minute drive from the Champs-Élysées. Once behind the wheel of his Peugeot, Mazzieri radioed the information to Broussard, whose fleet discreetly escorted his vehicle to the new rendezvous.

Mazzieri arrived at Le Murat at 3:40 p.m. Once again, the phone call from "Charlotte" turned into a palm-sweating interrogation. The voice on the other end asked who was the head of this or that company within the Empain-Schneider group. Mazzieri kept silent. New questions about the group's organigram. More silence from Mazzieri. The caller insisted. Finally Mazzieri improvised, playing the role of a frightened company underling.

"Look, I'm just a simple employee of the group. They asked me to give you all this money. I thought you would take it right away. Why all these questions?"

"You could be a cop."

"I never thought of that."

Instead of pressing the matter, Mazzieri's interlocutor sent him to a new rendezvous.

Thus began a complicated scavenger hunt that would send Mazzieri crisscrossing Paris from one café to another, to an underground parking lot, to a sidewalk trash can, to an emergency telephone stand along a highway. At each point, he would receive new telephone instructions or find various notes and hand-drawn maps directing him to the next rendezvous. In his command car, Broussard received periodic radio messages from Mazzieri, then relayed orders to the vehicles that made up the stealthy police armada.

The scavenger hunt was the brainchild of Daniel Duchateau, who had spent weeks working out the details, driving through Paris, studying maps, investigating possible drop-off points. He had laboriously typed or handwritten the notes and drawn the maps and diagrams that accompanied them. Caillol, who wanted to keep the operation as simple as possible, found the whole exercise a waste of time.

Actually, the Rube Goldberg arrangement did serve to complicate matters for the police, who had to regroup at every stage. It also managed to exasperate Mazzieri. At one café, he waited more than an hour for the expected call. When it came, the voice on the other end resumed the interrogations about the company organigram. Mazzieri blew his stack:

"Listen to me! I'm starting to lose my courage. I regret that I ever got involved in this damn thing. I don't think I can go on with it. I'm going to crack. I'll take the money back. They'll have to find someone else to replace me." The voice on the other end suddenly became conciliatory and sent him on to yet another rendezvous.

At 7:10 p.m., Mazzieri was instructed to drive to a parking lot in the southern suburb of Antony and locate a brown Renault 12 station wagon bearing the license plate 379 BGW 75. The car was left unlocked with the keys in the trunk. A written message under the seat ordered "Mazeaud" to transfer the ransom from his car to the Renault and drive it to another Parisian bar, Les Trois Obus (The Three Bombshells), leaving his own car behind. At 8:30 p.m., a new phone call dispatched him to the bar of the Hilton hotel at Orly Airport, some twelve miles south of Paris, to receive what was to be his final instruction.

Mazzieri wasn't the only one who was getting impatient with this seemingly endless exercise. Since late afternoon, Duchateau, Caillol, and the man he calls Mathieu had been waiting inside the hollow wall along the A6 highway, the spot they had chosen a year earlier for receiving the ransom. With a metal service door on the highway side, and another door opening onto a quiet suburban street, it would allow the kidnappers to escape with the money and dash to a waiting getaway car driven by Idir. The police vehicles—for they fully expected a police presence—would be blocked on the highway. If necessary, the kidnappers would use the emissary as a human shield to cover their escape. "We will cuff his hands behind his back and place him in front of the door," Caillol told his comrades. "If the cops show up, they won't be able to shoot because their buddy will be the only target." The prime consideration was to avoid direct contact with the police.

Huddled inside the dark concrete tunnel, the conspirators had brought with them a formidable arsenal: a Remington pump rifle, a Schmeisser assault rifle, two Scorpion automatic pistols, two Herstal 9mm pistols with twenty-round clips, and a Colt Python .357 revolver. For good measure, Caillol and Duchateau each had a defensive grenade in his pocket—an arm that can be lethal up to eighty meters. But the scavenger hunt had dragged on far longer than expected. Caillol finally decided to postpone the operation until the next day.

When Mazzieri arrived at the Hilton shortly after nine p.m., the caller informed him that it was too late to continue. Mazzieri was instructed to leave the Renault in the hotel parking lot and haul the money bags back to Paris in a taxi. He was to return to the Hilton with the ransom the next day at six thirty p.m. The "taxi" that drove him away from the hotel was in fact a police vehicle driven by an Antigang agent.

THOUGH THE OPERATION had been postponed, the kidnappers were in a festive mood that night. From inside his tent, Wado heard movement and muffled conversation in the apartment upstairs. He overheard someone say, "The delivery of the ransom will happen tomorrow, Good Friday, at seven p.m." One of the men descended the creaking wooden stairs leading to the basement and ordered him to put on his mask. Wado heard the sound of a cork popping. Through the tent opening, someone handed him a chilled glass. "Take this. Be careful you don't spill." He recognized Bertoncini's Marseilles accent.

Wado slipped off his mask. He was holding a glass of Champagne.

Bertoncini knelt by the tent. "It's happening," he said, his voice even more jovial than usual. "We're going to get the ransom and finally be able to free you. To your health, Édouard!"

Wado was dubious. "Free me? When?"

"Listen, first we have to prepare our retreat, our hiding places, all that. It will probably happen tomorrow night."

FRIDAY, MARCH 24. When Mazzieri woke up that morning, he no longer believed in the operation. Thinking the kidnappers had taken fright and given up, he could not put himself mentally in the role he was supposed to play. In his mind, he was no longer an Empain executive but a cop with a Smith and Wesson .38 in the pocket of his overcoat. Still, he went through the motions, ready to deal with the gangsters if they showed up but assuming that they would abort the mission as they had done in Megève.

At midafternoon, he drove to the Orly Hilton and transferred the heavy sports bags to the Renault station wagon that he had left overnight in the parking lot. Then he nursed a Vittel at the bar and waited.

The call arrived at 6:40 p.m. The voice on the other end sounded relaxed, almost friendly, even asking if "Mazeaud" had slept well.

"Not a wink," said Mazzieri. "I was too nervous to sleep."

"Keep cool, you're in no danger. Everything will be fine." The speaker instructed Mazzieri to fill the tank of the Renault at a nearby service station and come back to the bar for further instructions. He added: "Drink a shot of whisky before you go. It'll relax you." Mazzieri did not tell the caller he was a teetotaler.

The next call came at 7:55 p.m. Now the voice sounded stressed. Mazzieri was instructed to drive north on the A6 highway in the direction of Paris. He was to fetch a note hidden under a rock at the emergency telephone stand B16. Mazzieri didn't realize it at the time, but this order deviated from the kidnappers' original plan. The initial idea was to rendezvous at stand B12, which was situated right next to a door in the wall. Caillol and Duchateau would grab the ransom bags and escape through the door, emerging on the other side and hopping into the waiting getaway car. That's what should have happened had the operation been completed on Thursday evening. After deciding to postpone the handoff, however, Caillol suddenly changed the plan and decided to meet the delivery man at stand B16, two kilometers away from the B12. Presumably the two kidnappers intended to take "Mazeaud" hostage there and drive the Renault to the spot where they could grab the sports bags and disappear through the door. It was one complication too many.

At 8:10 p.m., Mazzieri pulled into the breakdown lane next to the B16 stand and flipped on his warning lights. He was discreetly accompanied by two dozen unmarked police vehicles of various types, some in front of him, some behind. Broussard was in the command car, accompanied by the Antigang's Marcel Leclerc and the Crim's André Bizeul. Thanks to Mazzieri's two-way radio, they were in constant contact with him and relayed instructions to the other units. It was sweaty-palm time, even for these seasoned professionals.

Before Mazzieri could get out of the car and retrieve the message, a tow truck pulled up behind him. Mazzieri opened his window and made a brusque sign to the driver to move along, but the truck did not budge. Exasperated, he got out of the car and went to dispatch the driver more forcefully. Caillol and Duchateau, watching the scene from the top of a roadside embankment, took the tow truck for a police vehicle. Scrapping their original scenario, they launched into a desperate improvisation. Wearing black ski masks and blue workers' overalls, they scrambled down from the embankment and made a dash for the station wagon. Mazzieri had made a big mistake by leaving the keys in the ignition.

Caillol slid in behind the wheel and tried to open the other door for Duchateau, but it was locked. He laid his 9mm pistol down on the passenger seat and leaned over to trip the lock. The door swung open and Duchateau jumped in, sitting on Caillol's weapon. The car squealed off in a cloud of dust and gravel. Clutching his automatic pistol, Duchateau leaned over the seat and checked the rear compartment. "It's good," he said. "The bags are in the back. Let's get the fuck out of here!"

Meanwhile, Mazzieri ran to an unmarked police vehicle that had been tailing him, hopped inside, and radioed to Broussard: "Mazeaud is safe. They took my car. They are heavily armed." Police vehicles—cars, vans, motorcycles—took off in hot pursuit. Broussard's command car had gotten too far ahead of the action. They were forced to take an exit and loop back, breaking through a toll barrier as they raced to the scene. Meanwhile, Caillol was speeding along the breakdown lane, parallel to the wall, heading for the B12 phone stand and the door that would allow them to escape.

Arrived at the B12, Caillol hit the brakes, but the car was too close to the guardrail and Duchateau couldn't open his door. Caillol tried to throw the car into reverse but couldn't find the gear. A police car swerved around the station wagon and screeched to a halt, pinning it against the wall. Meanwhile, another masked man, the one Caillol calls Mathieu, burst through the metal service door and opened fire on the police in an attempt to cover Caillol and Duchateau. (According to police accounts, at least three men began shooting at them, including two on top of the wall.) As the cops returned fire, Duchateau began spraying bullets through the windshield with his machine pistol. Unable to grab his own gun, Caillol tried to drive off but his tires had been shot out. Within seconds, more police cars arrived and an all-out gunfight erupted. Two cops fell wounded, which fired up their colleagues with a sort of bloodlust as they rained bullets on the immobilized station wagon.

Suddenly Mazzieri jumped out of a police vehicle and waved his arms. "Hold your fire," he shouted. "Stop the carnage! We need to take them alive."

The guns fell silent on all sides. Duchateau was mortally wounded. Caillol, hit twice in the arm, held up his hands in surrender. A swarm of enraged cops converged on him and pulled him out of the car, kicking him in the ribs, punching him in the face, and pummeling his head with their weapons. They stripped him naked, underwear, socks, and all, and grabbed his wallet looking for an ID. His papers and money flew all over the highway.

In the middle of the melee, inspector Éric Yung, an enormous bear of a man, jumped off his motorcycle and grabbed a fistful of Caillol's hair. He yanked Caillol's head back and shoved the barrel of his .357 Magnum into his mouth. "You asshole," he growled, "look at your buddy. He's dead. Tell us where the baron is, or I'll blow your fucking head off." Caillol, overcome with pain, choking on exhaust fumes, barely conscious, whispered, "Shoot, you'll do me a favor." Yung re-holstered his gun. Caillol was the key to finding the hostage; there was no question of shooting him. Meanwhile, Mathieu and his accomplices had escaped through the hollow wall and fled in a getaway car. Police later found the vehicle abandoned on a quiet suburban street.

The firing had just ended when Broussard's car arrived on the scene after his forced detour, his headlights slicing through a blue-gray haze of gun smoke and exhaust fumes. He climbed out and took stock of the situation. The station wagon was riddled with more than seventy bullet holes, its tires shot to pieces and the windshield blown out on the passenger side. Caillol was lying on the ground naked and bleeding with his hands cuffed behind his back. Duchateau's body was stretched out in the emergency lane, face-up, the front of his jacket soaked in blood from a fatal chest wound. The night air smelled of blood, gunpowder, and gasoline. Sirens were blaring. Police radios squawked and beeped. Traffic was closed off in this northbound lane, but the southbound side was jammed with vacationers leaving the capital for the long Easter weekend. Rubbernecking brought the heavy flow to a stop as people got out of their cars to gawk at what they took for a horrific automobile accident.

Among the scattered police vehicles and motorcycles were not one but two tow trucks. Police had intercepted the first truck and roughed up its driver, assuming he was an accomplice of the kidnappers. While that was going on, a second tow truck from the same company pulled up behind it. Its occupant managed to convince the cops that his colleague was a legitimate driver who had just happened to show up at the wrong time, wrong place. Everything was in disarray.

IN HIS OFFICE on the Quai des Orfèvres, Pierre Ottavioli and his colleagues had followed the whole operation in real time. Not only did they have Broussard's radio reports; Mazzieri had left his Motorola in the station wagon, so they heard the cacophony of the shootout as it happened. They had not expected to hear gunfire. If all had gone according to script, Mazzieri would have overpowered the kidnappers with his bare hands. But from the moment the tow truck appeared, nothing went according to plan. It was the perfect illustration of Murphy's law: Whatever can go wrong will go wrong.

Shortly after the shootout ended, a call came in on Ottavioli's direct line. It was Max Fernet, the retired police chief who was acting as an adviser to the Empain-Schneider group. Ottavioli filled him in: one kidnapper dead, one captured, two policemen down, and still no idea where the baron was. Fernet's laconic reply: "Not exactly brilliant, Ottavioli."

Ottavioli did not need to be told that. The president and the interior minister had also voiced their displeasure over the bloody and inconclusive result. At that moment, the chief felt abandoned by everyone. As he sped to the scene at the wheel of his own car, escorted by two motorcycles, he reviewed the situation in his head. He was the one who had insisted on the fake ransom strategy. If Empain were killed, Ottavioli would have to face the consequences. His one chance to avoid a potential fiasco was to force the prisoner to reveal the baron's whereabouts and secure his release before some idiot popped him.

Meanwhile, Caillol had been placed in a fire-brigade ambulance with an IV drip in his right arm. His broken left arm, shot in the elbow and shoulder, lay bandaged at his side. When Ottavioli arrived on the scene, André Bizeul met him by the rear door of the ambulance. They both knew that the wounded man inside held their best hope of saving the baron.

The two men approached the fire captain in charge of the ambulance. "We have to interrogate the prisoner immediately," said Ottavioli. "The baron's life is at stake. You need to leave us alone with him in the ambulance for a moment." The officer was reluctant to allow this highly irregular demand, but finally ordered all the medical personnel out of the ambulance. Ottavioli and Bizeul entered the vehicle and closed the door behind them.

Ottavioli subjected Caillol to what he called a "stormy" interrogation. That was an understatement. Caillol insisted that he knew nothing about Baron Empain and had nothing to do with the kidnapping: He had simply been recruited by Duchateau to help him recover the ransom for a fee of 500,000 francs. This preposterous story further infuriated the two police officers. Bizeul grabbed and twisted Caillol's wounded arm, then Ottavioli sat on it with all his weight. Caillol cried out in pain.

"Duchateau is dead," said Bizeul. "We could kill you right here and no one would care. Where is the baron?" Caillol said nothing. Reluctant to push any further with what was at this point an extralegal interrogation, the officers withdrew and let the ambulance take the prisoner to Hôtel-Dieu Hospital, located just a few hundred yards from police headquarters.

CHAPTER 16

"Can't I Call from Here?"

Caillol was a mess when he arrived at Hôtel-Dieu. One bullet had plowed through his left elbow like a drill bit through Sheetrock. The other one had hit him near the shoulder, slicing through muscle but missing the bone. Both eyes were swollen shut. His ribs were bruised. His battered skull was riddled with lacerations and contusions. Doctors sutured his wounds, installed a drain, then sent him to the Cusco ward, a secure section reserved for patients under police jurisdiction—otherwise known as the jailbird wing.

Caillol got little rest at Cusco. As he later recalled, "The ballet of inspectors around my bed started right away, like bees at the entrance to a hive. I knew that I was now in total security, unassailable. I also clearly realized that my life had just flipped upside down and that I had no future."

Under French law, the police had no right to interrogate him about the kidnapping because a judicial inquiry had been opened under the authority of an investigating magistrate. They got around that technical obstacle by charging him with attempted homicide—the wounding of the two police officers—and continued to grill him over the next two days. But they were getting nowhere. "He's no fool," one frustrated detective told his colleagues. "You can talk to him, but he will do all he can to help his accomplices evade capture."

ON FRIDAY EVENING, Wado realized that the mood had changed since Bertoncini had toasted him with Champagne the night before. On the floor above the basement, he heard footsteps, voices, doors slamming. The telephone rang fifteen times in one hour. On the street outside, cars came and went. At one point, Bertoncini trundled down the stairs and barked an order in a tone that had none of his usual joviality: "Put on your mask. We're taking everything away." As soon as Wado had covered his face, Bertoncini removed the television, transistor radio, reading lamp, and other objects from the tent. Assuming all the agitation was a preparation for evacuating the hideout, the captive, enshrouded in darkness, settled into a troubled sleep.

On Saturday morning, someone shoved a newspaper through the tent flap.

"Read this." Wado recognized the voice. It was the same man who had earlier promised to kill him "cleanly" if it came to that.

The headlines recounted the gunfight on the A6, the death of Duchateau, the capture of Caillol. The news was catastrophic for Empain. How could his captors spare his life now? He regretted that they hadn't killed him right after his capture and spared him his sixty-three-day ordeal.

Wado again heard the voice.

"Listen. You've read what happened, you understand the situation. There are only two solutions: kill you or free you. It's become too dangerous to keep you here. The ransom is screwed. There are different opinions about how to proceed. So we're going to get together and vote. I'll come back and tell you the result."

That night, Wado did not touch the meal Bertoncini served him. Neither did he manage to sleep. He was gripped by fear, facing what he thought was a likely death sentence. And he was tormented by the thought that he was responsible for the death of Daniel Duchateau, whose name he had just learned from the papers. Duchateau had been killed by Empain's "people"—the police working for his liberation. His mind still twisted by Stockholm syndrome, he felt that he had somehow betrayed Duchateau and caused his death. For that alone, he deserved to die.

THE MORNING AFTER the shootout, Caillol's lawyer arrived at Cusco to take charge of his case. Monique Smadja-Epstein, age forty-five, was a legend among French criminal lawyers. She resembled a character in a noir film: tall, faux blond, well dressed, with a web of fine wrinkles around her eyes and no makeup. (One cop said she looked like Mick Jagger in drag.) She had the raspy voice of a chain-smoker and spoke like the toughs she associated with—not only as their legal counsel.

Smadja was the mistress of Michel Ardouin—aka "The Aircraft Carrier"—erstwhile henchman of Public Enemy Number One Jacques Mesrine. In the past, she had been involved in an abortive plot to kidnap then–presidential candidate François Mitterrand and exchange him for the imprisoned Mesrine. That caper had fizzled and she was never charged, but her involvement with gangsters of Mesrine's ilk was no secret. She was considered the quasi-official lawyer of the *milieu*—the French mafia. Caillol was a longtime client.

When she entered Caillol's hospital room and saw his battered face, she put her crocodile-skin briefcase down on a chair, took a deep breath, raised her hands to her mouth, and gasped: "*Oh, mon Dieu!*" This from a woman who had seen her share of gangland horrors. When she recovered from her shock, she asked Caillol what he had told police. Nothing at all, he replied. Nodding her approval, she told him she was heading over to the courthouse to see what the judge had in his investigative file. If there was no evidence linking Caillol to the actual kidnapping, she would try to get him off with a lesser charge. Outside the hospital, she told the waiting journalists that her client's "only concern" was the health of his wife and son. Right.

After Smadja's departure, the detectives resumed their insistent interrogations. Caillol stuck to his story about being a hired delivery boy who knew nothing about Empain's whereabouts. "Bullshit!" as one cop crudely put it. Police had forensic proof that his friend Duchateau had been involved from the beginning: Fingerprints lifted from his corpse matched those found on documents sent by the kidnappers. Meanwhile, the investigators were already following leads based on Caillol's and Duchateau's known contacts.

One prime suspect was François Caillol. There was no evidence against him at that point, but his checkered past suggested he was likely involved in his brother's caper. On March 26, just one hour after the shootout ended, Inspector Michel Desfarges was dispatched to Grenoble, where François lived with his wife and their infant son. Irène Caillol told him her husband had left home on March 22 and had not returned. In fact, she said, he had made a number of mysterious trips since December, never telling her where he was going or why. When she heard of Alain's arrest on the news, she was troubled by the fact that her husband had not called her. "The more I think about it," she told Desfarges, "the more I have the feeling he was mixed up with his brother in the kidnapping of Baron Empain. There are too many coincidences, all his absences, and his silence since

Alain's arrest." That evening, Irène called Desfarges at the Judiciary Police headquarters in Grenoble. She had just heard from her husband and begged him to turn himself in. "I'm in Italy," he replied. "I don't want to go to prison." At that point, François Caillol was considered a fugitive from justice. But he wasn't in Italy.

Other detectives went to question Alain's wife, Pierrette, at the Caillols' pied-à-terre apartment in Paris on March 25. She had been partying all night with a friend and was not home when the police arrived. They left her a note summoning her to the Quai des Orfèvres. She arrived there at ten thirty a.m., looking a bit frazzled after her wild night. One detective who took part in the interrogation recalls the thirty-five-year-old blonde as "a beautiful woman—despite some wear and tear." Questioned about her husband's recent movements, Pierrette said he had left the apartment around two p.m. on Friday, March 24, the day of the shootout. She learned of Alain's arrest from radio reports the next morning. When the detectives showed her Daniel Duchateau's photo in the newspaper, she claimed not to know him, which left them more than a bit skeptical. The official deposition ended there. But according to Alain Caillol, the cops continued talking to his wife off the record. They played on her jealousy, saying her husband had been cheating on her during his long absences. She exploded and told them about Caillol's secret trip to Palma the previous summer. That vital piece of information would potentially allow them to identify at least some of his accomplices.

BACK AT POLICE headquarters, Ottavioli was losing patience. The clock was ticking, and every second increased the danger that Empain's enraged jailers might execute their hostage. In desperation, he outlined a daring plan to one of his men: "Look—you go to Cusco and grab Caillol," he said. "I have a friend who has a house in the suburbs. We'll hide him there and, believe me, we'll make him talk!" The suggestion that the police could illegally exfiltrate and torture the prisoner met with a firm refusal on the part of Ottavioli's colleague. For once, the chief backed down.

Meanwhile, Caillol was recomputing the situation in his head. He now knew that his confederates would never see the ransom and feared that their rage over Duchateau's death might lead them to kill their hostage. He was especially worried about an impulsive action by Bertoncini, who had "a chickpea for a brain," as he later told an investigator. Caillol himself was facing up to twenty years in any case, but his fate would be far worse if Empain were killed. Another consideration was the very real possibility that his hysterical wife might divulge the names of his co-conspirators to police. She knew nothing about the kidnapping plot, but she had attended dinners with Caillol and his pals and knew their names. Caillol's fears were heightened when a detective burst into his hospital room and demanded, "What were you doing in Palma last summer?" If Pierrette had told the cops about that, what else might she reveal?

That's when Caillol decided to take the initiative. He told his interrogators that he didn't know where Empain was, but maybe he could make a call and try to get him freed. He had one condition: They must take him to a random public phone booth, on the assumption that it would not be tapped and that the call could not be traced. Ottavioli assented but said he would need the judge's authorization. While awaiting judicial approval, they drove the prisoner to police headquarters around four p.m. on March 26, Easter Sunday.

Still dressed in his hospital gown and slippers, Caillol had to stagger up three flights of stairs to Ottavioli's office, his right hand handcuffed to the wrist of a police officer. Groggy and virtually blind in his left eye, he was escorted down a long, dark hall and passed through a padded door into Room 315, the legendary command center of the Criminal Brigade. It was a large office with cream-colored walls and a slightly stained beige carpet, furnished with a massive wooden desk and two imitation-leather armchairs. Two tall windows looked out on the heart of Paris: the Seine, the Pont Neuf, the Place Dauphine. The walls were devoid of decoration except for a large painting of the Corsican port of Ajaccio and the official portrait of President Giscard d'Estaing with his unconvincing comb-over.

Caillol was greeted by a dozen cops from the Crim and the Antigang squad. Among them: Ottavioli, Bizeul, Cancès, Leclerc, and Broussard. All the men wore business suits except for Broussard, the Antigang cowboy, who sported his usual jeans and leather jacket. Ottavioli, his eyes red and his features drawn tight with fatigue, spoke first. "The situation is simple," he said. "It is in your interest, Monsieur Caillol, that we recover the baron safe and sound. You understand that if things turn bad, you will bear the sole responsibility." Translation: If your buddies kill Empain, you will pay the price, up to and including the guillotine, the revolutionary death machine that was still used in France until capital punishment was abolished in 1981.

Caillol remained silent for a long time. His handcuffs had been removed and he was free to move about the room. He stood by a window and gazed out at the Seine, trying to clear his head. "I squinted as hard as possible with the half of an eye I could still see through, trying to get a grip on myself," he remembers. "I turned around and faced the dozen or so men who formed a semicircle around the desk. We were supposed to go call from a telephone booth in some Paris street. But then I saw the telephone on Ottavioli's desk, and I said to myself, if there's one phone that's not tapped, it can only be this one . . . I asked, 'Can't I call from here?'"

If the cops were surprised by the request, no one showed it. Not a smile, not a sidewise glance. Ottavioli nodded and handed over the rotary-dial phone. Caillol slipped it under his arm sling and stepped away from the desk as far as the cord would go. He turned his back and faced the window so no one could see the number he dialed. In fact he dialed four numbers. He claimed he had a mental block and couldn't remember the correct number, but in fact he was trying to call different accomplices. On the fourth try, a woman answered the phone.

"It's Alain," said Caillol. "Don't speak. Listen, I made a fair deal with the police. . . . The baron must be liberated immediately, alive, because the ransom will never be paid and otherwise this will all end with carnage."

Several minutes later, he called again, this time speaking to a man. After listening briefly to his interlocutor, he hung up and told the police, "It's good at ninety-nine percent. They're going to release him."

In fact, the conspirators had voted earlier in the day to free the baron, but they were still holding him at Bertoncini's place in the suburbs. Caillol's call sped up their timetable. They now knew they had to release the hostage in short order and abandon the hideout, lest the police learn their whereabouts and converge on the house with their heavy artillery.

After he made the call, Caillol, exhausted, slumped down in one of the armchairs facing Ottavioli's desk. The chief looked him in the eye and said, as if to console his prisoner, "After all, that was the only thing you could do."

Caillol nodded. "When I saw the determination of your guys, I understood that we'd never touch a cent. Better that it ends like this."

Ottavioli leaned back in his chair, hands clasped behind his head. "In fact, Caillol," he said, with a trace of a smile, "why did you choose Empain?"

Caillol answered without hesitation. "Because he was the easiest. We thought of Dassault, Rothschild, and Liliane Bettencourt. Then we studied Empain. He had regular habits, one chauffeur, no body-guard, and lived on a service road that made it easy to trap him."

Then he shut up. He knew he had said too much. That was the side of Caillol that made some people, cops and crooks alike, consider him something of a showboat. He wasn't exactly a braggart, but he craved respect, even for his misdeeds. And along with his good looks went a certain dose of vanity. Robert Broussard, who was present at that moment, thought then that Caillol could not have been the real mas-termind behind the plot because "he talks too much to be a leader." Caillol was savvy enough to know that his off-the-cuff remark, which was tantamount to a confession, was inadmissible in court because it had not been made before a magistrate. But Ottavioli and his men had heard it, and they would not forget.

Caillol had made another fatal error. He had been careful to conceal the telephone dial when he called, but he didn't realize that Ottavioli's phone was linked to a tape recorder in André Bizeul's office next door. There, technicians from France's counterespionage agency, the DST, were able to capture the conversations and the electronic clicks emitted by the numbers Caillol had dialed. It took them some time to decipher the data, but they finally managed to identify the ad-dress: 19 Rue Marcellin Berthelot, Savigny-sur-Orge. The house had been rented in the name of a certain Marc Le Gayan, whose sister, Marie-Annick, was Bertoncini's companion. It was Marie-Annick who had answered the phone. (The male voice that answered the second call was never formally identified, but Desfarges is convinced it was François Caillol.)

AFTER CAILLOL WAS escorted back to the hospital, Ottavioli and the other officers waited for a long time in the chief's office. Their hopes for a quick resolution gave way to rising doubts with every minute that ticked by. If Caillol's comrades did not carry out their promise and instead killed the hostage, the results would be disastrous. Not only for the baron but also for Caillol, who risked the guillotine, and for Ottavioli, whose bold gamble on the fake ransom would have crapped out. Caillol had estimated the chances of that outcome at 1 percent. Pretty good odds, but still not a done deal.

Around ten thirty p.m., the chief's phone rang. It was Inspector Jean-Claude Murat, the officer who had been embedded at Silvana's apartment for nearly two months. "Empain just called from the Opéra," said Murat. "I'm going with Silvana now to pick him up." Ottavioli ordered Murat to bring the baron straight to police headquarters. Then he hung up and informed his colleagues that the hostage had been liberated. According to one of the men who was with him that night, he smiled, stretched out his palms, raised his eyes to the ceiling, and said simply, "Voilà!" The other officers shook hands with one another and congratulated the chief. They still had a big job ahead—rounding up the rest of the gang—but with the baron free and one culprit in custody, the real investigation could finally begin.

CHAPTER 17

From One Prison to Another

*E*arlier on that Easter Sunday, Bernard Guillon had good news and bad news for the baron. The good news was that the band had decided to spare his life and liberate him. The bad news was that there was a condition: He must agree to pay the ransom himself once he was freed.

"I will pay," Empain said.

"Okay," said Guillon, speaking through the tent flap, "but we don't have to take your word for it. Here's what we're going to do. We know how to get ahold of you whenever we want. So we're going to make you sign three IOUs, for a total of 45 million francs. We're going to allow you some time to gather the money. Our code name will be Marika. Listen to this well: If, after our first call, you don't pay within twenty-four hours, we will kill some random person in the street and pin your IOU on their back, and so on until we get to the third IOU."

The baron signed.

On Sunday afternoon, Bertoncini threw a new green tracksuit and a fresh pair of sneakers into the tent and told him to put them on. Still chained by the neck and wrists, Empain could not execute the order so he remained in his soiled pajamas. Bertoncini later returned and peeked into the tent.

"Why aren't you dressed?"

"The chain."

"Put your mask on!"

For perhaps the thousandth time, Wado pulled on his blindfold. Bertoncini removed the chains and helped him change into the tracksuit. Outside the tent, he heard the metallic click of a machine pistol being armed and readied.

"This is not the time to try to run away." Wado knew that voice well. It was the man who had made him sign the IOUs—the same one who had promised him a painless death.

Bertoncini reattached the chain and handcuffs and left the baron alone in the tent for a couple of hours. Since learning of the shootout, Wado had been on an emotional roller coaster, going from the fear of immediate execution to relief over the vote to spare him to hope at the prospect of his forthcoming liberation. But nothing was certain. After all, a number of his jailers had voted to kill him in order to protect their identities. Would they feel bound by some arithmetic tally? Never, since the beginning of his captivity, had he felt such a primal, gut-gnawing fear.

Around nine p.m., his minders led Wado out of the basement and installed him in the rear compartment of a Renault 4L minivan. Though he was blindfolded, he realized that the driver was circling the same block three or four times in an effort to disorient him. After a half-hour's drive, he heard one of the men say, "Look for a deserted street." Why a deserted street? Was it to free him or kill him?

The car came to a stop. The two men hoisted Empain out of the van and removed his handcuffs. One of them grabbed his hand and gave him a wadded-up banknote. "Wait one minute before you take off your mask."

Wado heard the van drive off and turn a corner, but he was so used to obeying orders that he waited for seven or eight minutes before daring to unveil his eyes. Finding himself in a dark, empty street, he headed toward a well-lit intersection a hundred yards away. After two months spent mostly in darkness, his vision was dimmed. His atrophied legs felt like rubber, causing him to sway and stagger like a drunk. The only person he passed in the street crossed to the other side. He must have been frightening to behold with his matted two-month-old beard and his long, unkempt hair—not to mention the smell of his unwashed body.

He emerged onto a broad avenue that he did not recognize. Definitely not one of the chic Parisian neighborhoods he was used to. Finally he saw a Métro station and read the illuminated letters over the entrance. It was the Porte d'Ivry, in a working-class section of southeast Paris. He descended the steps, bought a ticket with the ten-franc note he'd been given, and boarded the first train that rumbled up to the platform. He hadn't the faintest notion where it was headed. Accustomed to his chauffeur-driven cars, Monsieur le Baron never took the Métro. Yet, ironically, it was the Métro—the proudest creation of his own grandfather—that would take him to freedom. Suddenly overcome by a sense of relief, he wanted his Métro ride to last a long time so he could savor this moment of liberation.

Wado watched the unfamiliar station names flicker past his window—Place d'Italie, Les Gobelins, Pont Marie, Châtelet . . . Finally, there was a stop he recognized: Opéra. That's where he got off.

He emerged onto the Place de l'Opéra, one of the most beautiful spots in all Paris. The whole quarter was alive with light and

movement as cars crisscrossed through the busy intersection and pe-
destrians strolled along the sidewalks on this festive Easter evening.
Stretching out before him was the Avenue de l'Opéra, a broad thoroughfare lined with cast bronze lampposts that led to the Musée du
Louvre some eight hundred yards away. Behind him stood the ornate
Opéra National de Paris, a neo-baroque creation of architect Charles
Garnier that some wags compared to a three-layer wedding cake when
it opened its doors in 1875. To his right was the Café de la Paix, a historic brasserie once frequented by the likes of Zola, Maupassant, and
Oscar Wilde. To his left stood Le Drugstore, a 1960s-era complex of
restaurants and boutiques that stood out like a sore thumb on the otherwise stately square. Wado entered and dialed his home number from
a phone booth, paying for the call with change from his ten-franc bill.

The person who answered was not his wife but Jean-Claude
Murat, a man whose voice he did not recognize.

"I'd like to speak to Silvana, please."

"Who's calling?"

"Her husband."

There was a brief silence on the other end.

"I said it's her husband," Wado repeated.

"Oh, excuse me, I'm with the police. Hold the line, don't hang up
whatever you do."

A few seconds later, Wado heard the voice of Silvana.

"I knew you would be freed tonight," she said. "Where are you?"

"Place de l'Opéra. Can you come get me? I'm wearing a green
tracksuit and white sneakers, with a two-month-old beard."

Wado felt good as he waited by the steps of the opera house. On
this holiday weekend, there were crowds of happy people milling
about, talking, laughing. He was free at last, no longer huddled in a
stinking tent and fearing a summary execution but free to embrace
the kind of joie de vivre he now watched unfolding in front of him,

free to resume the life of wealth and power that he'd been robbed of on the morning of January 23.

Twenty minutes later, he saw a Renault R12 sedan approaching along the Boulevard des Capucines. As it pulled up alongside him, the rear door opened and Wado tumbled inside. Inspector Murat was behind the wheel with Silvana at his side. She hardly spoke a word.

Exhausted and troubled, Wado noticed that the car was not headed in the direction of his apartment on Avenue Foch.

"Where are we going?" he asked.

"Quai des Orfèvres."

"No way," Empain shot back. "I want to go home."

Murat swung around and looked at his passenger. "Listen, I've told my colleagues I'm bringing you in. They are waiting there."

Wado exploded. He wrenched open the rear door and threatened to jump out unless he was driven home. Murat relented and radioed the change of plans to police headquarters. For the first time since he was grabbed on the street two months earlier, Wado cracked, collapsing onto the car seat and crying like a baby.

WHEN WADO ENTERED his ninth-floor apartment, he was greeted by his two daughters. Patricia, the eldest, vividly recalls that moment. "Since Papa's phone call, we were all waiting for him. Suddenly I see him walk into the entry hall and—what a shock! Papa was always in a business suit, impeccably groomed, his hair combed. Now he had a beard and long hair, he's limping, he's lost thirty or forty pounds and he's wearing a sweat suit. This was not the same man we were hoping to see. We were extremely happy to have him back, but it was like— what happened to him? We did not have a big family gathering in the living room with everybody around. I remember kissing and hugging him, then going back to my room."

There was no time for family bonding in any case. After a quick shower, a shave, and a change of clothes, Wado found Pierre Ottavioli and a half dozen policemen in the living room waiting to debrief him. Time was of the essence, Ottavioli explained. "We need to move as fast as possible to catch the scumbags who put you through this ordeal."

Robert Broussard, who was with Ottavioli that night, was shocked by the baron's feeble appearance. "Empain was visibly relieved to find his family, his walls, his home, but he was not euphoric. He was deeply marked by what he had gone through, like someone who comes out of the hospital after a long illness. He was very thin, and what really struck me was the way he held himself. Before all this, he was a big, strapping, good-looking guy. But now, he was all stooped and bent over."

Wado was in no mood to sit through an interrogation. It was nearly eleven p.m. He was exhausted and depressed by the absence of any sympathy or affection from his entourage. He insisted that his black Labrador, aptly named Love, be brought to him from his country house near Bouffémont, a good forty-minute drive from Paris. While waiting for the dog's arrival, he slumped down in an armchair and told his story. Or at least part of it, for he was still wary of the police and, strange as it seems, felt the need to protect his former guards.

He said he had never seen the kidnappers and could not identify them. When asked to describe the house in Savigny-sur-Orge, he gave only two details: There was a baby that cried and a large dog that barked on the upstairs floor. (The baby, it turned out, was the infant son of Bertoncini and his girlfriend, Marie-Annick Le Gayan; the dog was Bertoncini's German mastiff.) He also told the investigators about the IOUs he had signed, which made little apparent impression on them.

The reception he got that night was, in Empain's words, "strange, totally lacking in warmth. I had the impression that I was a mere object as I talked about what had happened to me to these men, who were silent as stones." Silvana hardly spoke to him. His mother talked to him briefly on the phone without a trace of emotion. Not a word from his stepfather Édouard or his colleagues. For two months, he had dreamed of his liberation, imagined a joyous welcome—"like the return of Monte Cristo"—with hugs and kisses and cheers from the balcony. Instead, he felt he was being treated with suspicion and even blamed for the trouble he had caused by getting kidnapped.

Patricia Empain denies that her father was "badly received" by his family. "I hugged him and kissed him and I cried, but there was a distance from the beginning. The problem is that the police wanted to question him immediately, so we did not have that family time together to get close to him. Certainly not my mom." It was not the family who created the distance, says Patricia. "He was distancing himself. We always wanted love, forgiveness, to be one happy family again. But Papa had a hard time figuring out where he stood with everyone. If he had accepted us back with open arms, as we were all ready to do, we could have turned the page and gone on. But too much had happened to him. He knew he could no longer be the legend he was before."

When his Labrador arrived at the apartment, Wado sat with him on a couch, stroking his thick black coat and basking in the unconditional affection that he felt was lacking in his human companions. Then, for the first time in three months, he took a long, soaking bath. It lasted for three hours. He slept like a rock.

The next day, the telephone rang off the hook. Reporters surrounded the building and clamored for interviews. No fewer than two thousand telegrams arrived at the apartment. But the police, backed by Silvana and René Engen, insisted that he talk to no one. He was not even allowed to read the telegrams. It was not the moment. He needed to rest and let the investigators do their work. "All of a sudden I understood that I was now a prisoner of the police, of my family, my colleagues. I had simply changed jailers."

AND YET, WADO had escaped the worst. On April 10, the body of Belgian industrialist Baron Charles Victor Bracht was found in a Brussels garbage dump. In what may have been a copycat action inspired by Empain's kidnapping, Bracht had been snatched from his car in an underground garage in Antwerp on March 7. His body bore signs of violent injuries, possibly inflicted during an escape attempt. On May 9, the bullet-riddled body of former Italian prime minister Aldo Moro, kidnapped by the radical Red Brigades nearly a month earlier, was found in the trunk of a car in central Rome. And if Caillol's comrades had followed his advice, that's how Wado would have wound up. A bullet in his head would have put a brutal end to the dynasty founded more than a century earlier by one of the most remarkable movers and shakers of his era.

PART V

The Empain Legacy

1900–1971

Father and Son:
Baron Jean Empain and baby
Wado in Heliopolis, c. 1940

*Empain family collection,
courtesy of Diane Empain*

A Family Affair:
Wado, Diane, and
Rozell at the Château
de Bouffémont, 1957

APRH/Bertrand

CHAPTER 18

The Baron's Progeny

In spite of his short stature, the first baron Empain was a man who commanded respect. The insistent gaze of his blue-gray eyes and his loud, deep voice projected an air of authority. When annoyed, he could explode in tirades of vulgarity. Though he exuded an air of toughness, he had an almost neurotic fear of microbes. Any colleague who showed up to work with a cough or sniffle would be reprimanded and sent home. A lifelong hypochondriac, he would panic at the sight of the slightest blotch or pimple and always slept on his side on the dubious theory that he would be less vulnerable to germs in that position. Though he smoked abundantly—cigarillos and Havana cigars—he avoided excessive eating and drinking. He also eschewed the card table and the gaming establishments, though he enjoyed an occasional game of billiards.

Bizarrely, considering his fear of microbes, the baron was a regular visitor to bordellos, where he could satisfy his sexual needs without wasting time on courting or sentimental entanglements. And yet, this inveterate bachelor would find himself ensnared in an intimate relationship around the turn of the century when he fell in love with a certain Jeanne Becker, thirty years his junior. It is not clear exactly how and when they met—one writer hypothesized improbably that their first encounter took place in a Brussels park, where Jeanne retrieved Empain's hat on a windy fall day—but the comely young woman soon became his mistress and his lifelong companion.

Jeanne Becker was the daughter of a Brussels distiller. Educated by nuns, she showed an early talent for singing and studied briefly at a Brussels conservatory, followed by private lessons. She learned arias from popular operettas and a few grand operas, which she enjoyed singing in private settings though she never performed in public. Just as well, for Empain kept their liaison discreet—even after she bore him two sons, Jean, born in 1902, and Louis, born in 1908. She was known within Empain's family as "Aunt Jeanne," and he would refer to his sons as the children of his "sister" or his "niece." On their birth certificates, the boys bore the names Jean and Louis Becker.

Why Empain chose to maintain this unorthodox relationship is a mystery, since he could have made an advantageous marriage thanks to his fortune and prominence. His younger brother François made an excellent match in 1912, marrying Ghislaine Albérique Descantons de Montblanc, daughter of a Belgian count. François in fact owed everything to his brother, who had encouraged his studies and paid for his university education. When François graduated with a law doctorate in 1884, Édouard took him into the family business and thus ensured his fortune. For good measure, Édouard prevailed on Albert I to confer a separate barony on François in 1921. And yet, François nursed a smoldering sense of jealousy toward his benefactor. With his doctorate and his marriage into an aristocratic family, not to mention his election to the Belgian Senate in 1913, François was accepted in social circles that considered his nouveau-riche brother a vulgar parvenu. And when Ghislaine gave birth to a son, also named Édouard, François began to nurture the secret hope that his legitimate offspring would one day inherit the family empire instead of his brother's bastard children.

Édouard had always said he was too busy to marry. And as the years wore on, it seemed increasingly unlikely that he would do so. Imagine François's consternation when he learned that, against all expectations, his brother finally married Jeanne Becker in April 1921. Sixty-nine years old, ill with pneumonia, he had apparently done so to legitimize his sons, then nineteen and thirteen, and thus ensure that his progeny would take over command of the Empain empire when he was gone.

Unaware of his brother's crushed hopes, he asked François to take his oldest son under his wing and teach him the workings of the family business. Under the guise of avuncular affection, François undertook to spoil young Jean (now Empain) by playing on his weakness for alcohol and gambling. Jean, nicknamed Johnny, was an easy target. Handsome, charming, and excessive in every way, he naturally preferred pleasure and dissipation to the drudgery of sitting in an office and learning about the business. François would wink at his nephew's profligacy while in fact teaching him very little. The general finally realized what was going on and exploded in anger against his brother's perfidy. François kept his positions within the group but, shorn of the baron's confidence, he was effectively sidelined. From that point on, a breach opened between the two branches of the Empain dynasty. It would have consequences.

In September 1923, Jean Empain married Christiane Rimoz de la Rochette, nicknamed Tita, the daughter of a noble French family. In rapid succession, Christiane gave him two daughters, Janine and Huguette—a frank disappointment to a father and grandfather in search of male descendants. Rather than settle down into a respectable married life, Johnny continued to pursue his career as a serial philanderer, openly cheating on his wife without the least qualm.

Along with female flesh, his biggest weakness was gambling, with a particular predilection for poker and baccarat. Johnny played frenetically and obsessively, betting and losing astronomical sums then begging his father to bail him out. The general, who detested gambling, reluctantly did so, hoping Jean would grow out of this ruinous habit. Shortly before his death, he allegedly handed his son a check for 100 million gold francs (then worth more than $20 million) to cover his gambling debts, and gave the same amount to his younger son, Louis, in the name of equal treatment.

ON THE MORNING of July 21, 1929, Édouard Empain died at his home in the Brussels suburb of Woluwe-Saint-Pierre. The seemingly indefatigable tycoon had long been in declining health and finally succumbed to a heart attack at age seventy-seven. Laid out in his general's uniform with all his medals, he was temporarily buried in the local cemetery accompanied by an entourage that included representatives of King Albert I, Crown Prince Leopold, Egypt's King Faud I, and dozens of Belgian dignitaries.

On February 8, 1930, in accordance with his wishes, the baron's body was transferred to Heliopolis. By all accounts, Cairo had never seen such a funeral. Thousands of people jammed the streets to get a look at the black horse-drawn carriage with silver trim that carried the casket to the Hindu Villa, where it lay in state in the main hallway. The general's military cap and sword were placed atop the ebony casket, surrounded by floral wreaths and dozens of candles whose flickering light was reflected by the marble walls and columns. At the grand entrance, Jean, Louis, and their mother stood at the top of the steps to accept the condolences of the government ministers, prelates, diplomats, and ordinary citizens who lined up for blocks.

Led on foot by prime minister Mustapha El Nahas Pasha and a large delegation of Egyptian dignitaries, the cortege proceeded from the villa to the basilica for the funeral mass and burial. Marching alongside the horse-drawn hearse was Empain's faithful friend and business partner Boghos Nubar Pasha, wearing his customary red fez and looking even more mournful than usual. After the mass, the casket was lowered into the crypt. A black marble plaque on the wall listed the baron's distinctions and decorations, so numerous that the final line merely read "ETC . . ."

The solemn occasion apparently did little to dim Johnny's ardor. After a night spent at the sumptuous Palace Hotel, he left for Luxor the next morning with his mistress of the moment, who had accompanied him to Egypt for the funeral: Josephine Baker, the sizzling American dancer and singer, known as the "Black Venus," who would later be an agent of the French Resistance and a U.S. civil rights activist.

Jean and Louis Empain inherited an immense fortune from their father. The exact monetary amount is impossible to know for sure, but one estimate puts the current value at some $2 billion. In addition to cash holdings and liquidities, the family fortune included a number of châteaux, mansions, and landed estates, not to mention the stock that made Jean and Louis the group's principal shareholders.

The two brothers wasted no time seizing control of the family empire. First, they consolidated the group's main entities into a single Belgian-based holding company, Electrorail, with Johnny as president by virtue of his seniority. Next, they unceremoniously relieved their uncle François of his functions, thus completing the excommunication that their father had not quite had the heart to carry out. Though he remained an important Electrorail shareholder, François withdrew to his château in Enghien, Belgium, where he sank into depression and alcoholism and died in 1935 at the age of seventy-three. His only son, Édouard, namesake and godson of the founder, continued to live in the château with his mother well into middle age. Johnny, who scorned and loathed this Édouard, called him *"cousin fausse-couche"*—Cousin Miscarriage.

The general's two sons were as different as Jacob and Esau. Jean, athletic and seductive, remained an unabashed hedonist. Louis, dumpy, bucktoothed, and bespectacled, was a somber introvert who would eventually detach himself from the business to pursue personal projects in Canada. After narrowly escaping drowning during a storm on the Saint Lawrence that nearly capsized his yacht, he embraced religion, philanthropy, and good works. He devoted his career and his fortune to Catholic charities, running a Christian youth organization, and writing numerous books about religion, education, and ecology. (Among other things, he campaigned against "the widespread vice of masturbation.") Moved by his rigid adherence to Christian values, Louis embraced progressive social ideas like profit sharing, income equality, and workers' rights that were sharply at odds with his father's capitalist ethos.

Johnny, for his part, had no problem with capitalism and its bountiful fruits. Well seconded by his father's ex-lieutenants, he proved to be a competent if not brilliant businessman. But his main activity was indulging his passion for women, yachts, horses, and Champagne. At the Château de Bouffémont near Paris, which he had inherited on the general's death, he was famous for hosting nonstop parties reminiscent of the Great Gatsby's fictional extravaganzas. Guests, including government ministers, financiers, movie stars, con men, and courtesans, were treated to punch bowls full of Champagne, fireworks, magic shows, dusk-till-dawn dancing, and even—on one occasion—a boxing match. But they were ill-advised to wander in the enclosed six-acre park surrounding the château: It was populated by wild animals, including lions, pumas, and bears. The château itself, which contained eleven large bedrooms, was filled with antique tapestries and mounted trophies of wild game that Johnny, an avid hunter, had shot on African safaris. The center of the main stairwell was occupied by a stuffed giraffe whose neck reached to the second floor. In its extravagance, if not its scale, the château recalled *Citizen Kane*'s Xanadu. It was against that exotic backdrop that Johnny and his guests would frolic in the drawing rooms—and in the bedrooms.

When he was tired of partying on land, Johnny would head out to sea aboard the *Héliopolis*, a long, narrow luxury yacht that had originally been built for Kaiser Wilhelm. It was captained by the former commander of the *Queen Mary* and manned by a dozen uniformed crew members. Accompanied by an entourage of friends, sycophants, secretaries, and lovers, Johnny would cruise for weeks at a time, gorging on Champagne and caviar and sleeping with a different woman every night. Shipboard photos from the mid-1930s show him sitting proudly on the deck, whisky and cigar in hand, dressed in a monogrammed blue blazer, spotless white trousers, and a commodore's cap.

A man of average height with a receding hairline and a strong nose, Johnny boasted a trim, muscular body, a killer smile, and dazzling blue-gray eyes that one mistress likened to mother-of-pearl. With his animal magnetism and gregarious bonhomie—not to mention his ostentatious wealth—he seduced effortlessly. In addition to Josephine Baker, the revolving list of his mistresses included a former Miss France, a famous Egyptian model, and, not least, Miss Siegfried Resch Knudsen, a beautiful young Swedish woman known as "Baby" for her girlish face. Johnny had met her in Deauville, gave her a ride to Paris in his roadster, and for a time made her his regular companion.

Knudsen, said to be a dead ringer for Marlene Dietrich, eagerly embraced the role, co-hosting Johnny's parties at Bouffémont, sharing his cabin aboard the *Héliopolis*, and lavishly spending his money on jewelry, furs, and designer clothes. By this time, Johnny had divorced his first wife and the road seemed open for Baby Knudsen to become his next baroness. But he soon started looking for greener pastures.

In desperation, Knudsen began consulting a well-known Parisian clairvoyant, a certain Madame de Thanis, who read cards, communed with dead spirits, and provided her client with an assortment of magic powders and potions guaranteed to rekindle Johnny's passion. For her occult services, dispensed over several months, Thanis billed the equivalent of some $70,000. When Johnny finally dropped her, Baby Knudsen sued the clairvoyant for fraud. Widely covered by the tabloid press, the case ended with Madame de Thanis's conviction—but only for tax evasion. The naïve Swedish beauty did not recover a cent. And none of it helped anyway. Johnny had moved on.

In January 1935, the *Héliopolis* steamed into the port of Southampton. Johnny and his entourage motored on to London and checked into the Dorchester. Over cocktails in the hotel's nightclub, they took in the floor show, a girlie dance revue that was nothing special—until the house lights went down and a young woman emerged from behind the curtains clad only in gold paint, the contours of her nude, well-toned body glistening under the spotlight. As she slowly turned and twisted to the languorous music, Johnny Empain gazed at this nymphlike figure and held his breath.

CHAPTER 19

Goldie

he lady in gold was Rozell Rowland, an eighteen-year-old American dancer who had recently arrived in England with a touring burlesque show. Rozell, Rosy to her friends, was born in Columbus, Ohio, a flat, drab Midwestern town that was scorching in the summer and freezing in the winter—a good place to leave from, as she put it. Rozell—whose name was variously spelled Roz Zell, Roz Elle, or Rose Zell—was the youngest of four sisters. Uninterested in school, she dreamed of a big career in show business. With her older siblings Dian and Betty Jane, she started taking dance lessons as a teenager, performed at local talent shows, then went on the road as a sister act with touring vaudeville troupes.

All three girls were pretty and perky, with supple, well-proportioned bodies and "skin like satin," as one reviewer put it. At first, they did their regular sister act, but soon started going on as singles and peeling off their clothes to the bump-and-grind rhythm of the stage bands. Their devout Christian Scientist parents, Alvah and his wife, Ada, were horrified—Alvah, a parole officer, was so strict that he wouldn't even permit his wife to wear a bathing suit on a public beach. "But he soon came around," Betty Jane remembered. "Dad ended up keeping scrapbooks on all three of us girls."

The Depression temporarily put the Rowland sisters out of work until an agent got them into the chorus line at the Old Howard Theatre in Boston in 1932. One night a New York impresario caught the act and recruited the girls to perform at the Paradise, one of Manhattan's top nightclubs. Their new employer was none other than Nils Thor Granlund—better known in the showbiz world by his initials: N.T.G. The Swedish-born Granlund had been a sportswriter, a publicist for Loews Theatres, and a popular radio announcer who brought the likes of Al Jolson and Eddie Cantor to the listening public in the 1920s. A sometime singer and performer himself, he composed the 1924 foxtrot "What Does the Pussy Cat Mean When She Says 'Me-ow?'" During the Prohibition years, Granlund ran some of Manhattan's most popular speakeasies, rubbing shoulders with movie stars, mobsters, and millionaires. When Prohibition ended, he replaced his dark, smoky gin joints with classier establishments featuring girlie floor shows, dance bands, crooners, and wisecracking comedians. By the mid-1930s, Granlund was known as the king of the Broadway nightclub scene—some even credited him with inventing the nightclub. As an impresario, he was famous for spotting and nurturing female talent. To be discovered by N.T.G., as Rosy soon learned, was a big break for an aspiring showgirl. It would not be the last time she would use her body to attract the attention of a powerful man.

It was at the Paradise Club that Rosy created the act that made her famous and gave her the nickname "Goldie": It consisted of cavorting onstage covered only with a thin coat of gold paint like the character that would appear decades later in the James Bond film *Goldfinger*. A promotional picture by the famous celebrity photographer Murray Korman depicts her as a gilded nymph, one arm raised majestically over her head and trailing a sheer veil, her shimmering, well-toned body the very image of erotic womanhood.

Goldie's act was an instant hit. Describing her "Golden Girl" routine in the Brooklyn-based *Kings County News*, one showbiz reporter fairly drooled on his typewriter keys. "This dainty little eyeful, who is a headliner in acrobatic terpsichore, will have the males all agog, agogga by the expressive grace, agility and charm she exudes while tripping the 'light fantastic.'" The article went on to announce that Granlund would be "taking his troupe, bevy of beauties, including Rose Zell to 'Merrie Ole England' shortly, where they are booked to perform for the ritzy Londoners at the swank Dorchester Hotel."

Rozell jumped at the chance to perform in Europe, but her sisters chose to remain in New York and continue their careers in the burlesque business. After a tearful goodbye at dockside, Goldie boarded the *Île de France* bound for England. She was seventeen years old, blond and beautiful, and the world was her oyster. She never looked back.

The girls were lodged at the newly opened Dorchester, a favorite haunt of the rich and famous, and performed in its nightclub. Despite the luxurious digs, Goldie found London, with its low buildings and narrow streets, a bit disappointing compared to the dazzling Broadway lights she had left behind. After six weeks there, she was starting to get bored. And then Baron Jean Empain checked into the Dorchester. "Johnny arrived with his Rolls-Royce, his chauffeur, his secretary, his friends, all his entourage," she later told a Belgian journalist. "He was magnificent. Handsome, elegant, athletic."

His eyes glued on the Golden Girl, Empain caught her act every night and waited for her at the end of each show. After four days, he invited her to dinner and asked her to come with him to Southampton, where his yacht was docked. She said she would need to ask the show's manager for permission to take a few days off. "Well, go ask him," Johnny replied. "I'll wait in my car for half an hour. If you don't join me, that means it's a no."

The manager and the other girls tried to dissuade her, saying a rich playboy would throw her away like an old sponge once he'd had his way with her. But Goldie decided to go for it. She wasn't exactly in love with this titled suitor, but she decided this might be her big break. "I'm sick of scuffling around," she told them. "I want to get ahead in life. I'll take a chance with him."

The next day, Goldie found herself on the deck of the *Héliopolis*. She had plenty of company. Johnny traveled with an entourage of friends and lovers, including a regular girlfriend that he was growing tired of. Though it was Goldie that he installed in his stateroom, he continued to visit the cabin of her predecessor, along with a clutch of other women he had brought along for the ride. Goldie quickly figured out the deal and gracefully put up with his overt bed-hopping. "I have the best place for the moment," she told herself, "but the others have a right to live too!" And live they did. Champagne for breakfast, gin and tonics at lunch, fine French wines at dinner, plus music, games, and all manner of frolicking into the wee hours.

After a brief stop in Ostend, the yacht steamed southward to Heliopolis, Egypt. "When we arrived," she recalled, "I realized that everything belonged to the baron: the train, the strange [Hindu] villa, the hotel, the racetrack, the city, everything! . . . There were so many domestics, I could hardly even blow my nose by myself. My head was spinning." Eager to impress her family back home, she sent them a postcard of the Palace Hotel and scrawled on the back: "The Baron owns this hotel too." As for the racetrack, not only did Johnny own it, he was the president of the Heliopolis Racing Club and boasted a stable of more than thirty world-class thoroughbreds, judged to be "one of the best in the country" by a prestigious racing almanac.

In spite of the dire predictions of her friends back in London, Goldie's affair with Jean Empain did not end with a cold fare-thee-well from the millionaire baron. She became his constant companion as he pursued his peripatetic life of pleasure. Photos show them bundled up alongside an English country road in February 1935; inspecting Johnny's horses at Bouffémont in June; aboard ship in July; lunching with friends at the Heliopolis racetrack in September; camping together in the Congo in early 1936. One shot shows Goldie in a safari suit sitting in front of a locomotive on a rail line built by the general. So visible was their relationship that the tabloids started bruiting a forthcoming marriage between the baron and the "Liquid Gold Dancer."

Those reports were premature, but when Goldie became pregnant in early 1937, her lover was delighted. "If it's a boy, I'll marry you," he promised. "If it's a girl, I'll take financial responsibility and you will want for nothing." But gallantry only went so far with Johnny. His sexual appetites required constant satisfaction, and he was not overly attracted by the swelling belly of a pregnant woman. Before embarking on a long tour of China with another girlfriend, he made arrangements to set Goldie up in Budapest to await the arrival of their child.

Why Budapest? The choice seems odd, but Johnny explained that he had funds in Hungarian banks that he could not export. He proposed to lodge her in a luxury hotel there, accompanied by a maid and a Saint Bernard, and let her draw down his Hungarian forints. So off she went, a twenty-year-old American girl planted in a strange city whose language she didn't know, with no friends or distractions but the sounds of gypsy music that wafted up from the gardens near her hotel. It was there that she passed what she called "the longest months of my life."

On October 7, 1937, she gave birth to a healthy baby boy in a Budapest clinic. His birth certificate identified him as Edes-Janos, the Hungarian version of Édouard-Jean. Several days later, Johnny showed up with two rings in his pocket. They were married on November 4 in the office of the clinic's director and hopped on the *Orient Express*, heading to their honeymoon in Egypt. Little Wado was left in the care of Jean's first wife, Christiane de la Rochette, whom he had divorced, à la Henry VIII, because she had failed to give him a male heir. (Tita remained on good terms with Jean and even became a friend of Rozell's.)

When they returned from Egypt, the newlyweds settled down at the Château de Bouffémont, the nineteenth-century mansion that the first Baron Empain had bought before World War I. With the infant Wado in the care of his nanny, the couple were free to resume their frenetic social life. Rozell settled easily into her new role as a baroness, catered to by servants, hobnobbing with Johnny's rich and famous friends, and riding thoroughbred horses as if she were born in a saddle. Dressed by Parisian couturiers, covered with furs and jewelry, little Rosy had come a long way from Columbus, Ohio—and still had a long way to go.

CHAPTER 20

Disgrace

*F*or all his devotion to fun and frolic, Johnny also had professional responsibilities as the titular head of an international conglomerate in the face of a worldwide Depression. Fortunately for him, the hands-on management was handled by competent lieutenants, and the group's key sectors—transport, energy, metallurgy, and mining—resisted the shocks of the economic downturn. In fact, the group's Belgian-based holding company, Electrorail, did quite well during this turbulent time: Profits grew steadily throughout the 1930s, and remained comfortable even after the outbreak of World War II in September 1939.

As a Belgian citizen and a member of the army reserve, Johnny, then thirty-seven years old, was liable to be called up in the general mobilization decreed by the government at the outset of the war. According to "friends" cited in an article by the *New York Times*, Baron Jean Empain allegedly left Egypt and joined the Belgian Army on

April 3, 1940. The article claimed that he had been "wounded while fighting in Belgium and was a prisoner in Brussels." Yet there is no record of Jean Empain ever fighting in the war, being wounded, or taken prisoner. Perhaps the *Times* confused him with his younger brother, Louis, who did enlist, was captured at Dunkirk, and was later freed.

In fact, Johnny spent the early war years at Bouffémont, where he continued to host his Gatsby-style extravaganzas as before. The only difference was that the guest list now included uniformed German officers. Johnny not only welcomed them to his decadent parties, he also invited them to extravagant Champagne dinners at Maxim's, Lucas Carton, and other famous Paris restaurants. In return for his amiability, he was allowed to frequent a bordello reserved for German officers and given an *Ausweis*, a pass that permitted him to circulate freely throughout occupied Europe at the wheel of his Mercedes-Benz. More important, the industrial activities of the Empain group in occupied France and Belgium were allowed to continue largely unhindered—which may in fact have been the main reason for his chumminess with the Germans. (To be sure, there were occasional moments of friction: When a bear escaped from Johnny's zoo and chewed up the upholstery of a German roadster, the car's owner shot the beast with his sidearm. Johnny, laughing hysterically, had the bear stuffed and put it on display in his entry hall along with his hunting trophies.)

Like most French capitalists at this time, Johnny abhorred the rise of bolshevism and saw the German Reich as a bulwark against its advance. There is no evidence that he actually embraced the National Socialist ideology, but it was good business—and good fun—to hobnob with the Germans who had become the masters of Europe. Yet his relationship with the occupiers went far beyond the bounds of courteous hospitality. According to one historian of the Occupation, the couple befriended Reichsmarschall Hermann Göring, hosted him at Bouffémont, and even helped prepare a reception in his honor in Paris in June 1941. (Göring was unable to attend due to the German declaration of war against Russia.)

Goldie herself was rumored to be more than friendly with the Germans. "In 1941," according to a French police report, "she had been the mistress of a German captain, commander of an armored unit stationed next to the Château de Bouffémont." The unsourced report, apparently based on hearsay, signaled the couple's "particularly dissolute mores," describing parties and orgies at Bouffémont and at their house in Paris that involved not only German officers but well-known collaborators. (Diane Empain, for her part, insists that her mother was not a collaborator and even credits her with several acts of resistance.)

Among the collaborators in the Empains' circle were Jean Luchaire, a notorious pro-German journalist, and his daughter Corinne, a movie actress and sometime mistress of a German SS officer. In her memoirs, Corinne admiringly described the gatherings of the "elite of the artistic, literary, and political world" at Bouffémont. In particular, she recalled a glittering costume ball that Johnny hosted on Christmas Eve 1940, attended by dozens of German officers in uniform whose long cars filled the courtyard. After D-Day, Corinne and her father fled to Germany. He was later captured in Italy and extradited to France for trial. Convicted of collaboration, he was executed in 1945. Corinne was sentenced to "national indignity" and deprived of her civic rights. She died of tuberculosis in 1950 at the age of twenty-eight.

Johnny was also threatened by the wave of anti-collaborationist reprisals—known as the *épuration*—that began even before D-Day. In 1943, as the winds of war started to shift against the Reich, the baron began to receive threats from the French Resistance—including a miniature coffin affixed to the gate of his château—and fled to Franco's Spain. Safely ensconced in Madrid, where the Empain group owned the local tramway company and a chain of hotels, he continued to negotiate deals and party with the Franquista elite—until he fell ill with throat cancer at age forty-six.

Johnny's flight to Madrid did not prevent France's provisional government from examining his wartime conduct in the wake of the Liberation. Toward the end of 1944, the Ministry of Industrial Production directed the newly formed National Epuration Commission—the agency responsible for investigating acts of collaboration—to look into the case of Baron Jean Empain, suspected of a "clearly pro-German attitude, demonstrated, in particular, by his continual receptions for German officers at his property in Bouffémont." If his suspected collaboration was confirmed, the ministry recommended that he be stripped of all his corporate posts. Meanwhile, the French ambassador in Brussels wrote to authorities in Paris recommending the confiscation of Empain's assets.

Two French investigators were assigned to examine the charges but lacked the legal authority to compel witnesses. Their report, though sparsely sourced and inaccurate on some points, nonetheless painted a highly unflattering picture of Jean Empain's wartime activities. The French ambassador in Brussels denounced the baron as a "miserable personage" but provided the investigators with few specifics. Based on unofficial conversations with French and Belgian officials, they concluded that Empain was "very badly considered, a man of libertine habits, who, on a prewar tour of the Belgian Congo, created a scandal by his bad conduct (drunkenness, loose morals, like his wife). He socialized with the Germans during the war, receiving them at his open table in Bouffémont and accompanying them to nightclubs in Paris." Belgian authorities were said to have a damning dossier on Empain's wartime activities, but withheld their information because, according to the investigators, King Leopold III, Albert's son and successor, had important financial interests in the Empain group.

If French authorities were having trouble linking Johnny to specific acts of collaboration—defined as actively aiding the enemy's war efforts—they were more successful in their efforts to sanction one key piece of Empain's industrial empire: the Compagnie du Métropolitain de Paris (CMP). The Métro had enjoyed a special status during the war: Not only was it the only means of public transport (all the buses and taxis were requisitioned), but sixty-four stations served as public bomb shelters during Allied air raids. The Germans, whose soldiers were allowed to ride the subway for free, also made military use of the network, converting two stations into underground arms depots and operational centers. But the Germans encountered a hostile population among the thousands of Parisians who continued to take the Métro. Many of the Métro employees were sympathetic to the Resistance, whose members used its hidden corridors to meet and furtively left their tracts and clandestine newspapers in the stations. When one Resistance fighter assassinated a German naval cadet on the platform of the Barbès-Rochechouart station on August 21, 1941, Métro employees helped whisk the killer from the scene.

The conduct of the company officials, however, was more than complacent toward the occupiers. CMP directives required Métro personnel to provide special assistance to German soldiers and citizens. The company offered bonuses to security agents who apprehended anyone defacing German posters in the Métro stations; offenders were turned over directly to German authorities. Jewish employees, subject to curfew, were not permitted to work night shifts, and at least a dozen of them were fired. On orders from the German military authorities, the CMP banned "negroes and negresses" from its first-class cars. Jews wearing the yellow star were relegated to the rear car. In a May 1942 report to stockholders, the company's management declared: "We are committed to pledge our most total cooperation to the public authorities"—meaning the German occupation force and the collaborationist Vichy government.

Two months later, the company's "cooperation" took a more sinister form. On July 16, 1942, the CMP put its buses and drivers at the disposal of French police during the infamous roundup that herded Jews into the Vél d'Hiv velodrome and deported them to German concentration camps. CMP vehicles and drivers also carried Jews to Drancy, where they were loaded onto cattle cars and shipped eastward. In May and June 1943, a delegation of CMP directors and engineers accepted an invitation to inspect transport networks in Dresden, Munich, and Salzburg, where they were warmly fêted by their Nazi hosts.

After the Liberation, the CMP's leadership was targeted by the provisional government for its ready cooperation with the occupiers. Heads began to roll in January 1945, when CMP president Paul Martin was abruptly suspended, followed by twenty-seven other senior company officials. A National Assembly committee report charged the CMP with "guilty submission" before the enemy and noted that its principal shareholder, Baron Jean Empain, was under investigation for collaboration. A law of March 21, 1948, stripped the CMP of its concession and barred it from any future transportation activity in Paris. The Métro was folded into a new public company, the RATP, which consolidated the capital's subway and bus services under one administration. That marked the end of the Empain group's long, and lucrative, control of the Paris Métro. In another major blow, the group lost its position as France's preeminent producer of electricity when the government nationalized the sector in 1946.

BEFORE THAT DENOUEMENT, Johnny Empain was fighting for his life in Madrid. Racked with pain from his advancing throat cancer, his once-athletic body wasting away, he sent word to Bouffémont that he wanted to see his wife and son for perhaps the last time. When Goldie and Wado arrived in August 1945, she found Johnny so wasted by the disease that she could hardly recognize him. He was drugged on cocaine but couldn't resort to his favorite form of self-medication, whisky, because his throat was blocked by the tumor. He asked Goldie to administer a shot through his nose using a straw. Wado, eight years old, hardly remembered the father he had not seen in nearly two years. "He was very weak and thin," he later recalled. "He spoke to me with warmth and tenderness, father to son." After that brief meeting, Wado was escorted back to Paris by a colleague of his father's. Goldie remained at Johnny's side.

In December 1945, Johnny suddenly announced that he had to return to France. Goldie thought it was to deal with a tax problem, but it is more likely that he simply wanted to die at home. By that time, he was almost a stateless person. The Belgian embassy refused to renew his passport. Spanish authorities were starting to consider him persona non grata. In France, he was still under investigation for collaboration. It seemed there was no way for him to travel to Paris. But the ever-resourceful Goldie took matters into her hands. She visited an American airline pilot at his hotel in the middle of the night and persuaded him to smuggle Johnny into France on board his plane. They left the next morning.

Once arrived in Paris, Johnny settled into a borrowed apartment on the fashionable Boulevard Suchet, visited only by a few close friends and a doctor who treated him with radium needles inserted directly into his tongue. Guy de la Rochette, brother of Johnny's first wife, secretly drove him to Bouffémont in a covered truck so he could have a last look at his beloved château through the gates. Back in Paris, he asked to see his son again. When the boy arrived, accompanied by Rozell, he was shocked to find his bedridden father exhausted and emaciated. But Johnny managed to perk up a bit. "Ah," he said, "since you're here, let's play a little game of cards." He produced a deck, shuffled, and began to deal. The game was called Russian Bank, a sort of two-handed solitaire. Even at that tender age, Wado was apparently proficient enough at cards to beat his father. But Johnny didn't like losing. "If I was in good health, I'd never have let you beat me. No one has the right to beat me."

Jean Empain expired on Thursday, February 7, 1946. He was buried in the uniform of a reserve lieutenant in the Belgian Army. After a sparsely attended funeral in the tiny village church of Bouffémont, he was temporarily buried in the local cemetery. His remains were later transported to Egypt and laid to rest in the crypt of the Heliopolis basilica, next to his father.

Johnny's death ended the legal actions against him, leaving the charges of collaboration unproven though they continued to cloud his memory. For his part, Wado struggled to reconcile the unpleasant things he heard about his father with the "perfect and unalterable" image that he wanted to preserve. He finally resolved the contradiction by "deciding once and for all that my father was what I said he was" and that "anyone who thought different would have to deal with me."

THE READING OF Jean Empain's will came as a shock to Rozell. Half his estate went to Wado, and the rest was divided among Johnny's three daughters (two by his first wife, the third by a mistress). Though Goldie was given effective guardianship over her son until his adulthood, she received no legacy at all. Louis Empain, Jean's younger brother, was named head of a family council charged with managing Wado's interests until he reached adulthood. That was bad news for Goldie: Louis had never hidden his contempt for Johnny's "strip-teaser" wife. He had even threatened her at the bedside of his dying brother. "Who do you think you are?" he shouted, wagging a finger in her face. "You shall soon see, Madame, what will happen to you. If you think you are going to keep your son, you are sadly mistaken!"

In short, Johnny's death left Goldie out in the cold. But once again, she was saved by the protection of a powerful man. Johnny's first cousin Édouard, heir to the junior branch of the Empain dynasty, suddenly proposed to marry her—or perhaps it was Goldie who nudged him. This Baron Empain, the one Johnny called Cousin Miscarriage, had little to recommend him as a potential husband. Described by Johnny as "pigeon-toed and droopy-mouthed," with an enormous nose and beady eyes, he still lived with his domineering mother at the Château d'Enghien in Belgium. Politically far-right, he maintained contacts with the notorious Belgian fascist leader and rabid anti-Semite Léon Degrelle during the Occupation and was later accused of collaboration but never tried.

Excessively timid, he had never had a serious relationship with a woman, and some suspected he was a closet homosexual. His mother, who strongly disapproved of the match, warned Rozell that her son was impotent. But Cousin Édouard had three things going for him: a noble title, money, and power. As the only son of François Empain (the general's younger brother), he had inherited his father's substantial estate and stock holdings along with his barony. Since Johnny's exile in Spain, he had effectively assumed command of the Empain group. By marrying Édouard, Goldie would retain her title as a baroness and her access to the family fortune. Though she felt no attraction to this awkward cousin, she held her nose and entered into this loveless marriage.

"I was surprised when he proposed," she told the Belgian journalist Yvon Toussaint, who interviewed her in the 1990s. "At the time, I knew nothing about business, and wondered how I could ever manage to protect myself and my son. Louis detested me. The others [in the family] would have let him trample me without lifting a finger. What could I do? This offer was unhoped for. I could remain a baroness. Édouard told me Wado would be the son that he could never have, that he could adopt him, and that he would inherit from Édouard after inheriting from Jean." She added, for the record, that it was a pure "marriage of convenience," since Édouard, as his mother had warned, had sexual "problems."

The wedding took place in the town of Saint-Symphorien-le-Château, near Chartres, on November 13, 1947. Photos of the event show Rozell, then thirty, dressed in a full-length fur coat; Édouard, thirty-three, sports a white tie and tails with a top hat. The couple doesn't smile or even look at each other. Their stiff formality seems to reflect the true nature of this *mariage blanc*: It was a purely business arrangement. After the ceremony, Goldie returned to live at the Château de Bouffémont, while her new husband went back to live with his mother at the Château d'Enghien. "From time to time, I gave him the authorization to come," she told Toussaint. "But he wasn't very amusing . . . He was gauche, always in the way, and encumbered by his own awkwardness . . . In short, he came rarely and left early."

CHAPTER 21

The Inheritor

*W*ado's childhood was one of privilege, comfort, and profound loneliness. Only nine years old when his father died, and ten when his mother remarried, he grew up in a virtual cocoon at the Château de Bouffémont. There was no family life to speak of. His stepfather, who eventually adopted him, lived in his own château in Belgium. His mother, preoccupied with her own social life, was cold and distant. Wado admired her from afar, as if she were a visiting princess, but there was no warmth or tenderness between them. He always believed his mother never loved him. Her true feelings are impossible to divine, but she was such a strong-willed and self-centered creature that there was perhaps no room in her life for motherly instincts. As she would later tell a family historian, there was also a cruel calculation behind her coldness: "I was frightened to death of my son's [possible] homosexuality. That's why I was systematically rude with him. I thought—I didn't know much then—that when one is tender with a little boy he would become gay! I wanted him to be a man!"

The real maternal figure in Wado's childhood was his Irish nanny, Miss Julie. A jovial, big-boned redhead, Juju, as he called her, played the roles of surrogate mother and best friend. The boy was educated at home by private tutors, including a young priest, l'abbé Langlais, who taught him to read, write, and count, and even played soccer with him on the château's luxuriant lawns. A woman from the village gave him weekly piano lessons, which he hated but dared not refuse. He had only one playmate in those days, a boy named Bernard Moine, whose family worked the farmlands belonging to the estate. Despite their different social stations, the peasant lad and the young baron became friends for life. Moine would later be at his side at a critical moment.

When he was ten, Wado was sent to a Catholic boys' school in the town of Bury, some twenty-five miles north of Bouffémont. He quickly realized that his privileged position set him apart from his schoolmates. He would arrive each day like Little Lord Fauntleroy in a chauffeur-driven car, while his comrades came on their bicycles, on foot, or by bus. The others at first found him cold and arrogant, and he made few friends. Trying to blend in with the group, he eventually adopted their way of dressing, their tastes, their speech. He even made the chauffeur drop him off at some distance from the school so he could arrive on foot.

There was one young man who took Wado under his wing: Jean-Jacques Bierry, who served as the château's *régisseur*, or superintendent, in charge of the grounds, the stables, and the domestic staff. Bierry, the son of a Parisian architect, had come to Bouffémont in 1943 at age eighteen. He started off as an assistant to the then *régisseur*, but soon took over when his predecessor retired. It was a big job for a man so young, but Bierry had exceptional qualities: He was smart, efficient, orderly, and knew how to get along with everyone. He was also an exceptionally good-looking young man, standing six foot three, blond and muscular. In fact, he bore a strong resemblance to the man Wado would become.

Originally hired by Jean Empain as a favor to Bierry's father, he was now considered practically a member of the family. He lodged in an outbuilding next to the stables but spent much of his time in the château, where he kept his office. Rozell had a particular affection for him—and perhaps more, according to Bierry's son. Far from showing any jealousy, Édouard thought so highly of Bierry that he later offered him a position in the Empain group, where he would eventually rise through the ranks to a senior position.

To Wado, starved for a male role model, Bierry was like a big brother—a "perfect man," as he put it. When Wado moved on to a Catholic boarding school in Pontoise, some twelve miles from Bouffémont, it was Bierry who would drive him there and pick him up for his weekend visits. It was Bierry who first took him to Paris, introduced him to the theatre and the cinema, and acted as an adviser and confidant.

Meanwhile, Wado's mother was living her own life, and much of it was centered on her passionate love affair with Jacques Doyasbère, one of the most famous jockeys in French racing history. Rozell had approached him as he returned his sweating mount to the paddock after another of his countless victories. With his sultry good looks and elegant bearing, Doyasbère, nicknamed "Tarzan" for his resemblance to Johnny Weissmuller, had no end of female admirers. But he fell hard for this blond *Américaine* who gazed up at him with admiring eyes as he dismounted. Their affair had begun even before Johnny's death and continued long after her remarriage to Cousin Édouard, apparently oblivious to their liaison even though it was touted in all the gossip pages.

Édouard, who lived apart from his wife, did not even notice that she was pregnant. On October 11, 1949, Rozell gave birth to a baby girl she named Diane. Jacques Doyasbère recognized his paternity, but Rozell, apparently fearing possible reprisal from her husband, insisted that the infant be declared as being "born of an unknown and unnamed mother." So the child began her life as Diane Doyasbère and for her first few years lived in the Château de Bouffémont with her mother and her biological father—apparently unbeknownst to Édouard. Jacques spoiled her, gave her a pony named Bobby, and taught her to ride.

Diane was not the only product of that liaison. In 1953, Doyasbère gave Rozell a thoroughbred mare named Flicka. Born in 1949 (the same year as Diane), Flicka was a natural champion who would later produce a legendary progeny as a broodmare. Rozell fell in love with the horse. With her characteristic will and determination, she trained obsessively and went on with Flicka to win a string of prestigious prizes at show jumping competitions. She seemed to have an inborn talent for controlling her mount. In sport as in everything else, Goldie was determined to dominate.

TYPICALLY SECRETIVE AND distant, Rozell had not bothered to inform Wado that he had a baby sister. He came home from boarding school one day and discovered an infant in a baby carriage. "No one told him who the baby was," says Diane, "but he figured it out. In that milieu, with that education, no one talked. Our mother said nothing. But when Wado discovered the carriage, and saw my father standing by it, he understood that I was his sister."

Wado was twelve years old when Diane was born. Despite the age difference, the two became very close. Family photos show Wado giving her a ride on the back of his bike at Bouffémont with Goldie following close behind on horseback. From her summer vacation in Le Touquet at age nine, she sent her brother a picture of her playing on the beach and wrote on the back, in English: "Darling Wado, how are you, I am fine and had many lessons, ballet dancing, swimming, gym, and riding lessons which I love. Love and kisses, Diane." Despite their ups and downs, Diane and Wado would remain devoted to each other for life.

If he was happy to have a baby sister, Wado was thrilled to have a surrogate father in the person of this superstar jockey who now lived with them as a family. "He was a wonderful man," he recalled. "He taught me to hunt and fish, play cards, and ride a horse . . . He was marvelous at playing the role of the father I had never known . . . I wanted with all my heart for my mother to marry him." According to Diane, Doyasbère also wanted to wed Rozell, but there was a considerable complication: She was married to Édouard Empain, head of the family enterprise and the source of her wealth and title. No way she was going to give all that up for a mere love affair.

When Doyasbère finally understood, he left Bouffémont and took his daughter with him. Diane was delighted to be with the father she adored, to accompany him to the races and bask in the reflected limelight of his stardom. She lived with him in his lodging at the Chantilly racetrack, alternating with his apartment near the Auteuil hippodrome in the west of Paris. Today, Diane tears up when she talks about her father, who died of cancer in 1969. "Jacques Doyasbère was kindness, laughter, joy. He taught me that anything you do must be done well—but you had to win!"

Rozell was also determined to win. When Diane was five, Rozell decided she wanted her daughter back. Belatedly informed of the child's existence, Édouard not only forgave his wayward wife but pledged to help her gain custody of the child. Easier said than done: Doyasbère was the only officially declared parent and Diane bore his name. To make his wife happy, Édouard offered to adopt the girl. But Doyasbère stood his ground—until Édouard laid a hefty payment on him to renounce his paternal rights and allow Édouard to recognize her as his own daughter. Thus it was that Diane Doyasbère became Diane Empain and moved back to the family château at Bouffémont.

With Diane's return, Édouard became a more frequent presence there. It was the château's superintendent, Jean-Jacques Bierry, who had the delicate task of explaining the new situation to the girl. "Your father is no longer your father," he told her. "This man, Édouard, is your father." Rebellious and resentful at first, Diane came to adore him. And Édouard doted on her. "He was always fantastic with me, very affectionate," Diane recalls. Isabelle de Montagu, a childhood friend of Diane's who practically lived at Bouffémont for a time, paints a touching portrait of Édouard. "He was just the sweetest man on earth, like a grandfather," she says. She describes him as an eccentric figure, hypochondriac, somewhat doddering, with something "almost childlike" about him. He would give the kids candy and pocket money. Every evening, without fail, he would come to the girls' bedroom and give them a benediction, making the sign of the cross over their foreheads and reciting Bible verses in Latin. He was a timid man who didn't talk much, says Montagu, but he radiated a warmth and affection that contrasted with Rozell's cold reserve. Diane, who called him "Tonton" (Uncle), remained devoted to Édouard for the rest of his life, even as her brother scorned him as his father had done. Her loyalty would later pay off.

MEANWHILE, WADO COMPLETED his *baccalauréat*, the French secondary-school diploma, and began to take courses in law and accounting in Paris. At that point in his life, he took after his hedonistic father more than the endlessly energetic grandfather who had launched the family empire and made them all rich. The young man soon grew bored of his studies and plunged into a phase of postadolescent revolt, chasing girls, partying all night, roaring down city streets and back roads at the wheel of his sky-blue Austin-Healey. No longer a shy, lonely boy huddled in his cocoon, he had become a stunningly handsome young man, tall and muscular with the chiseled features of a film star. It was not only girls his age who fell for him but also married women seeking a discreet adventure but no binding relationship. Wado was fine with that. He was having too much fun to think about tying himself down. But the heart has a mind of its own.

In August 1957, as they did each year, his family rented a villa at Juan-les-Pins on the French Riviera, and Wado continued to pursue la dolce vita with his rich friends—waterskiing behind his speedboat, frolicking on the Mediterranean beaches, dancing in exclusive nightclubs. One day he found himself alone on the beach next to a beautiful Italian girl who was vacationing with her mother and sister. She was Silvana Bettuzzi, a long-legged, dark-eyed brunette with an accent like Sophia Loren. It was love at first sight. But this end-of-summer romance between a nineteen-year-old boy and a seventeen-year-old girl from different countries seemed destined to evaporate when Silvana returned to Milan in September.

Back at Bouffémont, Wado could not get his mind off this enticing Italian *ragazza*. With that mix of determination and hardheadedness that he would later display as a businessman, he suddenly decided that he would marry Silvana Bettuzzi. He declared his intentions to his stepfather, who reluctantly agreed to accompany Wado to Milan to ask the girl's divorced mother for her hand. Jean-Jacques Bierry came along for moral support. While Silvana showed Wado the sights in Milan—the Duomo, the Galleria, the Castello Sforzesco—Édouard and Bierry sat down in her mother's salon and, over coffee and biscotti, negotiated the terms of the future marriage.

Though she boasted no noble title, Aldina de Ambrosis was re-spectably upper middle class—elegant and sophisticated, an accomplished pianist fluent in three languages, and, at age forty-four, a beautiful woman in her own right. After separating from her husband, a doctor working in Africa, she had raised Silvana and her sister Fiammetta on her own. In the late 1940s, Aldina had opened an exclusive boutique selling high-end ladies' undergarments. Her business supported a comfortable lifestyle that included regular cruises on the luxury liner *Le France*, summers at the posh Hotel Carlton in Cannes, and, for a time, English boarding schools for her daughters.

When Wado and Silvana returned hand in hand to the apartment, they learned that the engagement would be announced the following month. The wedding took place on December 15, 1957, at the Château de Bouffémont—a modest little ceremony attended by two thousand guests. They could have honeymooned in some romantic getaway—the Isle of Capri, say, or Crete, or Sardinia—but Rozell was not having it. At her insistence, they flew instead to the United States to visit Rozell's family. Her rationale for choosing this honeymoon destination was her desire for Wado to present the bride to his American grandparents. In fact, it was a typical power play. Once she had learned of Wado's intentions, it was Rozell who pushed for a speedy marriage and dictated the guest list, and now it was Rozell who decided where the couple would celebrate their marital bliss. Wado did not resist: As usual, he was putty in his mother's hands.

The couple flew out of Orly Airport the day after the wedding. A photo taken just before their departure looks like some diplomatic delegation headed off to a summit conference. With an Air France Caravelle jetliner idling in the background, Wado, in a baggy gray suit, and Silvana, wearing a demure white scarf, look a bit bewildered by all the attention. Surrounding them are half a dozen men in business suits, including Édouard and Jean-Jacques Bierry—but not

Rozell. The newlyweds must have breathed a sigh of relief when they mounted the steps and heard the door of the aircraft close behind them.

After a brief stopover in New York, they headed on to Columbus, Ohio. One wonders what Silvana made of Rozell's family. Wado's grandparents, Alvah and Ada Rowland, were a modest couple, nice enough in their way but in fact rather boring. Compared to Milan, Columbus must have seemed to Wado's bride like a drab provincial backwater. From there, they flew to Los Angeles to meet Rozell's sister Betty Jane.

Known as "The Ball of Fire" for her flaming-red hair and hot dance moves, Betty Jane Rowland was a buxom stripper who owned a club in L.A. After Rozell broke up their sister act by leaving for London in 1935, Betty Jane had remained behind to pursue a long career as an exotic dancer, appearing in vaudeville and burlesque shows all over the country before settling down in California. Dubbed the queen of the "femme trade" by *Billboard*, Betty Jane led quite a colorful life. A longtime star at Minsky's Burlesque theater, she was once arrested for "lewd behavior" onstage, dated Orson Welles, and sued Samuel Goldwyn for allegedly stealing her act as a model for the 1941 movie *Ball of Fire*, starring Barbara Stanwyck and Gary Cooper. She lost the suit but managed to land a few minor film roles in her own right.

Betty Jane was still performing when Wado and Silvana visited her in Los Angeles—in fact she continued stripping into her eighties. It is not unlikely (though nothing proves this) that the young couple were invited to see her show. If so, one can only imagine what Silvana made of her new aunt-in-law. Wado, for his part, might well have been troubled to see Betty Jane cavorting half-nude onstage, for she bore a strong resemblance to his own mother. According to Diane Empain, Rozell and Betty Jane had the same mannerisms, the same Ohio accent, the same voice. But some strange quirk of fate had made one sister a baroness and the other a stripper. (Their sister Dian, who also pursued a career as an exotic dancer, died of a heart attack in 1944 at age twenty-nine after performing at a burlesque joint in Detroit. A fourth Rowland daughter, Lorraine, kept her clothes on, married a policeman, and lived a quiet life as a Columbus housewife.)

AFTER THEIR RETURN from America, Wado and Silvana settled into a Brussels apartment while he performed his fifteen-month military service in the Belgian Army. During this forced interlude, Wado worked at a boring desk job and gave little thought to his future role in the family business. Up to that point, the young baron had enjoyed his share of the Empain fortune but showed no curiosity about the far-flung activities of the group and no burning ambition to assume a hands-on role. Until the day when, warned by a friend, he realized that his birthright was about to slip through his fingers.

Over lunch at a Brussels brasserie, the friend gave Wado some unsettling news: A large private bank was buying up stock in the group's central holding company, Electrorail, and apparently plotting a takeover. If the raiders succeeded, Wado would be eliminated from any future managerial role and the Empain family would be reduced to the status of minority shareholders in the empire founded by his grandfather. Like a sleepwalker who suddenly awakens at the edge of a cliff, Wado was gripped by an existential panic.

In a desperate effort to understand his position, he rushed to the group's Brussels office and buttonholed his stepfather's executive assistant. His interlocutor sat Wado down and patiently walked him through the Russian-doll assemblage of interlocking companies that comprised Electrorail. It turned out that Édouard, who was supposedly running the group as a sort of regent until his stepson came of age, had cleverly shifted Wado's stock holdings so that the young baron commanded no majority in any of the hundred-plus companies. The result was that the 98,000 Electrorail shares that Wado had inherited from his father conferred no power upon him. The wily Édouard, long scorned as Cousin Miscarriage by Johnny, had exacted his revenge by imposing his control over the family group, marrying Johnny's widow, and finally confiscating the power of Johnny's son. It was a modern industrial remake of *Hamlet*. But Wado, like Hamlet, finally struck out at the usurper.

His first stop on the road to redemption was the Château de Bouffémont, where he had it out with his mother. Goldie, wrapped up in her own concerns, and in fact understanding little about business, had given her husband free rein to manage Wado's interests as he saw fit. Now she was accused of treachery by her enraged son—no longer the timid and obedient adolescent she knew but suddenly emerging, at age twenty, as a young warrior girding up for battle. After a stormy argument with his mother—one of many that would follow—Wado headed for the Paris suburb of Neuilly, where Édouard maintained a residence in a three-story town house near the Bois de Boulogne.

Warned by a phone call from Goldie, Édouard was waiting with his right-hand man and confidant, Raymond Brissaud. During a heated fireside discussion that lasted all evening, Édouard and Brissaud tried to convince Wado that they had been acting in his best interests by diversifying his shares and spreading the risks. Wado wasn't buying it. He laid down a stark ultimatum: Either Édouard would recognize him as the rightful successor to the presidency of Electrorail—that is, the entire Empain group—or Wado would sell his shares to the bank that was plotting a corporate takeover and the family dynasty would be history.

While the flames danced in the marble fireplace, Édouard stared at his stepson. Was this young upstart bluffing? Would he really, like a modern-day Samson, bring the house of Empain crashing down around his own head? Unthinkable, but then, impetuous like his father, he just might do it. After a long silence, Édouard folded. *"Très bien,"* he muttered and told Brissaud to draw up a letter of understanding. The eight-paragraph document, informally dubbed the "Neuilly accord," called for Édouard to cede the presidency to Wado upon his demand. In the meantime, he pledged to take his stepson under his wing and teach him the business pending the future transfer of power. At this moment of triumph over his father's ill-loved cousin, Wado felt only "pity for this man who never knew joie de vivre, who lived a lonely and solitary life."

At age twenty, Wado had much to learn before he was ready to take over the helm of this enormous flagship. During his long apprenticeship, he attended board meetings at the side of Édouard and Brissaud, observing but rarely intervening in the discussions. He was introduced to the heads of the group's numerous companies, forming his own opinions of their qualities even as they sized up this callow youth who might one day be their boss. But for the time being, he took no part in formulating decisions or plotting strategy. Rather than a president-in-waiting, he considered himself for the moment an "interested spectator" and an "éminence grise."

Meanwhile, he and Silvana began to raise a family. Their first child, Patricia, was born in 1958, followed by Christine in 1961, and Jean-François in 1963. To all outward appearances, the Empains formed a happy family, blessed with wealth, privilege, and security. With the regularity that was Wado's hallmark, they spent each Christmas vacation together at Megève and each August at a rented villa in Juan-les-Pins. The family shared a love of winter sports, horseback riding, and waterskiing. Wado also made regular visits to local casinos, where, like his father before him, he developed a passion for the gaming tables. "I can see them now, driving off in the Maserati," their son Jean-François recalls. "She'd be in an evening gown and he'd wear a tuxedo—like James Bond."

It was a comfortable life, balancing fairly low-pressure professional activities with personal pleasures financed by the Empain fortune. But this phase came to an abrupt end in November 1967, when Raymond Brissaud came to Wado with a disturbing message: Édouard, though only fifty-three, was showing signs of senility. Increasingly hesitant and fumbling, he was making bizarre decisions, sometimes no decisions at all, seemingly overwhelmed by events. On behalf of the group's senior hierarchy, Brissaud implored Wado to "save us." Translation: You must take over the presidency now or all is lost.

Wado had just turned thirty. Was he ready to take on this burden? Was he capable of running the gargantuan empire that his grandfather had built? Would Édouard resist? He asked Brissaud for time to think it over and promised an answer when he returned from his annual ski vacation. After two weeks in the Alps, his decision was made: He would grab the ring. On Monday, January 8, 1968, he confronted Édouard and invoked the Neuilly agreement that promised him the presidency on demand. His stepfather was not happy about it, but he knew this day would come. Reluctantly, but loyally, he signed the requisite documents. By Friday, Wado was the fourth president of the Empain group.

No sooner had he settled into his chair than the new chief executive decided to replace the senior hierarchy, mostly appointees of his stepfather, with fresh blood loyal to him. His new right-hand man, René Engen, was named director general in early 1968. As Empain described him, Engen was a man interested only in business, who saw vacations as a waste of time, had no social life, arrived early to work and left late, dressed always in made-to-measure Lanvin suits. He demanded quick, decisive action from his colleagues, and those who didn't meet his standards were shown the door. Engen's method, Empain said, was "to be pitiless." In short, René Engen was just the man the baron needed at his side as he pursued his path of conquest.

UNLIKE HIS DEFERENTIAL stepfather, Wado immediately asserted an in-your-face style that did not sit well with the powers that be. In 1969, just one year after taking over, he sent shivers up the backs of the French political leadership by offering to sell a preponderant share in two major electrical equipment companies he controlled to the American giant Westinghouse, which was avidly seeking a foothold in Europe. (The Pittsburgh-based company already had a close relationship with the Empain group, which had licensed its pressurized water technology for the construction of nuclear power plants.) Fearing an American takeover of its nuclear sector, the French government blocked the sale. In Paris's ruling circles, the episode reinforced the view that this young Belgian baron—half American at that—was a loose cannon ready to sell out French national interests to the Yanks whenever it suited his purposes. Some even saw Empain as a "Trojan horse" for the Americans. But Wado was not one to knuckle under to political pressure, as he would soon prove with the most spectacular coup of his career.

CHAPTER 22

Wado's Triumph

$\mathcal{I}$t was the crown jewel of French industry. Founded in the eastern city of Le Creusot by the brothers Adolphe and Eugène Schneider in 1836, the company had started out building locomotives and tracks for France's nascent railroad network. Following France's military defeat by Prussia in 1870, the Schneiders moved heavily into arms production, churning out cannons, mortars, and steel armor that soon rivaled the output of Germany's Krupp industries. Schneider emerged from World War I as one of Europe's greatest industrial complexes, with diverse activities that included naval construction, civil engineering, energy, and banking. After World War II, Charles Schneider (grandson of co-founder Eugène) moved the group in a lucrative new direction: the construction of nuclear power plants. It was a prescient choice: Lacking its own oil resources, France would eventually opt for an all-nuclear energy program.

The Empains had long had their eye on Schneider, both as a

competitor and a potential ally. Though rivals in some sectors, in others their activities were complementary. Schneider had earlier teamed up with the first baron's company in the construction of the Paris Métro, and other joint ventures had followed. But with both groups firmly in the hands of their founding families, there seemed little chance of a corporate takeover—in either direction.

All that suddenly changed in July 1960, when Charles Schneider slipped and fell on his yacht while cruising off Saint-Tropez. He died several days later of a brain hemorrhage, leaving his wife Liliane in charge of the group. A former silent film star, Liliane Schneider, née Volpert, was then a handsome and statuesque lady in her late fifties. The granddaughter of a historic French socialist leader, Jules Guesde, she was imbued with paternalist notions about social responsibility and the well-being of workers. (During the war, her altruistic instincts had led Liliane and her husband to hide Jewish children from the Nazis.)

But the French government was not content to leave the management of this major industrial flagship in the hands of a former actress. Though Schneider was not a state-controlled industry—the government, in fact, did not own a single share of its stock—the country's political leadership had a long tradition of *dirigisme,* or state intervention on economic and industrial matters in support of the national interest. On the orders of then-president Charles de Gaulle, a senior banking official was parachuted in as co-president alongside Liliane. He was supposed to manage the group in concert with the heiress, but in reality he was there as the eyes and ears of the de Gaulle government and acted at their behest. The result was a simmering resentment on the part of Madame Schneider that grew more intense as time went by.

Meanwhile, in early 1963, Charles Schneider's sister decided to sell her 7 percent share of the company. At that point, Wado's stepfather, Édouard Empain, still in charge of the family group, decided to snap up those shares in hopes of getting a foot in the door of a rival conglomerate and eventually gaining control. Not content with that 7 percent, the Empain forces secretly proceeded to buy up all the available Schneider stock through five different intermediaries. Over the next four years, they amassed some 23 percent, making them by far the principal shareholders. Jubilant over their coup, the Empain crowd were about ready to start measuring the draperies for their new offices at the Schneider corporate headquarters at 42 Rue d'Anjou. But they would soon learn that their dominant shareholder position could not guarantee control of a historic industrial dynasty that the government considered central to French prestige and strategic interests.

Already in 1963, senior government officials had begun to sound the alarm about a possible takeover of Schneider by the Belgian group. In July of that year, de Gaulle penned an urgent note, stamped "Top Secret," to prime minister Georges Pompidou. "The Schneider affair is too important, too symbolic and too characteristic of our industry for 150 years for us to let it fall under the control of foreign interests," he wrote. "Our objective is to see that it remains French." In October, following a flurry of alarmist ministerial memos and stern warnings to Empain officials, Pompidou wrote to finance minister (and future president) Valéry Giscard d'Estaing, echoing de Gaulle's insistence that "the Schneider group holds too important a place in the French economy and in our national defense for us to allow a foreign group . . . to play a significant management role." Giscard had another, more personal reason to oppose any attempted takeover: His wife was a descendant of co-founder Eugène Schneider and herself a significant shareholder.

As long as the Empain forces remained in a minority position, those fears remained hypothetical. But when French officials learned that the Belgians had stealthily gobbled up a preponderant stake in

Schneider, they summoned Raymond Brissaud to the presidential palace and read him the riot act. Brissaud, Édouard's loyal lieutenant, was summarily ordered not to acquire a single additional share of Schneider. Moreover, the Empain side was forced to accept an agreement limiting them to four seats on a twelve-member board of directors under a government-appointed president, Roger Gaspard, former head of the state-owned power company EDF. Respectful of government authority, and fearful by nature, Édouard signed the agreement that appeared to quash his takeover bid. Wado, still in his heir-apparent role, thought he should tear it up and send the pieces back to the Élysée. In his view, the document was illegal and unenforceable.

Once they were in charge, Wado and Engen continued the pursuit of Schneider in defiance of government orders. In addition to various behind-the-scenes financial maneuvers, Wado hit on a brilliant idea for turning the tide in his company's favor: He began courting Liliane Volpert, Charles Schneider's widow, a major shareholder and an influential member of the board of directors. During his monthly visits to the dowager's Paris mansion, Wado, then in his early thirties and endowed with his movie-star looks, would sit by the fireplace in her immense salon and chat with her over tea. When she talked about the need to protect "her" workers, provide them with good benefits and job security, Wado assured her that he shared her paternalistic ideals, adding that his illustrious grandfather had always looked after the well-being of his employees. When she complained about the imperious ways of her company's state-appointed president, Wado commiserated and touted the virtues of unfettered free enterprise.

What might seem like a cynical attempt at manipulation in fact developed into an improbable friendship. Wado was genuinely fascinated by this "precious elderly lady, rather tall, very elegant, soberly made up, sophisticated in her speech." He compared her to "some rare species of bird" who "seemed to have emerged from another culture, another time." And he felt that she came to look on him as "the son she never had." For his part, how could Wado not see a parallel between this movie actress who married into an industrial dynasty and his own mother, the former exotic dancer who wed a millionaire baron?

Wado's yearlong charm offensive finally won Liliane over to his side. When the time was ripe, he made his move. At a regular board meeting, one of his colleagues suddenly interrupted president Gaspard and proposed a motion to remove him from office. Gaspard sputtered indignantly, pounding his fist on the table and shouting that only the government could replace him. Wado and his supporters ignored his protest and proceeded to a vote. In addition to the Empains' four board members, Liliane Schneider and two of her allies raised their hands in support of the motion. Red-faced and vowing to seek redress from the highest levels of government, Gaspard practically had to be carried out kicking and screaming.

In the aftermath of their mutiny, Wado and his confederates were summoned by senior state officials and roundly rebuked for violating their earlier nonaggression pact—the finance minister even threatened to escort Empain back to Belgium and bar him from reentering the country. But in the end the government was legally powerless to overrule the board of a private corporation. Like the savvy poker player that he was, Wado had called their bluff and won. In 1971, at the age of thirty-three, he took over the presidency of Schneider, renamed his group Empain-Schneider, and moved his headquarters to the Rue d'Anjou. For himself, he chose the former office of Charles Schneider.

In the wake of that spectacular coup, the baron launched a frenzy of takeovers and acquisitions, bringing dozens of new companies under his tent and even branching out beyond his industrial base onto the less familiar terrain of consumer goods. Like a gambler sitting behind a heady pile of chips, he was driven by his taste for high-stakes risk-taking and the prospect of ever-mounting wealth. But it was about more than money: As a foreigner who lacked the advanced university degrees of his colleagues and competitors, he was seen as a perpetual outsider who had inherited a family dynasty but didn't really belong to the exclusive club of France's leading industrialists. Even as they respected his power and wealth, many of those who inhabited the corporate boardrooms and gilded ministerial suites nursed a secret contempt for Baron Empain as a sort of usurper in their privileged domain. For Wado, growing his empire was the best revenge.

His ultimate goal, as he put it, was to become "master of the universe," and he pursued it with a my-way-or-the-highway ruth-lessness. He described himself as "a Wild West capitalist" who "per-sonally fired at least two hundred people without the least difficulty." Which made him the perfect target for a man like Alain Caillol, who scorned and resented his capitalist arrogance even as he coveted his fortune. Ironically, it was Empain's vertiginous rise to power and prominence that put his life in peril.

PART VI

Endgame

1978–2018

Starting Over: Wado and his second wife, Jacqueline

Francis Apesteguy/Getty Images

CHAPTER 23

Aftershocks

The shootout on the A6 highway ended Wado's harrowing sixty-three-day captivity, but it was only the beginning of the real investigation into the who, why, and how of France's most notorious kidnapping. For two months, Ottavioli's elite detectives had been spinning their wheels. Now, at last, they had some serious leads: one perp in custody (though not talking), the identity of his dead comrade, and an address that had been traced from Caillol's phone call to his fellow kidnappers. That was a good place to start.

ON TUESDAY, MARCH 28, 1978, at six a.m., Inspector Michel Desfarges drove up to a modest two-story house in the suburb of Savigny-sur-Orge. He was accompanied by another detective and three commandos from the Antigang.

They knocked on the door, guns drawn. Suddenly an enormous

dog—Bertoncini's German mastiff—appeared in the courtyard, barking furiously and baring his fangs. The cops retreated behind the gate.

"Shoot him!" said one of the Antigang boys.

"No," said Desfarges. "We'll call a dog handler."

When the civilian dog handler arrived, he took one look at the beast, then got back in his car and drove away.

An elderly woman opened the shutters of the house next door. "That poor dog's been all alone for two days," she said. "I've been feeding him." Showing more courage than the cops and the dog handler combined, she emerged from her house and calmly approached the drooling beast. He licked her hand and followed her into her yard.

Once inside, Desfarges and his colleagues observed signs of a hasty departure—scattered furniture; books, records, and cigarette butts on the floor; dirty dishes in the sink. In the basement, they found a bolt in the wall, presumably to attach Wado's chain. In one of the bedrooms, Desfarges discovered a trove of documents in a dresser drawer: photos, bills, some counterfeit 500-franc notes, and, most intriguing, a clutch of receipts for the plane tickets to Palma. "That was an incredible find," Desfarges tells me. "They had left this stuff behind in their haste to get away. The ticket receipts provided names that put us on the trail of the kidnappers."

Two DAYS AFTER his liberation, Wado insisted on going to the American Hospital for a checkup. Partly because he felt weak, but mainly to escape the "unbearable" atmosphere of the family apartment. As it turned out, there were good reasons to be concerned about his health. He had lost nearly fifty pounds and now suffered from high blood pressure in addition to stomach and liver problems. He had lost considerable muscle mass. But the thing that had caused the most worries initially, the amputated finger, had healed as cleanly as if it had been severed by a surgeon's scalpel. The doctors predicted that his robust constitution would, in time, permit a full recovery.

On Thursday, March 30, Ottavioli, Bizeul, and Desfarges showed up at the hospital and asked Empain to accompany them to Savigny to see if he could identify the house. To evade the journalists who besieged the hospital, Wado, now clean-shaven and freshly barbered, was dressed in a doctor's white tunic and whisked out a side door into a waiting police car. Upon arriving at the house, the baron knew immediately that this was the place of his third incarceration. He recognized the smells, the sound of footsteps on the stairs, the bark of the dog. On the basement floor, he found a crushed pack of Winston cigarettes that Bertoncini had given him. There was a fork with two missing prongs, which he had used to eat his last meal there, and a book that he had dog-eared.

The neighbors had not noticed anything unusual during all the time Wado was imprisoned in their midst. They knew nothing about the occupants of the house, except that "Monsieur Jo"—Bertoncini— walked his dog every day. But police quickly identified the person who had rented the apartment: Marc Le Gayan, brother of Bertoncini's girlfriend Marie-Annick Le Gayan. Ottavioli's detectives now had even more evidence and were ready to track down the rest of the kidnappers.

The Crim's initial interrogations were focused on specific details that could help police apprehend the perpetrators. It was the job of Judge Louis Chavanac, the magistrate in charge of the judicial investigation, to piece together the whole complex story of the kidnapping and construct the dossier for an eventual trial. Then in his midfifties, short and stocky, Chavanac was one of the most experienced and well respected of France's corps of *juges d'instruction* who play a key role in the country's justice system. The *juge d'instruction*—"the most powerful man in France," in Napoleon's famous phrase—can compel witnesses, order wiretaps, launch surveillance operations, and place suspects in preventive detention. This special magistrate is tasked with examining the pros and cons of a case, and ultimately deciding whether to charge defendants and send them to trial. He or she does not, however, prosecute the case or preside over the trial.

Chavanac was considered intelligent, dedicated, and scrupulously honest in his work. But he was also stiff-mannered and, in the words of one colleague, could be "difficult in his dealings with others." Early on in the Empain case, the judge had a bitter clash with Ottavioli over control of the investigation after the headstrong chief told Chavanac to stand down and leave it all to him. The judge, clinging to his oversight role, stopped talking to Ottavioli after that.

Not the most diplomatic of magistrates, Chavanac immediately got Wado's back up when he questioned the baron shortly after his release. The prickly judge grilled him like a suspect: *You said you read books during your captivity—what books, titles, authors? First you said you were in the trunk for a half hour, then you said it was forty-five minutes—which was it? Why did you get off the Métro at the Opéra station when you could have changed trains and gone straight to Avenue Foch?* The most unbearable thing was the judge's persistent fixation on the self-kidnapping theory—the notion, aired early on in the press, that Wado had organized the whole thing himself in order to pay off his gambling debts with ransom money. Outraged at this suggestion, Wado waved the stump of his severed finger under the judge's nose. "You think I did that to myself?"

Chavanac's hostile questioning, like the initial police interrogations, reinforced Wado's inclination to withhold or even distort details about his captivity. His reaction was partly the psychological residue of Stockholm syndrome, but it was also based on a very practical consideration: He was afraid that the kidnappers who were still at large, the ones who had made him sign the IOUs, would seek revenge if he helped the authorities pursue them. So he continued to tell the judge that he saw nothing, heard nothing, noticed nothing.

WADO'S GREATEST REENTRY trauma was his wife's lack of sympathy. He sensed it in her cold tone of voice when he called from the Place de l'Opéra, especially her matter-of-fact remark, "I knew you would be freed tonight." As he later told an interviewer, "That reception and that phrase marked a total break between me and my wife. In my mind I was already divorced from that moment."

Over the next few days, when he was most in need of comfort and consolation, all he got from Silvana was reproach about the gambling debts, the secret love nest, and the mistresses. Of course, she had known about at least some of his infidelities before that—his liaison with Shahnaz Arieh had begun practically under Silvana's nose on the beach at Juan-les-Pins. One time, she found lipstick on Wado's collar and told her mother-in-law. Rozell was unmoved: "Darling, if there is lipstick on his collar, it means he didn't take off his shirt." It was the police who had opened her eyes to things she'd rather not have known about, including Wado's secret apartment on the Rue Lord Byron (named, fittingly enough, for the English romantic poet and serial seducer).

All that was troubling enough for the baroness, but when the sordid details wound up in the newspapers, she was subjected to a public humiliation that she could not get over—or forgive. Her confidence in her husband was forever shaken. Adding insult to injury, the puritanical René Engen had scolded Silvana for not preventing her husband from indulging in such reprehensible behavior.

It was not only about the debts and the mistresses. Wado's long captivity was a source of intense emotional stress for his wife. There was the fear that he would be killed or further mutilated. There was the financial worry over raising the ransom money, and the shock of discovering that Wado's personal fortune was not what she had imagined. When the authorities froze Wado's bank accounts, Silvana suddenly found herself starved of cash. There were times when her maid would look in the empty fridge and say, "Madame, I don't know what we're going to eat today." Her mother-in-law, living in the family château at Bouffémont, was not in the least inclined to bail her out. Fortunately, Silvana's sister, Fiammetta, wife of a wealthy business executive, was there to help.

In short, Silvana was as much in need of comfort and understanding as her husband. But, as Wado later admitted, he was so wrapped up in his own anger and distress that he was incapable of giving. "The mother of my children was almost as shattered as I was: We could no longer do much for each other." Their separation became inevitable from the time of Wado's return, though their divorce was not finalized until July 1990.

The baron's relationship with his children was no less catastrophic. "With Patricia and Christine, there was a terrific clash," recalls Wado's sister, Diane Empain. "After the kidnapping there was nothing. They couldn't understand the money situation. They were terrified." Jean-François, then fourteen, remained in boarding school for the duration and was largely sheltered from the trauma that rocked his older sisters.

Relations between Wado and Patricia were especially troubled, due to the bad blood that developed between the baron and his American son-in-law, Terrell Braly. On his mother's side, Braly hailed from a wealthy family that owned 2 million acres of ranchland in Texas; his father was an air force colonel and onetime aide to Dwight D. Eisenhower. Terrell and Patricia had met while she was attending Pine Manor Junior College in Chestnut Hill, Massachusetts. No doubt inspired by the Empain family fortune, Braly pursued a rapid courtship that led them down the aisle in June 1977. Perhaps his head was turned by the grand reception at the Château de Bouffémont, with its big white tent and eight hundred guests, but Braly apparently assumed that he would soon be offered a lucrative job with the baron's multinational—why not a cushy position with its U.S. branch? No such offer ever materialized, so the couple moved to New York and Terrell, increasingly resentful of his father-in-law, began looking for a job.

That's where things stood when Patricia, newly pregnant, received a phone call from her mother on the afternoon of January 23, 1978. "I knew from her voice that something was wrong," she recalls. "Mom said, 'Your dad just got kidnapped.' I screamed and cried and told her, 'I'm coming to Paris!'" The couple caught a flight that night. Upon their arrival the next morning, they moved into the family apartment on Avenue Foch.

The household was already in a panic when they arrived, but the ransom demand that was received later that day touched off what Patricia describes as a "nonstop feud." Everybody was yelling at one another—Rozell, Silvana, Diane, the girls. But Braly was in the middle of some of the most violent arguments. "When they told him the family didn't have 80 million francs, he said, 'Of course you do. Everybody's lying.'" During one particularly heated exchange, he called Rozell a stripper and told Diane she was not even a real Empain!

After Wado was released, there was a clash between him and Braly. "My son-in-law is not my friend," he later told an interviewer. "In their eyes, I was guilty of having been kidnapped." According to Wado, Braly also grilled him about his shaky finances. His message, in the baron's paraphrase: "We've checked with your bank, there's not much money there. You must have hidden it in secret accounts. Tell us where it is so if you're kidnapped again we can find it."

Braly, for his part, called the whole thing a "misunderstanding" and blamed the group's leadership for poisoning the baron's mind against him. "The day after his liberation, while he was still groggy, they sent him a dossier that presented me as an opportunist who had tried to take advantage of the situation to seize power." In the face of these accusations, the couple cut off ties with Wado and returned to New York. "I had to choose between my husband and my dad," Patricia told me. "I chose Terrell." Their estrangement would last for years.

On Thursday, March 30, Wado decided to return to his company headquarters on the Rue d'Anjou. The doormen and chauffeurs greeted him warmly—"Bienvenue, Monsieur le Président"—but the colleagues he encountered on the higher floors spoke only curtly if at all. Entering his own office, he found himself in the middle of an empty room. All his files and papers had been boxed and stored. Only an immense desk remained, like a sarcophagus in the middle of a mausoleum.

In an adjoining office sat René Engen, who had been running the baron's vast empire during his absence. Empain's erstwhile protégé briefed him on what had transpired during the previous two months. First, he explained his position on the ransom payment: In the beginning, he had acquiesced in the family's wishes and unblocked 30 million francs. But following the kidnappers' refusal and Ottavioli's return from the United States, he had accepted the police chief's view that no ransom should be paid. And the results proved him right, no?—Empain was safe and no one had paid a cent to the kidnappers. As for the group's affairs, Engen reported with undisguised satisfaction that he had managed quite well without the baron at the helm. Despite the distraction caused by the kidnapping, overall sales were up by 17 percent over the previous year.

But there was a problem. The revelations about Empain's private life—the gambling debts, the mistresses, the secret apartment—were damaging to the group's reputation, shocking to the stockholders, and unacceptable in the eyes of the government. "You have an image inside the group that must be totally reconstructed," Engen said bluntly. "And to reconstruct it, you must go away." He suggested that the baron take an open-ended vacation in the U.S.A. to clear his mind, restore his health, and think over his situation. "I will keep you informed about the evolution of things here, Baron," Engen reassured him. "I will tell you when to return and take up the helm of command."

Wado didn't hesitate. Disgusted with his family, the authorities, and his own colleagues, he was ready to leave it all behind him. "I wiped the slate clean: no more family, no more children, no more job, no more group, no nothing." He would seek peace and happiness across the ocean with a woman at his side who adored him, understood him, and felt his pain, a woman he called "both my nurse and my mistress." She was Shahnaz Arieh, the beautiful Iranian émigré whom Wado had met in the early 1970s on the beach at Juan-les-Pins. Now that Wado and Silvana were separated, she was only too happy to join her lover on this journey of renewal. It seemed like she was finally getting her wish.

Shahnaz offered what no one in Wado's entourage had provided: unconditional support and sympathy. "This woman loved everything about me, the good and the bad. For the first time since my return, I heard a voice speak to me the way I needed. She told me I was a good man, that I was intelligent, that I had led a dazzling career, that I had to get ahold of myself and recover my old form. I eagerly listened."

In early April, he and Shahnaz flew off to New York together. Shortly before their departure, he went to the Rue d'Anjou and signed over the powers of the presidency to René Engen. The arrangement was supposed to be temporary, but in Engen's mind it was a one-way trip. After Empain left, he told Bierry: "He's finished, he's no longer credible. Whatever happens, he must not return." Bierry reluctantly agreed.

That opinion was shared by President Giscard d'Estaing, who privately told Engen that the baron should be encouraged to sell his shares and move on. According to Giscard's former chief of staff, Claude Pierre-Brossolette, the president favored the "definitive eclipse" of the baron, who he felt could "no longer run the group with a sure hand." The kidnapping and the revelations about Wado's private life had in fact been a boon to the president. Though he was outwardly friendly with Empain, Giscard had long nursed a secret grudge going back to Wado's corporate raid on Schneider. As finance minister, Giscard had opposed this "foreign" takeover of a key French industrial group. Yet his resentment went deeper than that. Not only was his wife a descendant of the Schneider family and a shareholder in the company, but there were those who thought Giscard himself had nursed hopes of one day becoming its CEO. Wado's takeover had blocked that path.

Though Giscard went on to win a far more prestigious job in the 1974 presidential election, his resentment against Empain continued to simmer. Wado was well aware of it, and quipped that he and Giscard were "two roosters on the same manure pile." The kidnapping had eliminated one of those roosters. Some even speculated that Giscard had encouraged the abduction in order to wrest France's nuclear program from the control of this bothersome baron. That theory proved baseless, but the president could not be unhappy over Wado's fall from grace.

Upon their arrival in the States, Wado and Shahnaz settled into a grand hotel in Manhattan, where they spent a week decompressing. Then it was off to Bermuda to lounge on the powder beaches and soak up the sun. After that, they crossed the continent to the West Coast, with a stopover in Las Vegas. In addition to gambling in that city's glitzy casinos, they may actually have gotten "married" in one of Vegas's instant wedding chapels (an illegal ceremony, if it did take place, given that Wado was still married to his first wife). From there they headed to San Diego. Ensconced in a luxury hotel next to a golf course, they spent an idyllic month, swimming, relaxing, playing golf—and making love like newlyweds.

Their California idyll was interrupted by the unexpected arrival of Wado's mother. She had come with the express purpose of giving her son a dressing-down. "I just spent ten hours in an airplane," she told him. "I wrote down everything I had to tell you." Reading aloud from her own handwritten pages, she proceeded to recite a litany of charges against her son: His behavior had done great harm to his family and to the group; the press was full of scandalous gossip and rumors; he was neglecting the education of his son, who would one day take over the industrial dynasty; his reproachful attitude since his liberation was unjust and intolerable . . .

As she read these accusations in her indelible Ohio accent, Wado immediately suspected that René Engen had put his mother up to making the trip and had even dictated the points she should make. Rozell's concern for the group's financial health, combined with her low esteem for her son's leadership abilities, made her a willing emissary of the man who wanted to replace him. She later admitted as much to a Belgian journalist: "After his liberation, I felt that my son was not doing well. One day, I went to see him so he could confide in me, but he pushed me away and that annoyed me. So when Engen told me that it would be better for him to abandon [the presidency] and just enjoy his money, I thought maybe he wasn't wrong. I agreed to go see Engen and, obviously, he briefed me. He had even prepared a paper that I copied myself and gave to my son. It contained all the arguments why he should not come back."

Rozell's message so enraged her son that he cut off all communication with her—a rift that would last for the next six years. The carefree joie de vivre he had savored in San Diego now gave way to a new spiral of depression. He and Shahnaz flew back to New York, where his morale sank even further. Gripped by fears and recurrent nightmares, he spent hours walking alone in Central Park and finally had to consult a psychiatrist.

It didn't help his morale when René Engen arrived in New York and summoned him to a tête-à-tête at the Waldorf-Astoria hotel. The ostensible purpose of the meeting was to brief the baron on the group's affairs. Engen cited reams of facts and figures that did not particularly interest Empain at that moment, but his main point was that he had the situation in hand, thank you very much, and that the baron could perhaps think about returning "in a few years."

The unctuous manner with which Engen delivered that message was belied by the brutal memo he sent the baron in July. "I can assure you that if I hadn't been here, if I had had any ambition other than serving the general interest, there would no longer be any Empain-Schneider group today," he wrote. "Because there are things that destroy the respect and moral authority that we need." Engen added this blistering personal attack: "Gambling, on the scale that you practice it, is incompatible both with your important official functions and with your position as principal shareholder . . . You give the most abominable image of the capitalist: an inheritor who is an incompetent, lazy, gambling, credulous braggart, surrounded by a coterie of parasites, do-nothings, and vultures!"

The change in Engen's tone was stunning. No longer the discreet and dutiful number two, he had come to see himself as the group's natural leader. His presumptions were nourished not only by his own ambition but also by the heady spheres he inhabited as the de facto boss of one of France's biggest industrial conglomerates. The honors and deference formerly paid to Empain now went to René Engen. The powers that be, in fact, were far more comfortable working with this competent and conventionally pedigreed executive than with the unpredictable Belgian baron who played by his own rulebook and as often as not defied their directives. During Empain's absence, Prime Minister Raymond Barre decorated Engen with the coveted Légion d'honneur. It was with that kind of high-level encouragement that Engen made his power play.

Indeed, there were others who thought that Engen would be a far better helmsman than Wado. It was Engen, they argued, who had the diplomas, the discipline, and the work ethic required to lead this sprawling multinational. "Engen was a remarkable captain of industry," says Inspector Michel Desfarges, who had multiple dealings with him during the investigation. "A real intellectual, a man of superior intelligence. Empain had the image and the name, but it's not serious to claim he really led the group." That view was partly echoed in the specialized business press, with some analysts questioning Wado's lack of "assiduity" while praising Engen as a "meticulous" and "tenacious" manager. That, too, went to Engen's head and emboldened him in his pursuit of the top job.

The double whammy of his mother's admonitions and Engen's riot act made it clear, more than ever, that Empain had nothing to expect from his family or colleagues. What he really needed was uncondi-tional moral support and affection from people he really cared about. One of those people was Shahnaz, with her gift for listening and comforting. The other was Wado's best friend since childhood, Bernard Moine, the son of a farmer who worked the family's lands at Bouffémont. Now, in this moment of emotional need, the baron called Moine to his side.

Wado phoned Bierry in Paris and asked him to order a plane ticket for his friend. When Moine went to pick it up, Engen called him into his office—and not just to wish him bon voyage. He wanted to enlist Moine in his campaign to keep Empain in New York. "His mother is American, isn't she?" he said. "You understand that it's in our interest for him to be happy. His future is in the United States, so we should all push him in that direction." In Engen's eyes, Moine was a useful pawn in a corporate chess game aimed at felling the king.

As soon as Moine arrived in New York, Wado's mood changed. The two men slipped easily into their old friendship, laughing, joking, playing pool and Ping-Pong, and attending baseball games at Yankee Stadium. They even watched the World Cup final (Argentina 3, Netherlands 1) on a giant TV screen at Madison Square Garden. During their ten days together, Moine avoided any mention of the kidnapping, the scandals, or the affairs of the Empain-Schneider group. Instead, he let his friend do the talking. Until the moment when Wado, nursing a beer in a Midtown bar, leaned over and said, "Listen, Bernard, I think I'm going to stay in America."

Moine shook his head. He told his friend about Engen's briefing, his determination to keep Wado in the States and away from the levers of power on the Rue d'Anjou. Moine advised him to rush back to Paris and reclaim his birthright. Shahnaz agreed. "You really intend not to return?" she asked. "All those people are mocking you; they've despoiled you, that's all they care about."

Suddenly, as if waking from a troubled dream, Wado remembered that he was still Baron Empain. He was still the principal shareholder in the Empain-Schneider group. He was still the grandson of the man who had built that formidable industrial dynasty. And he would not give it up without a fight. In late August, he and Shahnaz boarded the *Queen Elizabeth 2* and sailed for Europe.

CHAPTER 24

Exile's Return

*E*mpain's first stop was London. Like the hunter he was, his instinct was to track his prey from a distance, sniffing the air and judging the terrain before giving chase. He set up his staging ground in a hotel suite overlooking the Thames and began to work the telephones. On the other end of the line were people he considered his friends and allies—people he had been systematically cut off from after his liberation. They all advised him to return to Paris, rout the usurpers, and reclaim his throne. His resolve tightened to the sticking place, he decided to make his triumphal return in early September. "I intended to smash everything. It was no longer the Stockholm syndrome but the Monte Cristo syndrome."

He called Jean-Jacques Bierry, his childhood friend turned colleague, and announced his intentions. Relations between the two men had become strained since Bierry, putting company interests over personal loyalty, had supported Engen's efforts to distance Wado from the leadership. But Wado was not calling to ask Bierry's advice. Instead, he instructed him to book a suite at the Plaza Athénée, just off the Champs-Élysées, one of the most elegant and expensive hotels in Paris.

Word of the baron's planned return from exile quickly spread, like the news of Napoleon's escape from the Isle of Elba. When Wado and Shahnaz landed at Orly, they were momentarily detained by the border police. "Monsieur Empain," said a passport officer, "we have instructions to inform the interior minister in case you seek to enter France. I must call him immediately." Clearly, the minister, and the president, wanted to know if and when Baron Empain planned to reassert his leadership of this major industrial group. Now they knew.

On the phone the next morning, René Engen could hear the determination in Empain's voice. This was not the cowering creature who had left the country five months earlier with his tail between his legs. It was the voice of a fighter—a fighter who also happened to own more than one-third of the group's shares. Though clearly unhappy over Wado's return—and perhaps still hoping to outmaneuver him—Engen opted for the better part of valor: "Of course, Baron, I was here as an interim leader and I did the best I could. There is no problem. Your place is waiting for you."

Those assurances were well and good, but Empain wanted all the world to see that he was back in power. He called a press conference at the group's headquarters on Thursday, September 7, 1978. The ground-floor conference room was jammed with journalists jostling for position with their microphones and cameras. At eleven a.m., the baron strode into the room wearing an elegant glen-plaid suit. Smiling, fit and tanned, his movie-star looks restored, he took a seat behind a microphone and made a five-minute statement before opening the floor to questions. Speaking without notes, he exuded such confidence and determination that *Paris Match* grandiloquently compared him to "a conquering gladiator wrapped in Caesar's toga."

He gave few details about his incarceration. His harshest criticisms were reserved for his personal entourage, those who "in place of the warmth, friendship, comfort, and love I had hoped for rubbed my face in certain facts about my private life and demanded explanations." He slammed the police for revealing his personal secrets and the judge who "grilled me like a suspect." With Engen sitting meekly at his side, Empain made no direct allusion to his colleagues, but his message was clear: "I am the principal shareholder. It is not possible to run the Empain-Schneider group against Baron Empain . . . Since I'm back, they'll have to make room for me." He had not returned in order to "make heads roll," but he clearly intended to clean house. As for Alain Caillol and his band, Empain voiced a surprising magnanimity. He himself knew what it was to suffer the loss of freedom for two months, but his kidnappers were looking at long years behind bars. "I tend to think that our society imposes punishments that are too harsh and unbearable . . . I think that I'd go as far as forgiving them." Empain's two-hour performance was almost unanimously applauded by the French press. To all appearances, the baron had survived his ordeal and come back stronger than ever.

WADO'S RETURN OCCURRED at a difficult moment for Empain-Schneider. Faced with stiff competition from foreign steelmakers, the group's main metallurgical subsidiary, Creusot-Loire, was hemorrhaging more than 150 million francs a year and headed for an apparently inevitable bankruptcy. Other sectors—capital goods, nuclear construction, banking—were on more solid ground, but the baron found himself increasingly obliged to put out fires, poring over balance sheets, dealing with unions, and sitting through tedious board meetings at a time when he had less and less patience for such details.

In fact, he had never been a detail man. Empain wanted to play a role like that of the queen of England, who reigned but did not govern, alongside a prime minister figure who would take care of hands-on management under the monarch's authority. The problem was that his "prime minister," René Engen, in addition to his suspected disloyalty, was the object of mounting complaints from the heads of a certain number of companies within the group. Some had resented his high-handed management style in Wado's absence; others sensed an opportunity for promotion if Engen's head rolled. As for Empain himself, he had totally lost confidence in his number two in the wake of the kidnapping. Engen, now approaching his sixtieth year, saw which way the wind was blowing and offered to resign.

The baron's candidate to replace him as director general was Didier Pineau-Valencienne. A former executive of the Empain group, Pineau-Valencienne, forty-seven, was then the number two at Rhône-Poulenc, the chemical and pharmaceutical giant. A graduate of Harvard Business School and an exponent of "American" managerial methods, he had made a reputation for himself as a ruthlessly efficient cost-cutter and downsizer, hence his nickname "Doctor Attila." DPV, as he was known, readily accepted the offer. Engen spent several months briefing his successor on the group's far-flung activities before quietly handing over his post and riding into the sunset in November 1980.

Empain soon realized that he had invited the fox into the henhouse. Sensing the weakened position of the nominal president, who had plunged ever deeper into his old gambling habit with high-stakes poker games and casino binges, Pineau-Valencienne asserted more and more control over the group's affairs. He was not a man to play prime minister to Empain's monarch: He wanted the power *and* the throne. Meanwhile, the Giscard d'Estaing government was still pushing behind the scenes to replace the problematic Belgian baron with a reliable French manager at the helm of this industrial juggernaut. "I felt quite clearly," Wado concluded, "that I was no longer needed in this company."

The final straw was the perfidious trick that Pineau-Valencienne played on Empain following Engen's departure. During his negotiations with Engen, the baron had agreed to pay him a hefty sum as part of his retirement package. Empain had written and signed a letter specifying the amount of this "golden parachute." But when it came due for payment, Pineau-Valencienne refused to authorize the funds, saying the document was not written on company letterhead and was therefore Empain's personal responsibility. Complaining that DPV had put him "in the shit," the baron wound up having to pay Engen out of his own pocket.

Disgusted and disheartened, Wado decided to sell all his shares and walk away. On February 24, 1981, the Paribas bank bought his 35 percent stake for 30 million francs plus the repayment of his debts, estimated at some additional 15 million francs. Wado was the last Baron Empain to run the industrial empire founded by his grandfather. All that was left of his link to that illustrious past was his gold signet ring bearing the family crest and a trove of family mementos.

The Empain-Schneider group itself soon disappeared from the map—indeed, the very name of Empain was dropped within a few years of Wado's departure. Framatome, the group's profitable nuclear power subsidiary, was gradually absorbed by state-controlled agencies. Creusot-Loire, the historic keystone of the group's metallurgical branch, was liquidated in 1984 after years of catastrophic losses. In the wake of that failure—the biggest industrial bankruptcy in French history—Pineau-Valencienne pursued a slash-and-burn policy, dismantling many subsidiary companies and concentrating the group's energy activities under the name Schneider SA. By 1987, overall sales had declined by 50 percent and Schneider had slid from twelfth to twenty-fifth place among leading French companies. Widely denounced as an "industrial gravedigger," DPV was burned in effigy on the streets of Paris by angry workers.

In the 1990s, he engineered a number of successful takeovers in the energy sector, but he ran afoul of the stockholders of two Belgian target companies in 1993 and spent twelve days in a Brussels prison on charges of forgery, abuse of confidence, and fraud. The case prompted comparisons to the Empain kidnapping and fed speculation that Pineau-Valencienne himself, like Wado, might be forced out in the wake of a scandal. He managed to hold on to power until his retirement in 1999, but his eventual conviction for fraud, even though it carried no prison time, remained a blot on his copybook. There was no small irony in the comeuppance of this French executive at the hands of Belgian justice after his Belgian predecessor had been rejected by the French establishment.

AFTER SELLING HIS shares, Wado entered a spiral of self-destructive drift, cut off from his family, shorn of any professional responsibilities, gripped by anger and depression. He continued to hunt and gamble as before, but his social life was chaotic. For reasons that are unclear, he ended his longtime affair with Shahnaz Arieh and threw himself into a series of casual relationships, relying on his still-stunning looks to pick up partners in the steaming cauldron of Parisian nightclubs and discothèques.

One woman who encountered Wado on the disco scene found him terribly attractive but difficult to approach. She had actually met him three years earlier, introduced by mutual friends, but nothing had come of it then. Now, in the wake of Wado's kidnapping ordeal and his separation from Silvana, she managed to pull him into her orbit. She was Jacqueline Ragonaux, an ex-model born in Senegal. Not only was she endowed with a dark, exotic beauty, like Shahnaz, but she also had the ability to comfort and reassure Wado—to mother him, in fact, as his own mother had never done. Neither one knew it at the time, but they were destined to be partners for life.

CHAPTER 25

The Dragnet

$\mathcal{A}$fter Caillol's arrest and Duchateau's bloody death, the other conspirators scattered far and wide. Mathieu and Idir, the getaway team who had been waiting on the other side of the wall, sped away from the scene and immediately fled the country—Idir back to his native Algeria and Mathieu to an undisclosed European destination, where, according to Caillol, he remains to this day. The rest of the band went into hiding, desperately hoping to evade the police dragnet that began tightening around them from the moment their hideout was discovered in Savigny-sur-Orge. Investigators had the names of at least five suspects thanks in part to the documents they had found in the Savigny house. On March 31, 1978, just five days after Empain's release, Judge Chavanac issued arrest warrants for François Caillol, Bernard Guillon, Georges Bertoncini, René "La Grise" Rigault, and Marc Le Gayan.

The first one they nabbed was Le Gayan, brother of Bertoncini's girlfriend Marie-Annick. He was the easiest to track down because he had signed the lease on the Savigny house. Le Gayan, a twenty-six-year-old café waiter and wannabe musician, was a friend of Bertoncini, who had helped him out financially. He returned the favor by renting the Savigny place plus a Paris studio that served as a safe house for the gang. He also loaned Bertoncini the Renault 4L minivan that was used to take the baron to the spot where he was finally liberated. On Wednesday, March 29, anticipating the official arrest warrant, police apprehended him at his apartment in the Paris suburb where he lived with his wife. He was charged with complicity in Empain's detention.

Le Gayan was a small fish, but bigger ones soon followed. After Alain Caillol's arrest, François Caillol and Bernard Guillon had driven together to the southeastern city of Nîmes on March 28. Three weeks later, Ottavioli got a tip from his network of Corsican mafia informers: Guillon was expecting an envelope containing forged ID papers at the central post office in Nice, and François Caillol was likely to be with him. Otta dispatched Claude Cancès, Michel Desfarges, and three other agents to Nice, where they mounted a weeklong stakeout. On April 19, Guillon, sporting a newly grown beard, showed up at nine thirty a.m. and retrieved his envelope from a post office box. Minutes later, the cops arrested him as he headed on foot in the direction of the Nice train station. François Caillol was a no-show that day.

Guillon, who had no police record, loudly protested his innocence, but investigators found some compromising items in his car. Among them: a publicity brochure for the type of tent in which Empain had been kept, and an ammunition clip for an automatic pistol identical to one used in the A6 shootout. Although there was no hard proof linking Guillon to the actual kidnapping, the baron would later identify his voice as belonging to one of his jailers. Police also suspected, but never proved, that it was Guillon who amputated the baron's finger. For the moment, the evidence was sufficient to charge Guillon with arms violations and complicity in Empain's detention. He was remanded into custody on April 21.

One month later, Desfarges led a team of detectives to Palma. Acting on evidence they found in the Savigny house and tips from people in Bertoncini's entourage, they zeroed in on a restaurant-hotel called La Baraka (the name means "benediction" in Arabic). The owner not only recognized key gang members by their photos but produced a hotel register showing that Bertoncini had reserved rooms for them in August and December 1977. The guest list was a virtual Who's Who of the Empain kidnappers: Caillol, Guillon, Duchateau, La Grise, and of course Bertoncini himself, who was well known on the island. By this time, it was clear to investigators that Le Marseillais was a central figure in the plot. But he was also a slippery character whose ratlike street smarts made up for his limited intellectual capacities.

Bertoncini had initially fled to Italy with his girlfriend Marie-Annick Le Gayan and their infant son, sailing from the French Mediterranean port of Menton in a Zodiac inflatable boat. From Italy, they made their way to Lausanne. Toward the end of May, Bertoncini flew to Costa Rica, where the couple was apparently preparing to settle. He had asked Costa Rican consular officials about residence requirements and had even shipped his Mercedes to Costa Rica—a well-chosen refuge since that country had no extradition treaty with France.

On June 5, Bertoncini flew to Lisbon to rendezvous with Marie-Annick and their nine-month-old son and prepare their move to Costa Rica. While searching the apartment of another suspect in Lausanne, French police intercepted a telegram indicating that Bertoncini and Marie-Annick were staying in Lisbon's Hotel Diplomatico. On June

10, André Bizeul and two other agents flew to Lisbon and liaised with Portuguese police, who apprehended the couple at the hotel that evening. They were taken into custody pending extradition to France.

Before returning to Paris, Bizeul warned Portuguese authorities that Bertoncini was a high security risk—he had tried to grab the gun of one of the arresting cops—and advised them to take special precautions. All for naught: On July 31, Bertoncini faked an asthma attack and escaped from the prison's hospital wing by sawing through the bars of his fourth-floor window and shimmying down to the ground using knotted bedsheets—hardly an original escape method, but one that apparently caught the Portuguese off guard. Marie-Annick remained in prison with her infant son and was later extradited to France.

Bertoncini's flight to freedom ended on November 21. Once again, it was Ottavioli's network of underworld informants that provided the key tip: The Marseilles pimp and car thief was holed up in the apartment of an eighteen-year-old prostitute in the twentieth arrondissement of Paris. The chief sent a team headed by Michel Desfarges to stake it out. "After two days," Desfarges recalls, "a guy comes out of the building and walks straight toward me. It's Bertoncini. It was the scariest moment of my life! I had my hand on my .45 and had some of my men behind me. When he was about three feet away from me, one of my guys hit him on the back of the head with his gun butt. Bertoncini collapsed on the sidewalk. When we picked him up and told him it was the police, he said 'Ouf!' He thought it was a score-settling hit by a French gang." Hauled before Judge Chavanac, his hair still matted with dried blood, Bertoncini was placed in preventive detention.

When they went to search Bertoncini's apartment on the Rue des Pyrénées, investigators found a machine pistol, five automatic pistols, a cache of counterfeit 500-franc notes, and a pile of fake documents.

At seven p.m., while they were still rummaging through Bertoncini's affairs and placing items into evidence bags, they heard a key in the lock. One of the inspectors ripped open the door and shouted "Police!" The two men on the landing scrambled down the stairs. One fled into the street and disappeared, but the cops managed to collar the other in the narrow stairwell. It turned out to be none other than François Caillol, who was promptly handcuffed and whisked off to police headquarters for questioning. Ottavioli was surprised and delighted by the day's second arrest, especially since François Caillol was then considered one of the gang's possible leaders.

Among the papers Desfarges found in the apartment was a document concerning a safe deposit box in Bertoncini's name at the Union de Banques Suisses in Lausanne. Desfarges flew to Lausanne and, along with Swiss colleagues, ordered the bank to open up the box. Inside, he found a trove of forged documents and some 50,000 francs in cash.

While Desfarges was on that mission, Swiss police tried to sell him on a bizarre theory. According to them, there was a link between Bertoncini and Shahnaz Arieh, Empain's Iranian mistress, who lived in Lausanne. Their theory held that Shahnaz was somehow in league with Bertoncini and the other kidnappers and had possibly provided them with information on Wado's habits as well as his finances. Shahnaz was known to frequent gaming establishments, where, according to the Swiss detectives, she could have encountered criminal elements seeking information on the baron. And Bertoncini's trips to Lausanne established a possible geographic link with Shahnaz.

The problem with this intriguing notion was that it was based on pure conjecture. Desfarges wasn't convinced. He decided not to interrogate the wealthy widow, fearing her deposition would cloud the investigative dossier and give the defendants an angle to exploit. So the Swiss hunch about Shahnaz was never fully examined. And yet, at least theoretically, the Iranian had a possible motivation: the hope that the ordeal would destroy the baron's marriage and make him hers.

With the arrest of Bertoncini and François Caillol in November 1978, Ottavioli's men had rounded up all the main players in the kidnapping drama. Three others were definitively out of reach: Daniel Duchateau had been killed in the A6 shootout; Jean "Willie the Crutch" Brunet was shot dead during a robbery in the Paris suburb of Créteil in December 1978; his friend René "La Grise" Rigault died of cancer in a Paris hospital in 1982. According to Caillol, the driver, Idir, was later killed by Islamic guerrillas in Algeria; the feckless Fredo met a gruesome end in Corsica, where "he had the bad idea of sleeping with the wife of a guy who was in prison." Neither man was ever identified by police. Most of the captured suspects cooled their heels in preventive detention pending trial. While in prison, Bertoncini and Marie-Annick took advantage of their forced leisure to get married.

STILL, WADO COULD not rest easy. In May 1981, François Caillol and Bernard Guillon were released on their own recognizance due to a baffling procedural error. Judge Louis Chavanac, who had conducted the judicial investigation for four years, was assigned to another post and replaced by a magistrate unfamiliar with the file. While the new judge was plowing through the thirteen volumes of investigative documents, he neglected to question any of the suspects. An article in the French code of criminal procedure stipulates that any imprisoned defendant who is not called before the investigating magistrate for a period of four months may request provisional liberty. Lawyers for Caillol and Guillon petitioned the court and obtained their freedom pending trial.

No sooner were they out on the street than the baron received an anonymous phone call: "Go buy a newspaper. You'll see that we're free. You must respect your engagements or die." The "engagements" referred to the three IOUs Empain had signed, promising to pay the ransom after his liberation. The baron, who had moved and changed unlisted phone numbers several times, was so scandalized by the release of his former jailers that he threatened to cut off all cooperation with the judge. It was not the first time that he had received threatening phone calls, but with Caillol and Guillon on the loose, he now had real cause for concern.

CHAPTER 26

The Reckoning

On Thursday, December 2, 1982, Baron Édouard-Jean Empain passed through the gilded gates of the Palais de Justice accompanied by his lawyers. He was immediately surrounded by a scrum of journalists shouting questions, sticking microphones and TV cameras in his face, and jostling one another for position like paparazzi stalking a movie star. "He was like Gary Cooper in his elegant, well-cut blue suit with these magnificent eyes," recalls Catherine Tardrew, who covered the trial for the daily *Le Parisien*. "I remember that he was smiling, calm, just a beautiful man."

Slowly Wado and his entourage pushed their way through the thicket of reporters and entered the august, wood-paneled chamber of the Paris Assize Court. The clicks, whirs, and flashes continued as they made their way to the plaintiff's bench on the left side of the courtroom. As Wado took his seat and adjusted the knot on his dark-blue tie, his eye fell on the table where various pieces of evidence were laid out in a glass display case. Alongside a veritable arsenal of weapons, he spotted something he had not seen since the night of his kidnapping: the top joint of his own finger floating in a yellow liquid inside a glass flacon. He registered no visible shock, but quickly resumed his nervous habit of chewing his remaining fingernails.

From a rear door, police led in the eight handcuffed defendants and seated them in the dock at the right side of the courtroom. The baron, who had never seen them unmasked during his sixty-three days of captivity, silently studied the faces of his former tormentors—Bertoncini with his graying mop of a Beatle haircut; Alain Caillol with his hollow cheeks and shifty blue eyes; François Caillol with his round, bald head, thick black eyebrows, and terminally bland face; Bernard Guillon, burly and scowling—"someone you wouldn't want to meet on a dark street," in the words of one cop. To look at them and their four accomplices, these men hardly seemed like criminal geniuses. "They looked tiny, shabby, mean," Wado said. "And yet, they had a certain power, because my life depended on them for two months."

At 1:20 p.m., Presiding Judge Xavier Versini and his two associate judges, all draped in their scarlet judicial robes, entered the chamber and took their places on a raised dais. After the seating of the nine-person jury (which happened to include the daughter of Charles de Gaulle), prosecutor Jean Libouban read out a sixty-six-page summary of the state's case. Incredibly, the three-and-a-half-year judicial investigation—comprising nine thousand documents—had amassed no evidence directly linking any of the defendants to the actual kidnapping. The formal charges included illegal detention (*séquestration*), various forms of aiding and abetting, and in Alain Caillol's case, attempted homicide related to his role in the March 24, 1978, shootout. Alain Caillol and Bertoncini admitted to being involved only at the end of the operation. All the other defendants proclaimed their innocence. Most of them claimed not even to know one another.

Alain Caillol was the first to take the stand. Dressed stylishly in a double-breasted blazer, speaking with almost exaggerated precision, he told the court he had decided to "play the card of truth"—then proceeded to recount a totally fabricated version of his role in the affair. Reprising what he had told the police the night he was arrested, he claimed to know nothing about the kidnapping itself. On February 24, 1978, he said, his friend Duchateau had met him in a café and asked him to help collect the ransom for a fee of 500,000 francs. "He told me I wouldn't have much to do, just drive the car. I accepted."

The prosecutor proceeded to cut holes in his story. How could he explain his numerous trips to Paris in the months before the kidnapping, the checks he had written to other members of the gang, or his presence with the others at Palma, where the plan was apparently worked out?

Caillol's lawyer, Georges Kiejman, attempted to change the subject by portraying the plot as a conspiracy aimed at bringing down the baron because he was considered too powerful, arrogant, and dangerous by the powers that be. "I'm not alone in believing that professional criminals were not the only ones interested in this kidnapping," he argued, slowly pacing back and forth in front of the courtroom. "The big question that hovers over this trial is this: Are those in the defendants' dock merely factotums for higher-level commanders seeking to ruin a man whose responsibilities were enormous in the economic and military potential of France?"

Kiejman returned to this theme repeatedly over the course of the two-week trial, sketching out an elaborate scenario whereby an initial team had snatched Empain at the behest of unnamed bosses, then handed him over to a second team once irreparable damage had been done to the baron's reputation. According to Kiejman's theory, the fact that this second crew continued to pursue the ransom served to disguise the conspiracy as an ordinary criminal operation. The true aim of the operation all along, Kiejman argued, was to force Empain to sell his shares and relinquish control of this strategic conglomerate. The main problem with his intriguing conspiracy theory was that, as Kiejman would later admit privately, there was not a "shred of concrete evidence" for it. (Today, he concedes with a shrug that it "was not the greatest plea of my career.")

Though Kiejman's argument seemed far-fetched, it could not be rejected out of hand. He was one of the most respected and eloquent members of the Paris bar, a prominent figure within the leftist intelligentsia, and soon to be a cabinet minister under the newly elected president, François Mitterrand. At age fifty, the bald, mustachioed Kiejman was famous for his high-profile cases—not to mention his numerous feminine conquests—and was one of the country's most renowned criminal lawyers.

How did a relatively low-level delinquent like Caillol wind up a client of this legal superstar? When Caillol was arrested, he was represented by the redoubtable Monique Smadja-Epstein, a tough-talking, chain-smoking lawyer closely linked to the French underworld. It was Smadja who had accompanied Caillol through all the phases of the investigation. On the eve of the trial, however, he suddenly dumped her in favor of Kiejman. "Smadja was good for pimps and hustlers," he explains, "but I thought she wouldn't swing enough weight at the trial. When I told her I wanted Kiejman to plead for me, she took it very badly. But I had to make the choice."

Looking back, Kiejman offers a wry explanation for Caillol's decision: "He considered himself an intellectual, and thought he had a right to have an intellectual lawyer." One of the most high-priced attorneys on the Paris bar, Kiejman soon realized that Caillol didn't have any money and finally represented him pro bono. The two men maintained friendly relations for years thereafter.

. . .

COMMISSAIRE ANDRÉ BIZEUL, who had overseen the original police investigation, took the stand and knocked a huge hole in Caillol's story about being a hired hand. Bizeul had been present in Ottavioli's office on the evening of March 26, 1978, when Caillol made the phone call that liberated the baron. After the call, as previously noted, Ottavioli had asked Caillol why they had chosen Empain as their victim. Knowing that the police could not legally question him at that point, since an investigative magistrate had taken over the case, Caillol apparently let his guard down. He told them that they had considered other targets, but settled on Empain because he had regular habits, one chauffeur, no bodyguard, and lived on a service road that made it easy to trap him. Ottavioli, characteristically shrewd, had pocketed the informal notes of the conversation. "Don't put it in the investigative file," he told his colleagues. "Let's spring it on him at the trial. We're free to say whatever we want in court."

As it happened, it was André Bizeul who was assigned to present the police brief to the tribunal on Tuesday, December 7. Looking more like a banker than a cop in his chalk-striped double-breasted suit, he held forth for three hours in his velvety baritone, methodically summarizing the police investigation point by point. Suddenly, unexpectedly, he sprang his trap by quoting Caillol's own words about how the kidnappers zeroed in on Empain. The courtroom exploded.

"That was just idle chatter," said Caillol.

"It's inadmissible," Kiejman shouted. "This is scandalous!"

Amid a crescendo of protests from the defense benches, Judge Versini tapped his gavel, adjourned the session, and retired to his chambers with his two associate judges. An hour later, they returned.

"The commissaire may continue his testimony," said Versini. "The jurors may take note of everything he has said."

"That was it!" Bizeul recalls with a grin. "The jury understood that Caillol was in it from the very beginning. He was looking at twenty years."

Any doubts that Caillol was a key member of the band, if not its leader, were pretty much dispelled on the sixth day when the police tape of his March 26 phone call was played over the courtroom loudspeakers. After several rings, the voice of Marie-Annick Le Gayan answers. "Alain here," says Caillol. "Don't speak . . . The baron must be released immediately, alive. Otherwise this will all end in carnage." The authority in his voice, the fact that Marie-Annick recognized him immediately, and the subsequent release of the baron proved that he was anything but a hired hand.

Compared to Caillol's edgy affect, Georges Bertoncini came off as the kind of jovial provincial character you might meet in a Marcel Pagnol novel. Short and pudgy with a round, red face and a lilting Marseilles accent, Bertoncini set off a few titters with his colorful language. The amusement came when he tried to explain how he unwittingly wound up being the baron's jailer in Savigny-sur-Orge. "It was Brunet and Duchateau"—both conveniently deceased—"who asked me if I could lend them my house to store some 'merchandise.' I said, 'sure,' and the next thing I know, they show up with the baron Empain. What do you want me to do? I couldn't call the police [laughter in the courtroom]. Sure I got involved in the affair, but I barely stuck my little toe in it."

Judge Versini asked if Brunet and Duchateau were his friends.

"They were no friends of mine," Bertoncini shot back. "They were dangerous. Look how they wound up! . . . Guys like that don't mess around. If you answer back, something real bad could happen to you."

Versini: "You could have gotten out of there and left them the house. Instead it was you who watched over the baron."

That was Bertoncini's opening to vaunt his humane treatment of the prisoner—his best chance of winning leniency. "Baron Empain can tell you, because he is right here, that I treated him like a friend. He always had a hot meal, I gave him whisky and pastis so he'd feel good, so he wouldn't feel like an animal in his cave . . . Listen, Monsieur le Président, anything he'd ask for I would have done for him, if it was in my power . . . It touched me to see him there like that . . . What I did for him came from my heart. All my life, I have respected people. I'm proud of what I did for the baron." To hear Bertoncini tell it, he had acted out of pure altruism.

François Caillol, as discreet and soft-spoken as his brother was intense, claimed to know nothing about the plot. True, he had spent a total of ten years behind bars for a string of thefts and break-ins, but he told the court he had put all that behind him after his last release from prison in 1973. He now lived a quiet life with his wife and four-year-old son near Grenoble, where he ran a branch of his father's furniture chain. Though there was never any concrete proof of François's involvement in the kidnapping, there were ample grounds for suspicion. When Judge Versini asked why he had made at least seven trips to Paris between January and March, François was unclear about the reasons—even though he was under court order, stemming from an earlier conviction, not to set foot in the capital. He admitted he was in Paris the day of the shooting, but only because his brother had asked to meet him in a café and hand over an unspecified "parcel"; according to François, Alain Caillol never showed up that day. If he wasn't involved in the plot, said Versini, why did he go into hiding after the showdown on the A6? "I was innocent," François replied, "but I knew the police would look for the brother of Alain Caillol."

In fact, the police strongly suspected that François was one of the shooters who had emerged from the wall and opened fire on them.

Bernard Guillon likewise denied any part in the Empain affair. Though no hard evidence linked him directly to the kidnapping, he admitted being friends with the Caillol brothers and told the court he had driven with François to Nîmes after the shootout. The biggest problem for his defense was that during the investigation the baron had identified his voice as belonging to one of his jailers—a fact that Empain would forcefully reiterate when he himself took the stand.

For twelve days, Baron Empain had passively observed the trial proceedings, neither speaking nor showing any emotion as he listened to the witnesses—including his former tormentors—give their testimony. On Monday, December 13, it was his turn to tell his story. Speaking with a quiet dignity, never raising his voice, he calmly recounted the details of what he called the "nightmare" that he had endured for two months. Apart from the sound of his voice, the courtroom was enveloped in a tomblike silence and jurors were visibly scribbling notes. He began by describing the circumstances of his abduction and his transfer to the first hiding place. Almost immediately, his abductors proceeded with the amputation. "There were five of them kneeling around me, all masked," Empain recounted. "Suddenly one of these men whistled. They pushed me down and administered a strong drug and I fell asleep. When I awoke I saw my hand was bandaged. I hardly need to tell you that it was very, very painful."

Empain had the impression that his jailers intended to hold him only three or four days, but as the vigil dragged on, he was moved to a second location, and finally to the house in Savigny-sur-Orge. He said he learned of the shootout from a newspaper thrust into his tent on the morning of March 25, 1978. "For me, that meant the end. I didn't see how they could release me alive." It was at that point that one of the kidnappers made him sign the three IOUs totaling 45 million francs. He would be contacted with the code name "Marika." If he didn't pay, they would kill a random person in the street—three people, in fact, one at a time, until he handed over the money. Empain signed his name, affixed his thumbprint to the documents, and promised to pay after his liberation.

Because of the Marika threat hanging over his head, he said, he had lived in constant fear of retribution. "Not all of my jailers are in the defendants' dock," he told the court. "Others are still free and they know that I did not keep my word." For that reason, he had been reluctant to provide much information about his abductors—especially after the investigating magistrate suggested he had staged the kidnapping himself to pay off his gambling debts. "When I heard that, I intended to say as little as possible."

Now, four years later, he said he was able to think "normally." Of the dozen or so distinct voices that he had heard during his incarceration, there were two that he could identify with certainty: those of Bertoncini and Guillon. Bertoncini, with his unmistakable Marseilles twang, had already admitted to acting as the baron's "host" during the last phase of his captivity. But Guillon had always denied any role in the caper. Now Empain identified Guillon "one hundred percent" and provided damning details. "This is the voice that I heard right after my amputation," he said, raising the possibility that Guillon himself had done the chopping. The same person had told Empain that, if it came to that, he would be the one to execute him and promised to do it "cleanly." Finally, Empain identified Guillon as the man who had made him sign the Marika IOUs just before his liberation.

With that, Guillon stood up in the defendants' dock. "That's false! Monsieur le Baron is mistaken!"

"Monsieur Guillon is mistaken," Empain replied calmly. "Ninety-eight percent certainty is not enough for me. I needed one hundred percent, and if I ever had any doubts, I can tell you that today they are completely dissipated." He added that he recognized the voices of at least two other defendants, but would not identify them for lack of absolute certainty.

When Empain stepped down after his four hours of testimony, it was clear that the trial had reached a dramatic turning point. After days of tedious procedure, countless investigative details, self-serving testimony by the accused, and bombastic oratory by their lawyers, the baron's serene, self-assured words weighed heavily against the defense. And for Wado himself, it was a long-denied moment of vindication for a man who had almost been made to feel guilty for the crime of being kidnapped. "When I finished speaking," he later wrote in his memoirs, "I felt that my deposition had erased all the scandal, all the invisible misery that had gripped me for so long . . . Through the trial of my kidnappers, I had achieved my public rehabilitation."

The next day, Empain's attorney, Jean-Yves Dupeux, delivered an eloquent plea, stressing the human cost of the plot to the baron and his family. After evoking the physical agony endured by his client during his two-month incarceration, Dupeux described the deeper wounds that followed his liberation. "Put yourself in his place for a moment," he told the jury. "He is free, the nightmare is over, he weeps . . . But then another kind of suffering begins. Because his private life was stripped bare, his secret garden was sacked. Today he is the object of an unhealthy curiosity. People approach him in the street to ask him questions and try to get a look at the stump of his amputated finger. Nothing can ever be as before after this incredible suffering, this useless cruelty . . . Empain's family life was shattered, his social life destroyed." In closing, Dupeux called the baron's testimony his "second liberation" and voiced the hope that "this trial will be the end of the long night that began on January 23, 1978."

The next day was devoted to final pleas by the various defense lawyers. Though their ranks included some of the top names in France's legal pantheon—including the future foreign minister Roland Dumas—most of them plodded through the unenviable task of defending an unsavory set of characters whose guilt seemed clear to everyone. The most memorable flight of eloquence came from Alain Caillol's lawyer, Georges Kiejman. As expected, the eminent jurist repeated his earlier claim that some high-level "mastermind" had hatched the plot in order to bring down the haughty baron. But even Kiejman knew his theory was far-fetched, so in the end he appealed to the jury's sense of fairness. "I tend to think that the punishments justice hands out are too severe," he said. "Don't forget that Alain Caillol is young. If you condemn him to spending twenty years in detention, he will be in his fifties when he gets out. All his adult life would be that of a living dead man."

Kiejman, a philosophical leftist, then appeared to attack the baron himself, whose rise, he said, was in itself a sign of social injustice. "What do you think of a society that accepts for a young man of thirty years, Belgian and privileged, to become, merely by virtue of his heritage, the emperor of an industrial empire? What do you think of a society that accepts for him to condemn fifty thousand people to the ranks of the unemployed? What do you think of a society that accepts for this man to gamble away, in a few days, 11 million francs—the annual salary of three thousand workers?" Kiejman's stunning flight of anticapitalist rhetoric, implying that in some way the victim of the kidnapping had it coming to him, won little sympathy for his client.

THE CASE WENT to the jury on Friday, December 17, 1982. After only five hours of deliberation, they handed their verdict to Judge Versini at seven p.m. All eight defendants were found guilty as charged. For the four main perpetrators, the sentences were harsh: Alain Caillol and Bernard Guillon, twenty years; Georges Bertoncini, fifteen years; François Caillol, thirteen years. The aiders and abettors got off easier: Marc Le Gayan, five years; his sister Marie-Annick, five years, with three suspended; Robert Matheron, a Bertoncini crony who had helped him escape, two years; Andrée Boniface, a young woman who had sheltered Bertoncini, received a suspended eighteen-month sentence.

When the judge gaveled the session to a close, Wado exited the courtroom with an attractive woman on his arm. She was Jacqueline Ragonaux, the ex-model he had met in a Paris nightclub a year earlier, and whom he would later make his second baroness. Speaking to journalists on the steps of the Palais de Justice, he had a charitable word for his former aggressors: "My faith helped me resist during my long hours of captivity, so if you ask a Catholic whether forgiveness exists, the reply is evident. Of course it exists."

CHAPTER 27

Afterlives

For Wado, the trial marked the beginning of what he called his "new life." He had only recently shaken off a long depression and recovered from a painful and debilitating ailment—a kidney stone the size of a peach pit, surgically removed in June 1982. His relationship with Jacqueline brought a measure of emotional stability to his personal life. (His old affair with Shahnaz Arieh had flamed out sometime after their return from the United States in August 1978, though she occasionally got in touch, causing the jealous Jacqueline to hang a voodoo image on the wall to ward off the spirit of this "unwanted soul.")

Wado felt he had entered a phase of redemption and renewal. He even went so far as to say that the kidnapping had "enriched" his life. From now on, the baron would live a simpler, calmer existence. As he told one interviewer, he no longer needed to drive a Ferrari or a

Maserati; he was happy with his compact Renault R5. Since his day in court, he said, he finally felt like "a totally free man."

Though his career as a captain of industry was behind him, he still needed to make a living. In September 1982, he started a business called Air Matériel, dealing in civilian and military aviation equipment. It was a modest affair with only a dozen employees, but things started out well enough. He rented prestigious office space just off the Champs-Élysées and, thanks to his name and address book, his new company quickly lined up major clients, including Air France.

But lady luck was not with him. On December 27, 1982, just ten days after the trial ended, he got some alarming news while vacationing with Jacqueline at the Megève ski resort: The office of Air Matériel had been bombed in the middle of the night, causing considerable damage but no injuries. Was it targeted by friends of the convicted kidnappers, some leftist political group, or Iranian agents out to punish the baron for his business dealings with Baghdad during the 1980–1988 Iran–Iraq war? Despite two ambiguous claims of responsibility—one by a murky anarchist faction, the other by an unknown group calling itself the "Internationalist Hooligans"—the authors were never identified. Whoever was behind the attack, Wado was spooked. Early the next year, he sold his share of the business to his partner and set himself up as an independent trader, acting as a go-between in discreet commercial exchanges involving various public and private entities.

Meanwhile, he continued to live in fear of retribution from his former kidnappers. The known perpetrators were in prison, but he was convinced that others were still at large. Though he changed addresses and phone numbers numerous times, he would receive harassing calls at all hours of the day and night—some of them pronouncing the dreaded code name "Marika" and demanding that he make good on the IOUs he signed just before his liberation. These could have been prank calls, for the "Marika" story had been recounted in the press—but how would the callers know his private number? The police placed a security patrol outside his residence for a time, but they didn't seem to take the threats seriously. The calls were never followed up by action, but they had a chilling effect on the baron, who would continue for the rest of his life to have nightmares related to his abduction.

Around this time, Commissaire Robert Broussard, former leader of the Antigang, happened to run into Empain at the Casablanca airport. "As my colleagues and I headed for the departure gate," he tells me, "we see a guy dragging his suitcase. It was Empain. I was sad to see him like that, I think I had tears in my eyes. Because this once-dashing figure was all bent over—I can still see the scene—he had a little rolling suitcase that he dragged behind him with difficulty. He came over and gave me a hug. For a guy like him, who we'd known under other circumstances, it was a very emotional moment."

Several years later, Wado invited Broussard to visit him at his country house near Bouffémont. "He needed to talk," says Broussard. "He was doing better, he was struggling, but this was a guy who had not fully recovered his faculties. He was enormously disappointed and told me he had received a second shock that was more painful than the first. The first was the physical suffering during his incarceration, the second was the emotional pain that came after his liberation."

In 1985 Empain published an autobiographical memoir called *La vie en jeu*. The title was itself quite revealing, since it could be translated either as "a life in the balance," or "a life of gambling." The second meaning, perhaps unintended, ironically pointed to the addiction that had tarnished his image in the wake of the kidnapping and would continue to hold him in its grips. The book recounts the whole arc of Wado's life, with flashbacks to the dynasty's founding, his childhood, and the dramatic story of his own rise to power as he wrenched control from his stepfather and engineered one of France's most spectacular corporate takeovers. Mostly, though, the memoir focuses on the kidnapping and its consequences. It describes the ordeal in gripping detail, but perhaps more striking is the story of its aftermath—his chilly reception by his family and by the colleagues who, instead of welcoming him, forced him to relinquish his hold on the empire built by his illustrious grandfather. It is both a confession and a score-settling—not against the kidnappers but against those who, in his view, conspired to bring him down.

WADO'S FAMILY LIFE never really recovered from the aftershocks of his kidnapping. His long separation from Silvana finally ended in an uncontested divorce in 1990, quickly followed by his marriage to Jacqueline in Monte Carlo. His relationship with his three children remained strained. Patricia lived far away in America. Christine, profoundly destabilized by the trauma, kept her distance. And Jean-François, only fourteen at the time of the kidnapping, grew into manhood, as Wado had done, without a father to guide him: "I didn't see him for three or four years after his return. He disappeared. I would come home [from boarding school], and it's 'Papa's not here. Papa is off on a trip. Papa needs to rest. Don't expect anything from your father,' which is pretty violent. Time passes, months then years—no news."

By far Wado's most troubled relationship was with his mother. He had never received much maternal affection from Rozell and felt betrayed by her in the wake of his ordeal. "She was not moved by my kidnapping," he told a documentary filmmaker. "She is a person I know, someone with whom I passed a certain number of moments and hours, but she never took care of me. So there is no love there.

Neither in one direction or the other." For long years, the two were estranged from each other with Diane acting as a go-between.

Goldie was Goldie, cold and self-centered, always the star of her own show. And what a show it was! From Columbus, Ohio, to the bright lights of Broadway; from the London burlesque stage to the bed of Johnny Empain; from Heliopolis to the Château de Bouffémont; from baroness to widow and back to baroness as the wife of Édouard Empain, aka Cousin Miscarriage.

As we have seen, her second union was a mere marriage of convenience: Édouard lived mainly at the Château d'Enghien with his elderly mother, while Goldie continued to entertain a succession of lovers at Bouffémont. Imagine her surprise when Édouard, presumably impotent, announced in 1966 that he had fallen in love with a twenty-three-year-old German girl named Rosmarie Lorenz. Goldie had no problem with that and even encouraged a relationship that kept Édouard occupied and out of her hair. But when Édouard asked for a divorce in order to marry his blond Fräulein, Goldie exacted a hefty settlement—plus a monthly pension of 25,000 francs—that Wado aggressively negotiated on her behalf. She always seemed to land on her feet.

Édouard and Rosmarie were married in 1975. Though she lived with him in his Belgian château, and was apparently an attentive partner, the young woman also insisted on having her personal freedom. In 1979, she returned pregnant from a solo vacation. When a daughter was born, Édouard refused to recognize the child and the couple eventually divorced. (Rosmarie was hardly left in the lurch: Her cuckolded husband granted her a monthly stipend of 115,000 Belgian francs, equivalent to some $7,000 today.) His health and morale declined quickly after that, aggravated by heavy drinking. He died in 1984 at the age of seventy.

Three years earlier, Édouard had revoked his adoption of Wado.

Relations between the two men had never been good, but what ostensibly triggered this legal action was Wado's statement in a *Paris Match* interview that Édouard had tried to usurp his power in the family group and that his stepfather's management was "catastrophic." That was the reason Édouard stated to the Brussels court that approved the revocation on September 30, 1981. In reality, it was apparently Rozell who pushed behind the scenes to have Wado disinherited by his stepfather. "After the kidnapping, she considered that Wado had lost his dignity," explains Diane Empain. "She thought he was dangerous for the group and convinced Édouard to renounce the adoption." Senior officials of the multinational quietly supported the move. And for good reason: If Wado had inherited his stepfather's stock, he would have remained a significant force within the Empain-Schneider group even after selling his own shares.

Wado did not contest the action, which left his half-sister Diane the sole heir to Édouard's estate. (The natural daughter of Rozell and the jockey Jacques Doyasbère, Diane had been legally recognized by Édouard as his own child.) In addition to Édouard's substantial stock holdings—11 percent of the Empain-Schneider group—the estate included the Château d'Enghien and its twenty-five-acre park. Diane subsequently sold it to the local municipality for 92.5 million Belgian francs (about $1.7 million, equivalent to some $4.4 million today)— minus a large mortgage debt. A year or so later, she sold the stock back to the group for a considerable sum. Unlike Wado, Diane had always remained close to the man she affectionately called "Tonton"— Uncle. Her loyalty had paid off handsomely.

The other Empain château, Bouffémont, had been inherited by Wado. But it, too, ultimately escaped the family's control. The sad, but perhaps predictable, reason was the issue that had contributed so heavily to Wado's fall from grace. Along with skiing and hunting, his favorite pastime was still gambling, which he continued to pursue with abandon, not only at his weekly poker games but also in the very casinos where he had lost a fortune before his kidnapping. "I don't have any great needs," he told *Le Monde* in 1985, "except for my gambling passion. And, believe me, that's expensive."

It was an addiction that he simply could not kick—nor, apparently, did he really want to. "For me, it's normal," he would tell his sister. "My father gambled in the casinos and partied all the time. It's not a vice." Over the years, his losses far outstripped his income as a trader and consultant. The 30 million francs he had received when he sold his Empain-Schneider shares was rapidly dwindling. In desperation, he decided to sell the château that the general-baron Empain had bought eight decades earlier, at the height of his glory, and turned into a proud family fiefdom.

By that time, in Diane Empain's perhaps exaggerated description, the château was a "ruin." Rozell, who had lived there ever since Johnny's death, had never bothered to maintain the place. (When relatives from Ohio visited in the late 1970s, they were shocked to find that they had to take cold showers because the water heater didn't work.) In 1986, Wado bought out his mother's usufruct rights and sold the building to a mason, who intended to fix it up and live there in grand style. The sale price was 2 million francs—equivalent to about $725,000 today—quite a bargain for a historic château but a reflection of its run-down condition. Apparently finding the restoration job too big for him, this buyer resold the château to a Russian oligarch ten years later. Most of the surrounding land was sold to a Japanese investment group that turned it into a golf course. Diane herself bought the stables and related outbuildings plus fifty-four acres of land. Having inherited Jacques Doyasbère's equestrian passion, she continued to live there and raise champion show horses.

· · ·

AFTER LEAVING THE château, Goldie moved in with her daughter in the stable complex. But their stormy relationship became so unbearable—Diane claims her mother once tried to run her over in her car—that Goldie was "invited" to move to a rented apartment nearby. In 1992 the dowager baroness built a large traditional-style country house for herself in Normandy, near the English Channel resort and horse-racing enclave of Deauville. Goldie had hoped to entice her older sister Betty Jane to move there so they could live out their final years together. Betty Jane, preferring to remain in L.A., said no thanks. Goldie eventually sold her Normandy property and moved to the South of France.

In 2004, she was hospitalized in Saint-Tropez after a series of panic attacks. Faced with her aged mother's mounting instability, Diane convinced Wado it was time to put her in a rest home. "She had become unmanageable," Diane explains. "I found a medicalized facility near Bouffémont that had room. Then I negotiated with my mother and showed her the catalogue. She listened to me—never to Wado. She finally agreed to go."

For the next two years, Diane visited regularly as her mother's mood grew increasingly somber. "She knew she was trapped and muzzled," says Diane. "She tried to run away several times and started to commit acts of self-mutilation."

At two a.m. on the morning of March 26, 2006, Diane received a phone call from the center's director.

"Your mother has defenestrated herself."

Shaken out of a deep sleep, Diane didn't understand. "What does that mean?"

"It means she has committed suicide."

Indeed, the baroness Rozell Rowland Empain, at eighty-nine, had performed the final act of her fabulous saga by jumping out of a third-floor window and smashing into the sidewalk below.

When Diane arrived at the center later that morning, she was escorted to the morgue and shown her mother's body. "Her face was not destroyed," she recalls. "She was still beautiful. I didn't cry, because of the shock. She had always said, 'One day, I will throw myself out of the window.'" Then Diane went to inspect her mother's room. "It was like something out of a Hitchcock film. There was a table stacked on top of another table, with the curtain fluttering in the open window. She left me a note: 'Darling, I love you. Your road is in front of you. Mamy.'" Diane is convinced that the date was not chosen at random: It was the twenty-eighth anniversary of Wado's liberation. Perhaps a lugubrious way of grabbing the attention of her son, who had not visited his mother once during her two-year stay in the rest home.

Six days later, after a simple benediction by the local priest, Goldie's ashes were dispersed according to her wishes. Half were scattered on the golf course around the 7th hole (her lucky number); the other half were sprinkled over the graves of her dogs on the grounds of the Château de Bouffémont. It was somehow a fitting end—but could a soul like Goldie's ever really rest in peace?

THE OTHER MEMBERS of Wado's family went their separate ways in the wake of the kidnapping. "It changed everybody's lives," Patricia Empain told me in the first of several interviews. "Not just Mom and Papa, but the kids were also marked forever." Silvana, remarried and widowed, now lives with her Siamese cat in West Palm Beach, Florida. Patricia, divorced from her American husband in 1989, moved back to Paris eight years later. Four times married, she now occupies a small apartment in the same building where her family lived when Wado was kidnapped. Her younger sister, Christine, also divorced, lives with her two grown sons near Paris.

Jean-François lives in Lausanne and heads a company that owns a chain of upscale dental clinics in Hungary, Switzerland, France, and Luxembourg. Lacking male heirs (he has two daughters), he is technically the last baron Empain, though his father was the last baron to head the family's industrial dynasty—hence the title of this book. In a 2019 documentary on the kidnapping, Jean-François was asked what he would like to tell his father that he never said before. His eyes reddening, he replied: "I'd tell him, 'I don't blame you.' I'd tell him, 'Whatever happened, I'm proud of you.' I'd tell him, 'It's a pity we didn't see more of each other.' But what a life! Hats off. All the suffering, all the horrors, all the joys, such a life for one man—incredible!"

The perps in the Empain kidnapping—at least those who were caught—have met varying fates since they were convicted in 1982. After serving his time, François Caillol returned to his home near Grenoble, where he lives in quiet retirement. Bernard Guillon, who always denied any involvement in the Empain affair, was not a happy camper in prison. In August 1984, along with six other prisoners, he sliced off the top joint of his little finger with a knife, apparently smuggled from the canteen, and mailed the bloody body part to the justice minister along with a demand for a retrial. This first-time-tragedy-second-time-farce mutilation was all the more remarkable since Guillon was the one police suspected of chopping off the baron's finger in 1978. Released in 1990, he is still living somewhere in France and presumably keeping his head down.

Georges Bertoncini, the loquacious Marseilles pimp and car thief, just could not manage to keep out of trouble. Released from prison in 1989, he was arrested in Brittany five years later for cocaine trafficking with the Medellín cartel. At his trial in 2000, he was sentenced to twenty-two years in prison. The following year, he was found dead in his cell at the Luynes prison north of Marseilles. The official story was that he had swallowed all his medicine to avoid being put in solitary confinement. According to Alain Caillol, Bertoncini had suffered a severe asthma attack, but the prison doctor refused to transfer him to the hospital wing for treatment, leaving Jo le Marseillais to die gasping in his cell at the age of fifty-eight.

And Alain Caillol? Well, Caillol deserves his own story.

CHAPTER 28

Light and Twilight

*A*lain Caillol, the presumed leader of the kidnap plot, remains the most enigmatic player in the whole Empain drama. The baron called him a "complex and interesting personality." Georges Kiejman, his former lawyer, describes him as "a cultivated man with social pretensions." But to Michel Desfarges, the retired police investigator who followed the band's trail to Palma, Caillol is "a piece of filth who took himself for Alain Delon."

Photos of the young Alain Caillol do bear a passing resemblance to the French movie star. Today, on the cusp of eighty, his tanned face, drawn and weathered, still bears a trace of his youthful good looks. The eyes are blue, the graying hair neatly brushed back, the face lean with angular cheekbones. As he puts it, "I look more like a little boy grown old than a tough guy in the movies."

I first met Caillol in the autumn of 2018 at a café near the Place de la Concorde in Paris. Despite his advanced age, he was vigorous and animated, dressed with the flair of someone who gives attention to his appearance: a blue blazer over a gray cashmere sweater, well-cut jeans, and tan suede shoes. My intention was just to have an initial get-acquainted meeting over coffee, hoping to win his confidence enough for him to open up with inside details about the case at subsequent meetings. That proved to be a pointless exercise. From his opening words, Caillol was off and running with revelations about his role in what the French press had dubbed "the kidnapping of the century." I pulled out my notebook and let him talk.

It was clear from this and many later conversations that Caillol remains obsessed with the case. He is tortured by what-ifs and if-onlys, constantly turning over in his mind the string of errors and bad luck that left his buddy dead and condemned him to long years in prison over what turned out to be a pile of worthless paper. Time and again he returns to what he considers the gang's biggest mistake of all: turning down the Empain group's initial counteroffer of 30 million francs.

"When we called Bierry two days after the kidnapping, he had 30 million in his safe," says Caillol. "He could have driven to a rendezvous and handed it over and we'd release the baron and disappear. It would have been a done deal! But we acted like a bunch of saps and refused the 30 million. When Ottavioli returned from New York, it was all over. He ruled out any payment and imposed his control over the family and the group. Once the police were in charge, it was hopeless."

Why did they turn down the counteroffer? "A sin of pride," says Caillol, his metallic voice laced with self-deprecation. "We refused to compromise on principle. It was the biggest mistake of my life, because I could have retired and bought a nice hotel on the Costa Brava." On other occasions, he has said he might have moved to New York or elsewhere. It is clear that he had no precise plan for what to do with his share of the ransom, other than hanging up his spurs and quitting the crime game. And even that is doubtful. For in Caillol's eyes, crime was a way of life. And he genuinely enjoyed it.

"First of all," he explains, "you don't have any fixed hours. You are your own man. I lived totally free. I could eat at three a.m., go to Pigalle [Paris's main red-light district], take a ski vacation when I wanted. Then there's the adrenaline rush. It's an exciting lifestyle." And dangerous—witness the bloody ends of his former comrades Mesrine, Duchateau, and Brunet. Caillol shrugs. *"Risques du métier"*— occupational hazards. He himself was lucky. Until the shootout on the A6, he had never taken a bullet, nor had he ever fired at anyone, except for a single warning shot during a bank job.

Apart from the sheer thrill of it all, the criminal life offered the promise of instant riches—or at least enough cash to make the risks worthwhile. Like the legendary Willie Sutton, Caillol robbed banks because that's where the money is. The paradox is that he made quite a decent living running his father's furniture outlet. But the business world, like family life, bored him. Rather than living on his comfortable salary, saving and investing like a responsible member of the bourgeoisie that he was born into, Caillol preferred to play the gangster and steal his money. Over the years, he reckons he and his buddies raked in maybe a couple million. Where did it all go? "Restaurants, travel, ski vacations. I bought a house in the South of France and a blue Jaguar. And clothes—Berluti shoes, cashmere sweaters. I always wore a suit and tie when I cased a joint. It was important to present well."

Caillol insists that he and his buddies never intended to harm Wado physically—beyond the initial amputation, of course. "The idea was to create a shock. Get their attention so the deal would be concluded quickly. The longer a kidnapping lasts, the more time the cops have to do research and try to track you down." So chopping off part of the baron's little finger was written down in the meticulous plan that Caillol and Duchateau drew up in the months before the abduction. "The guy who drew the short straw said, 'Oh, shit!' Nobody wanted to do that. We wanted to do the least harm possible, so we cut off the last joint of the little finger. It was not like the guys who sliced off Paul Getty's ear. That was nasty!" The idea of using a guillotine-style paper cutter and a mallet instead of a knife, says Caillol, was in order to do the job "cleanly and not damage the flesh."

Killing Empain was never part of the original plan. Yet when the affair dragged on with no end in sight, the band took a vote on whether to execute their prisoner. Caillol himself had voted to kill him. "There were only two solutions," he says. "Free him or kill him. If you free him, what do you do after that? Another kidnapping? Nobody would take you seriously."

The majority of the kidnappers, as we have seen, voted to spare the hostage. But had it gone the other way, they would have drawn straws to designate the executioner. If Caillol had drawn the short straw, he tells me he would have killed him "without hesitation—I would have had no choice." And how would he have done it? "Quickly, so he wouldn't even know he was dead. You know, bend over a map or a photo or something with him and talk to him, then shoot him in the head from behind. I wouldn't have wanted to frighten him." Looking back, he is glad they didn't kill their hostage. "Empain had become almost like a friend, because we all had esteem for him. His courage, his discretion, his dignity commanded our respect. He dominated us morally."

Though Wado was spared that time, Caillol admits that his fate would have been sealed had he and Duchateau escaped with the fake ransom and realized they had been duped. "We would have been so enraged that we would have killed Empain. I saw no other solution. Considering my psychological state at that time, there would have been no question of liberating him." Though Caillol and his confederates didn't physically eliminate their prisoner, they ruined his life nonetheless. "We killed him," he admits. "We destroyed him. We screwed his professional life and his social life. It all collapsed on him."

Caillol has spent much of his adult life behind bars. Even before snatching the baron, he had done nearly five years. Sentenced to twenty years for his role in the kidnapping, he was released for good behavior in 1989. Arrested again in 2000 for cocaine trafficking, he did another six years. Today he lives on a pension of €1,000 a month in a tiny apartment in the rough working-class suburb of Saint-Denis, north of Paris. The hundreds of thousands of euros that went through his hands during his heyday as a bank robber have long since evaporated, never mind the millions he'd counted on from the Empain caper that never materialized.

Though poor in monetary terms, Caillol developed a rich intellectual life during his long years in prison. He studied English and computer programing, played chess, and read voraciously—Sartre, Freud, Dante, Tacitus, Michelet, Kafka, Victor Hugo, and countless other authors. He also indulged his longtime passion for opera and classical music, amassing a large collection of cassettes and CDs. Taking university courses by correspondence, he earned a master's degree in history, then began research for a doctoral thesis on the nineteenth-century French novelist and feminist George Sand.

After reading an article by a university professor named Mireille Bonnelle, a specialist on Sand, Caillol wrote to her in 1984 seeking advice on his project. Their correspondence blossomed into an intense epistolary relationship. Fascinated by this bookish gangster, Bonnelle actually fell in love with him. When Caillol was released in 1989, they set up house together in Montpellier. Their cohabitation was short-lived. After revolting against his bourgeois roots and spending decades in prison, the last thing Caillol wanted was to be tied down in a conventional relationship. "The curtains, the bedspreads and floral cushions, it was all too much," he says. "It was not my style to be prim and proper like a stiff." The two have remained close friends, however. In 1990, Bonnelle published their prison correspondence under the title *Lettres en liberté conditionnelle.* The book, co-signed by Caillol and Bonnelle, spawned a theatrical production that had a brief run in the Latin Quarter.

Caillol's writerly efforts did not end there. In 2012, he published a book called *Lumière* (Light) in which he related his version of the Empain affair. Written in a novelesque manner with a certain literary flair, it revealed for the first time what the investigators and prosecutor could not prove at the trial: He and his team had in fact planned and carried out the kidnapping from the beginning. (The convictions were for illegal detention and, in Caillol's case, attempted homicide during the shootout with police.) The book was widely reviewed, often favorably, but sales were negligible. Caillol's hopes of hitting the jackpot with a literary Hail Mary pass were dashed.

WHEN HE WAS first released from prison in 1989, Caillol had contacted the baron to express his regrets. Wado invited him to breakfast at the grand manor house near Bouffémont that he had built in 1962. But Jacqueline, obsessively protective of her husband, was hovering around and the two men passed an awkward moment together. "It was like with my father. We sat there face-to-face and I didn't know what to say."

They had a more substantive exchange when *Lumière* was published in 2012. Caillol wanted to give Empain a copy so he would know the whole story behind the kidnapping. An acquaintance of Caillol's, screenwriter Gilles Malençon, reached out to the baron and asked if he would be willing to meet with him. Empain, then seventy-five years old, agreed but insisted on a discreet encounter far from the prying eyes and cameras of journalists. Malençon reserved a private suite in the Hôtel Arc de Triomphe, near the Parc Monceau. Caillol arrived first, nervously pacing around the suite's dining room, where coffee, fruit juice, and cookies had been laid out as if to host a business meeting. He was wondering what to say, whether he should shake the baron's hand, use the "*tu*" or "*vous*" form of address. He had brought a copy of his book but was unsure how to sign it.

Moments later, the baron walked in. Flashing a warm smile, he strode over to Caillol and held out his hand. "Alain," he said. "It's Alain, right? I remember." The two men shook hands then sat across from each other at the table. "I didn't want to run the risk of one of us dying before we had a chance to talk," Caillol began. Empain replied with elegance: "I am at peace with my kidnappers. I know what it is to be deprived of freedom." Once their conversation was under way, Malençon withdrew to the lobby and left the two men alone.

Two and a half hours later, Empain emerged from the elevator. "I am pleased," he told Malençon, "and I think he is too." After the baron's departure, the screenwriter returned to the suite. Caillol was almost euphoric. "He shook my hand, he told me to say '*tu*' to him right away." Empain had even asked for his telephone number. On the table, two empty bottles from the minibar bore witness to a small but remarkable event: The erstwhile kidnapper and his victim had shared a whisky together. And Caillol had finally decided how to sign the baron's copy of his book. Above his name, he scribbled a single word: "Pardon."

Caillol is reluctant to go into detail about what he and Empain discussed in private. "We talked about this and that," he says evasively. "Obviously about the affair." One thing sticks out in his mind. During the investigation, Empain was asked if he could recognize the voices of the defendants. He only identified two men: Georges Bertoncini and Bernard Guillon. But Caillol is certain that Wado also detected his own distinctive voice. "I was one of the first to talk to him," he tells me. "He recognized my voice for sure. But he never said it. He must have thought I was the nice guy."

Empain, for his part, never revealed the substance of his talk with Caillol, but he did have some kind words for his book. "Everything that Alain Caillol has written is a faithful transcription of what I went through," he told a journalist from *Le Figaro*. "He went as far as possible in admitting his own responsibility and expressed a degree of repentance. I consider that he has paid his debt and we are even." In spite of their cordial meeting, though, he made it clear that he would "never be a friend of Alain Caillol, even if I don't rule out the possibility of seeing him again." Two subsequent meetings did in fact take place, but they were staged by TV crews and were little more than photo-ops.

THE REALLY SIGNIFICANT encounter between the two men had taken place on the morning of the kidnapping, the moment when their destinies intersected and changed their lives forever. They had much in common: Both men came from privileged backgrounds, went to elite private schools, and suffered from a lack of parental affection. Wado inherited an immense fortune and went on to become, for a time, a "master of the universe." Caillol went off the rails and became a gangster. Yet for all Caillol's spouting of anticapitalist ideology, there was something about Empain's world that attracted him— perhaps a case of nose-against-the-glass envy, perhaps some kind of class identification with the milieu he was born into. Though Wado came about his wealth through different means, Caillol was seeking the same thing—indeed, he was literally trying to appropriate part of the baron's own fortune. As Caillol put it, "Each one of us saw in him the image of what we wanted to be: handsome, rich, powerful, and intelligent."

Though Wado was only four years older than Caillol, it is perhaps not too much of a stretch to imagine that, at some level, Caillol saw him as a father figure. Which might explain why, four decades after the fact, he sought a reconciliation with Wado in lieu of the paternal benediction that he never received. It seems far-fetched. And yet, Caillol himself said as much on the last page of *Lumière*, when an imaginary interlocutor tells him to go see Baron Empain. "Maybe he will reach out his hand, and then you can ask forgiveness of your father, and be reconciled with yourself."

By then, it was too late for Caillol to seek a reconciliation with his real father. On March 27, 1978, Pierre Caillol had suffered a severe heart attack in his Paris apartment, apparently triggered by shock and shame upon learning that his son had just been arrested for his role in the Empain kidnapping. Three years later, as the trial of his two sons was approaching, he attempted to commit suicide. He survived but apparently lost the will to live and died shortly afterward at the age of eighty-two. When Alain learned of his father's death, his Oedipal rage was compounded by intense guilt. "He was too ashamed of me, to the point where he let himself die before the trial."

It is not the purpose of this book to pass judgment. After all, Alain Caillol and most of his confederates have already been judged by the courts and paid their debt to society. Some of them, *requiescat in pace*, have passed before a higher jurisdiction. Yet it is impossible not to look on Caillol's life and wonder why it took the turn it did. It is impossible not to say that he did some terrible things—from breaking into people's houses and robbing banks at gunpoint to mutilating and torturing Wado and, in effect, ruining his life. It is impossible not to wonder why, after a long and supposedly edifying prison stay, he plunged back into criminality and got busted for a cocaine deal. And it is impossible not to see the mortal shame he visited on his own father, whatever Pierre Caillol's shortcomings as a parent.

When pressed on these points, Caillol blames his upbringing for not providing him with a moral compass. "I had absolutely no moral education," he tells me. "I can distinguish perfectly well between right and wrong, but it's something I never interiorized. Since I had a deficit of moral education, I guess I never found that within myself." It is hard to understand how such a cultivated and well-read man—a man who grew up in privilege and attended Jesuit boarding schools— can treat the ethical implications of his actions so lightly.

It would be too easy to call Alain Caillol a monster, as some have done. He is far too complex a character for such a neat judgment—"a prime candidate for psychoanalysis," as Georges Kiejman says. And yet it is equally wrong to see him as some kind of social avenger of capitalist evils or a romantic Robin Hood figure. When I first met him, he wrote this dedication on the flyleaf of his book: "For Thomas Sancton . . . His book will speak of me, here's hoping he will not be too severe." I told him then that I would present the truth as best I could and let others draw their own conclusions. As for Caillol himself, he has done his time and must live with his own conscience.

CHAPTER 29

Wado's Adieu

*I*n retirement, Wado and Jacqueline lived in La Chaumière, the grand Anglo-Norman-style manor he had built in 1962 on the grounds of the Château de Bouffémont. Under its steep thatched roof, the house contained seven bedrooms, five bathrooms, a billiard room, and an immense living room with an open fireplace. The interior was filled with antique furniture, paintings, hunting trophies, oriental rugs, outsize couches, and memorabilia celebrating the family's history—mostly the glorious exploits of the grandfather Wado always referred to as "*le général.*"

La Chaumière had originally served as a country home where Wado and his family spent nearly every weekend while the children were growing up. The kids loved going there—especially their visits to their grandmother, who continued to live nearby in the château. Though Wado hardly spoke to his mother, his children adored her. "Rozell was fun," says Patricia Empain. "She wore jeans and no makeup. We would make cakes with her and play Monopoly. We liked her very much. She had no rules." That lasted until the girls reached their teenage years, when the allure of their social life in Paris outweighed the rustic charms of Bouffémont. But Wado continued to use the house as a weekend retreat and finally settled in there full-time.

Wado and Jacqueline liked to travel. There were the annual Christmas vacations in Megève, summers on the Côte d'Azur, and frequent sojourns in Monaco, where for tax reasons the baron obtained Monegasque citizenship and kept a residence in the Loews hotel. He also spent much time—and money—in the historic Monte Carlo casino. For he never kicked his gambling addiction. And in the end, it devoured him. As his debts mounted, Wado put mortgages on his property, haggled with tax authorities, dabbled in dubious art sales, and borrowed six-figure sums from friends who were rarely, if ever, paid back. Whenever he hit bottom, he would call his sister and say, "Diane, help!" That meant he needed a new infusion of cash. Says Diane: "I would tell him, 'Wado, you're a crook,' and he would reply, 'No, I just cultivate human naïveté.'"

In his later years, the baron had plenty of time to reflect on his life and fate. He was not a serious reader or writer—his autobiography, though factual and highly personal, had been composed with the help of an editorial assistant. Nor was he naturally a contemplative or introspective sort. But as he struggled to make sense of his life, he was drawn more and more to the story of his grandfather and the glorious dynasty he had founded more than a century earlier.

That was the subject of a remarkable 2016 documentary, *Les Barons Empain*, in which Wado played a starring role. Produced by a Franco-Belgian team, it recounted the history of the Empains going back to the founder. Copiously illustrated by archival clips and family photos, the film used Wado's own reminiscences and explanations as its central thread. Unlike most of the interviews he had given over the years, this one hardly dealt with the kidnapping itself. It was all about the rise and fall of the dynasty.

Wado's sequences, filmed in the cluttered living room of La Chaumière, provide an intimate look at this man in the twilight of his life. In the frequent close-ups that fill the screen, one sees little resemblance to the lean, strikingly handsome face that, in his heyday, graced the covers of magazines. The blond hair has turned white and receded far back from his lined forehead. Rebellious gray brows bristle over watery blue eyes that have lost their luster. The prominent nose, inherited from his father, has swollen and thickened over the years. The jowls are heavy, the once-sensual mouth is a thin-lipped slash.

Yet there is still life and fire in that face and in the baritone voice that recounts the story of his once-proud family. "Nothing was impossible for him," Wado says, admiring a photo of his grandfather dressed in Bedouin robes. "No one could have imagined that, starting with nothing, he would construct this whole empire in thirty years." As if to underscore his link to this illustrious ancestor, he runs his hand over an image of the Empain coat of arms and compares it to the crest on his own gold signet ring. (The same shot also shows the stump of his mutilated finger, but he makes no mention of that.) He recounts the building of the Paris Métro, the Congo railroads, and especially the creation of Heliopolis. "That was the most astounding thing he ever did. I know of no one else who ever built a city by himself—a whole city, in the middle of the desert."

A brief, tender memory of his father sparks a truculent defense of Johnny Empain's alleged collaboration: "If you have to get a general drunk to keep your factories turning, well then, you get him drunk." As for his unloved and unloving mother, he describes her coldly as a "brood mare" that his father married only to produce a male heir.

Goldie's second husband, Cousin Édouard, is scathingly dismissed as "a strange personage . . . timid, mean, afraid of women and afraid of everything." With undisguised relish, Wado tells how he wrested power from this deceitful stepfather and engineered the takeover of Schneider, unquestionably his greatest triumph. "In the business world, conquest is the most fantastic thing," he says, chuckling and leaning forward in his armchair. "During my whole period of conquest, I was ecstatic—and proud of myself."

But Wado's days as a conqueror ended abruptly. Though there is practically no mention of the kidnapping itself, he reflects bitterly on the fate that befell him in its wake. "I was weak for a moment and people took advantage. When you're not there, people can say anything they want about you. I had no one to defend my skin. No one!" The moral of that story, he says, is, "Don't trust anyone. Live like you want, but don't trust anyone—never!" As the camera lingers over his face, he breathes heavily, clenches his jaw, and stares into the distance.

At the end of the ninety-minute film, Wado announces the final extinction of the Empain dynasty: Since his son has no male heir, the name itself will disappear. "But it's not a drama," he adds with a wistful smile. "Nothing is forever." Asked what he hopes to leave as a legacy, he bristles: "I couldn't care less about what happens after me. What good does that do?" Alternately truculent, tender, bitter, and stoical, it was a performance that any aging actor would have been proud of. It was also something of a swan song.

In November 2017, Wado fainted while getting out of bed and fractured his hip. After a brief hospital stay, he was transferred to a clinic in the Paris suburb of Saint-Ouen for physiotherapy. Dr. Raymond Abadji, a senior partner in the clinic, was assigned to oversee his treatment. Wado was considered a fragile subject, an eighty-year-old man with heart problems and chronic bronchitis that was aggravated by his heavy smoking. Yet he was a model patient, says Abadji, conscientiously doing his exercises and never complaining about anything—not even the mediocre clinic food. One day, though, the doctor entered his room and found Wado in tears. "It's nothing," he said. "It will pass." Abadji understood this upsurge of melancholy as a flashback to the kidnapping, as if he were back in his tent. "I think he lived his hospitalization as a second internment," says Abadji. "He was not independent. He was confined, and even needed help to put on his pajamas. He experienced that like a second kidnapping."

Shortly after Wado left the clinic at the end of December 2017, his wife Jacqueline passed away following a long bout with cancer. (She had outlived her rival Shahnaz Arieh by four years.) Wado was crushed. "He won't live long," Abadji told his sister. Diane didn't need convincing of that. She had watched Wado's physical decline for several years and now looked on in dismay as he self-medicated with alcohol. His only interests were crossword puzzles and, of course, gambling. "Every morning when he woke up," she says, "he would light a cigarette, go to his computer, and start playing liar's poker online."

The alcohol and tobacco aggravated a heart problem that had required the insertion of a pacemaker at the end of his clinic stay. There were times after Jacqueline's death when he seemed to rally, even visiting friends in Brussels and the South of France. But at other moments, he seemed to give up, gripped by grief and mounting financial woes. "I am just an old cardiac case, a ball and chain for the family who has remained faithful to him," he wrote to his daughter Patricia on January 29, 2018. "I know I won't weigh you down much longer." Two days later, he wrote to Diane, "Alone in my Chaumière I cry, but perhaps that doesn't move you." Of course it moved her. She stuck by her brother to the end, dealt with his myriad problems, and did her best to buck him up. Sometimes he thanked her, sometimes he lashed out with hurtful words to which she would respond in kind. But she was always there for him.

Toward the end of May, Diane paid her daily visit to La Chaumière and found Wado racked by a violent coughing spell. She wanted to take him to the hospital, but he defiantly waved her off and lit another cigarette. The next morning, his housekeeper phoned Diane. "Monsieur wants me to call an ambulance." Diane rushed over and found Wado gasping for breath. When the ambulance arrived, the medics administered oxygen as they wheeled him out onto the gravel driveway. He was shouting, "I don't want to die, I don't want to die."

Soon after he arrived at the hospital in nearby Pontoise, he sank into a coma. "He communicated with me, he squeezed my hand," says Diane. "He had large tears in his eyes. But that's as far as it went. He knew he was dying." On June 20, 2018, after three weeks in the hospital, Édouard-Jean Empain, the last baron to head his family's industrial dynasty, quietly gave up the ghost.

Wado had always said that he wanted to be buried next to his father and grandfather in the crypt of the Heliopolis basilica. His family decided otherwise and laid him to rest in Bouffémont. On June 29, some eighty mourners gathered in the eleventh-century St. Georges church to bid him farewell. His family were all there, of course—including Silvana, who had flown in from her home in Florida. So was André Bizeul, the ex-detective who had managed the investigation, along with a handful of journalists and a contingent of Wado's hunting friends and gambling pals. "It was like the Dead Poets Society," says Diane with a quiet smile.

Following the mass, the cortege proceeded to the local cemetery, where the oak casket was laid to rest in a polished marble tomb. Located on a wooded hillside on the outskirts of town, it is a peaceful spot with a panoramic view, a final resting place for generations of villagers going back to a time long before the château was built, before the Empains ever raised their standard here. The baron's grave is in the newer section, not far from the urn containing Jacqueline's ashes. The inscription on the headstone is stark:

BARON ÉDOUARD-JEAN EMPAIN

KNOWN AS "WADO"

7 OCTOBER 1937–20 JUNE 2018

The death of an eighty-year-old man is not surprising. But there was something ironic in the quiet demise of this once-powerful figure, a man who had dazzled the world with his title, wealth, and good looks; who had defied the powers that be and snatched up the crown jewel of France's industrial patrimony; who had suffered a terrible ordeal at the hands of a criminal band and, against the odds, managed to emerge alive. Or did he? Looking over his last four decades, one might say that his life really did end on January 23, 1978. Because of that event, his destiny was derailed, his image was tarnished, his career was shattered, his family ripped apart, and the proud Empain dynasty laid to ruin. Not a Greek tragedy, perhaps, for Wado did not quite have the stature of a Greek hero. But a human tragedy nonetheless.

Epilogue

Survivor: Diane Empain and friend at her stable in Bouffémont, June 2021

Photograph © Sébastien Soriano/Figarophoto

Bouffémont, February 4, 2020

$\mathcal{D}$iane Empain greets me by a crackling fire in her rustic lodgings next to the Bouffémont stables. Across the gravel courtyard, horses neigh and whinny in their stalls, successors to the champion steeds that Johnny Empain first brought here from Egypt in the 1930s. For the past four decades, Diane has raised and trained show horses here, some of which have gone on to win medals in Olympic competitions. Horses are her life.

Petite, blond, blue-eyed, she has inherited her stature from her father, jockey Jacques Doyasbère, and her features from Goldie. "I can't stand to look at myself in the mirror," she tells me. "I have the same face as my mother." Our long conversation, the first of many, goes all over the map, from her childhood to her brother's kidnapping to her fond memories of the father she adored. But she keeps coming back to the subject of the difficult mother she shared with Wado.

"My mother was diabolical," says Diane. "She never showed any affection. We called her the wicked one." All her life, Diane struggled with Goldie's determination to command and control everything around her. "When I was little," she says, "she would wake me up at five a.m. every morning and make me do gymnastics and skip rope. She'd tell me, 'You have to maintain your factory'"—meaning the body that had been the key to her own advancement in life. She considered Diane her "little thing"—*sa chose*—and tried to shape her daughter in her own image. Through a remarkable display of will and determination, Goldie had turned herself into a champion show rider and pushed Diane in the same direction. Not that the girl needed that much prodding—a love of horses was perhaps the one thing she and Goldie agreed on. Diane, practically born in the saddle, became a prizewinning member of the French national youth equestrian team. And yet, she always seemed to remain in her mother's shadow. Diane was so oppressed by the relationship that she underwent years of psychoanalysis. The analyst's conclusion: "Get away from your mother—she's dangerous!"

AFTER LUNCH, DIANE takes me to visit the château. Purchased in 2006 by a senior official of Gazprom, the Russian energy company, it is now rented out for weddings, receptions, and corporate events. From the outside, it looks pretty much the same as it did in the first baron's day, with its caryatids, porticos, double-helix staircase, and multiple iterations of the Empain coat of arms emblazoned on the façades. Inside, the décor is, well, Gazprom. It takes a leap of the imagination, aided by old photos, to see it as it was in the old days with its antique tapestries, hunting trophies, and a full-size stuffed giraffe in the central stairwell. This was the place where Johnny and Goldie hobnobbed with movie stars, millionaires, and Nazi officers;

the place where Wado grew up in the care of his Irish nanny, and where, many years later, he hosted the gala wedding receptions of his daughters. It was the Tara of the Empain clan.

Diane walks me through the bedrooms—"This was Wado's room . . . this was mine . . . this was my mother's"—without a trace of nostalgia. Living literally in the shadow of the old château, she never really left it behind. Soon, though, she and her horses will be leaving Bouffémont for another location: She is selling the stable complex to the chateau's Russian owner, who will convert it into luxury hotel units. Her departure will sever the last physical link between the Empain family and the property that the general bought more than a century earlier, thinking, perhaps, that his dynasty would last forever.

Nothing is forever, of course, but it might have endured another generation or two if Wado had not been grabbed on the Avenue Foch that fateful January morning.

Today, nothing is left of the industrial empire created by the first baron Empain. But its major works—including the Paris Métro and the fabulous city of Heliopolis—remain as testaments to its former power and grandeur. *Sic transit gloria mundi.*

ACKNOWLEDGMENTS

When Baron Édouard-Jean Empain was kidnapped in Paris on January 23, 1978, I was living in the suburb of Rueil-Malmaison. I was then submerged in research for a doctoral thesis in French history, but the sensational news headlines drew my attention to a dramatic event that was unfolding in real time. In the daily newspaper accounts, I was fascinated to read about the details of the abduction, the severed finger, the police investigation, and finally, the bloody shootout that led to the baron's release.

After that apparently happy ending, I didn't think much about the Empain story over the next four decades. In 2017, as I was finishing up a book called *The Bettencourt Affair*, a friend alerted me to an obscure fact he had run across on the Internet: the men who kidnapped Baron Empain had originally considered grabbing Liliane Bettencourt, the heroine of my book and at the time the world's richest woman. Intrigued, I did some digging and stumbled on interviews by a certain Alain Caillol, the supposed ringleader of the Empain kidnap plot. After spending many years in prison, he had published a gripping memoir about the caper. I knew immediately that I had found the subject of my next book.

But reporting a forty-year-old story presents special challenges— not the least of them actuarial. I obtained Baron Empain's phone number, but before I could contact him, he fell ill. His death at age eighty deprived me of my main interview subject and momentarily discouraged me from pursuing the project. But another key figure was still very much alive: Alain Caillol. Contacted through his lawyer, Georges Kiejman, Caillol readily agreed to talk to me. Our initial meeting in September 2018 was followed by numerous inter- views, phone calls, and email exchanges over the next three years. Caillol also handed me a trove of documents and newspaper clip- pings related to the case. "Don't send them back," he told me. "I don't want my heirs to find this stuff." Through him, I was able to get the inside story of the Empain affair from the kidnappers' vantage point.

The victim's side of the story was provided largely by the baron himself, through his fascinating 1985 memoir, *La vie en jeu*, as well as his numerous published interviews, trial testimony, and appear- ances in a half dozen documentary films on the case. Though I was never able to interview Empain directly, this wealth of material helped me understand what he went through physically and mentally as well as the toll it took on his life. Several family members shared valuable information and insights. Diane Empain, the baron's half- sister, was an extremely gracious source, not only through our inter- views and email exchanges, but also by giving me privileged access to documents and photos from the family collection. Patricia Empain, the baron's eldest daughter, kindly shared her personal memories and impressions in a series of interviews, telephone conversations, and emails.

My other prime sources were the police officers who finally tracked the kidnappers down and won the baron's freedom. André Bizeul, who had overseen the investigation, received me at his home in Nantes and shared a large number of documents and photos. (Our discussions revived his own interest in the case to the point where he wrote his own book on the investigation, as mentioned below.) Michel Desfarges, also a central figure in the investigation, met me at a Paris brasserie for a lengthy interview and followed up with phone calls and emails in reply to my numerous checking questions. Claude Cancès, the former head of the Criminal Brigade, shared his memories of the case and accepted my invitation to a memorable cops-and-robbers lunch with Alain Caillol. Robert Broussard, the legendary ex-chief of the Antigang intervention squad, did me the honor of coming to my home near Paris to recount his role in the investigation and his personal dealings with the baron. Jean Marc Mazzieri, the police martial-arts expert who played a key role in the final showdown, shared his vivid memories, and provided copies of his handwritten notes on the case. I must also thank a number of other individuals who granted interviews and provided useful information. Among them, lawyers Jean-Yves Dupeux and Georges Kiejman, Dr. Raymond Abadji, Hervé Bierry, Marie-France Fondère, Jean-Marc Leclerc, Isabelle de Montagu, Maguy Tran, and Alvah Werner.

Readers will find detailed information on my published sources in the endnotes, but I should single out a number of books dealing with the kidnapping and the Empain family dynasty. Among them: Alain Caillol, *Lumière* (Paris: Cherche Midi, 2012); Yvon Toussaint, *Les barons Empain* (Paris: Fayard, 1996); Christophe Hondelatte, *L'enlèvement du baron Empain* (Paris: Michel Lafon, 2006); Caroline Suzor, *Le groupe Empain en France* (Brussels: Peter Lang, 2016); André Bizeul: *Empain, le rapt: Le récit de l'enquête* (Paris: Mareuil Editions, 2021); Pierre Ottavioli, *Echec au crime* (Paris: Grasset, 1985); Robert Broussard, *Mémoires du commissaire Broussard* (Paris: Nouveau Monde, 2012); and Claude Cancès, *Histoire du 36 Quai des Orfèvres* (Paris: Editions Jacob-Duvernet, 2010).

Thanks also to my wife, Sylvaine, and my son, Julian, both of whom pored over successive versions of the manuscript and provided helpful advice and encouragement. (My son found time to do this while writing a book of his own.[*]) Finally, very special thanks to my editor at Dutton, Jill Schwartzman, for believing in this project and helping me make it better.

---

[*] Julian Sancton, *Madhouse at the End of the Earth: The Belgica's Voyage into the Antarctic Night* (New York: Crown, 2021).

NOTES

CHAPTER 1 PRIDE BEFORE THE FALL

5 **champion skier and horseman:** Baron Empain, *La vie en jeu* (Paris: Editions Jean-Claude Lattès, 1985), 218.

5 **an industrial empire:** "Présentation générale du groupe Empain-Schneider," French Ministry of Industry, 1979. Archives Nationales, 19910445/16.

5 ***le Krupp français:*** Christophe Hondelatte, *L'enlèvement du baron Empain* (Paris: Michel Lafon, 2006), 32.

6 **"international gentry":** René Tendron, "Pourquoi Empain," *Nouvel Economiste,* January 30, 1978.

6 **"work, family, property":** Tendron, "Pourquoi Empain."

6 **won a monopoly:** Empain, *Vie,* 104–106.

6 **"the shining symbol":** "Un héritier entreprenant," *Le Monde,* January 25, 1978.

6 **the very face of Paris was changing:** On the urban transformations of the 1970s, Bernard Marchand, *Paris, histoire d'une ville* (Paris: Seuil, 1993), chapters 5 and 6; Yvan Combeau, *Histoire de Paris* (Paris: PUF, 1999), 117–119.

7 **Claude François:** Claude Fléouter, "Une 'idole' des années 60," *Le Monde,* March 14, 1978.

7 **a spate of modernizing reforms:** "Les grandes réformes," france24.com, December 3, 2020, accessed online April 21, 2021, https://www.france24 .com/fr/france/20201203-les-grandes-réformes-que-la-france-doit -au-président-valéry-giscard-d-estaing.

8 **education went no further:** Empain, *Vie,* 32.

8 **photos of Empain with Brigitte Bardot:** Tendron, "Pourquoi Empain."

8   a natural timidity: Empain, *Vie,* 31, 219 and passim.

8   received his barony from Belgium's King Leopold II: Yvon Toussaint, *Les barons Empain* (Paris: Fayard, 1996), 98.

8   had long since been abolished: On the diminished status of nobility in Belgium, Georges-Henri Dumont, *La vie quotidienne en Belgique sous Léopold II* (Paris: Hachette, 1974), chapter 3; in France, Theodore Zeldin, *The French* (London: Collins, 1983), chapter 11.

8   "everyone was on their knees": Empain interview, *Paris Match,* March 20, 1981.

8   an "annoying young man": Michel Bôlé-Richard, "A la cour d'assises de Paris: Le baron Empain sur la sellette," *Le Monde,* December 6, 1982.

8   "mediocre shot": Empain, *Vie,* 124.

8   "suitcase without a handle": Empain, *Vie,* 124.

8   Empain's private life: Empain, *Vie,* 147–148.

9   But sometimes complications: Details of Empain's summer vacations and meeting with Shahnaz Arieh from Patricia Empain, interview with author, October 30, 2020.

11   the baron joined friends: Empain, *Vie,* 126–127.

11   players met that night: Details of poker games from Empain, *Vie,* 127–128; police depositions of his fellow players, February 2–6, 1978.

11   "He didn't receive us": André Marcarof police deposition, February 2, 1978.

11   the group sat down to dinner: Empain, *Vie,* 127–128.

12   "a strong-willed fighter": Bob Zagury police deposition, February 2, 1978.

12   "a passionate player": Yves Montand police deposition, February 3, 1978.

12   losing big-time: Bob Zagury police deposition, February 2, 1978.

12   "You look tired": Empain, *Vie,* 128.

13   The modernistic concrete-and-glass structure: Description of building and apartment from Patricia Empain, interview with author, October 30, 2020.

13   waiting by the rear door: Details of kidnapping from multiple sources, including Jean Denis police deposition, January 23, 1978; Empain police deposition, March 29, 1978; Alain Caillol interview with author, September 20, 2018; Empain, *Vie,* 128–130; *Le Monde,* January 25, 1978.

13   "He's completely crazy": Empain, *Vie,* 129.

14   "Do what we tell you": Empain, *Vie,* 129.

14   The driver headed up Avenue Foch: Details from Alain Caillol interview with author, September 20, 2018.

14   the stolen van containing chauffeur Jean Denis: Jean Denis police deposition, January 23, 1978; Caillol interview, September 20, 2018.

15   Giscard d'Estaing was furious: Hondelatte, *Enlèvement,* 42.

15 immediately formed a crisis cell: Claude Cancès, *Histoire du 36 Quai des Orfèvres* (Paris: Editions Jacob-Duvernet, 2010), 291.

15 pulled into a private garage: Caillol interview with author, September 20, 2018; Empain, *Vie*, 130.

16 "Are you a political group?": Caillol interview with author, September 20, 2018.

16 Hanns Martin Schleyer: "Schleyer, Key Figure in Industry, Once a Top SS Official in Prague," *New York Times*, October 20, 1977.

16 Aldo Moro would later meet: Robert Solé, "L'assassinat d'Aldo Moro," *Le Monde*, May 11, 1978.

16 press outlets received a communiqué: Hondelatte, *Enlèvement*, 46.

16 "It's not us!": *L'Humanité*, January 26, 1978.

17 "Keep your mouth shut": Caillol interview with author, September 30, 2018.

17 afraid of smothering to death: Empain trial testimony, December 13, 1982, quoted in *Le Matin*, December 14, 1982.

17 heard crackling voices: Empain, *Vie*, 130.

17 smelled the earthy odor: Empain, *Vie*, 130.

18 warren of underground tunnels: Caillol interview, September 30, 2018.

18 kidnappers had stocked the tunnels: Caillol interview, September 30, 2018; Alain Caillol, *Lumière* (Paris: Cherche Midi, 2012), 159.

18 One of the men helped the baron: Empain deposition before Judge Louis Cavanac, March 29, 1978; Caillol, *Lumière*, 159.

19 "I understand": Caillol, *Lumière*, 159.

19 "You asked if this was a political action": Caillol, *Lumière*, 159.

19 a ransom of 80 million francs: Caillol, *Lumière*, 160.

19 "We're going to cut off a finger": Caillol, *Lumière*, 160; Empain, *Vie*, 131.

19 "Eighty million?": Caillol, *Lumière*, 160.

19 Empain gave them the names: Empain, *Vie*, 131.

20 "now we're going to proceed": Empain, *Vie*, 131.

20 They handed Empain a bowl of red liquid: The account of the amputation is drawn from several sources, including Caillol's interviews with author, September 20, 2018, January 22, 2020; Caillol, *Lumière*, 160–163; Empain, *Vie*, 131–132; Empain deposition, March 29, 1978. Different versions vary on the details. Caillol says Empain was asleep and that the fingertip was severed with a paper cutter and a mallet; Empain says in some accounts that it was done with a knife while he was awake. However, in his trial testimony on December 13, 1982, he declared: "They gave me a powerful sedative and I fell asleep. When I woke up, my hand was bandaged." That would tend to confirm Caillol's version.

20 thought he was in his own apartment: Empain, *Vie*, 132.

21 "Pour all the alcohol on your bandage": Empain, *Vie*, 132.

21　**never voiced a word of complaint:** Caillol, *Lumière*, 164.

21　**an encouraging sign:** Empain interview with Christophe Hondelatte in Hondelatte, *Enlèvement*, 56.

21　**handed him a pâté sandwich:** Caillol, *Lumière*, 9–10.

21　**asked him if he was up to writing:** Caillol, *Lumière*, 163.

22　**Jean-Jacques Bierry was lunching:** Hondelatte, *Enlèvement*, 52.

22　**one of the baron's oldest and closest friends:** Empain, *Vie*, 29–31.

22　**In the locker:** Details of locker contents from Claude Cancès, *Histoire*, 36, 290.

22　**This one was gnawed down to the quick:** Toussaint, *Barons Empain*, 374.

23　**"Dear Silvana":** Hondelatte, *Enlèvement*, 53.

CHAPTER 2　～　YOUR MONEY OR YOUR LIFE

24　**interior of a red pup tent:** Details of tent contents and conditions of incarceration from Baron Empain, *La vie en jeu* (Paris: Editions Jean-Claude Lattès, 1985), 133–134; Alain Caillol, interviews with author, September 20, 2018, February 7, 2019.

25　**fell over and emptied the contents:** Empain interview in *Paroles d'otages*, documentary by Jean-Claude Raspiengeas and Patrick Volson, TF1 Vidéo, 1990.

25　**best chance of survival:** Empain interview in Christophe Hondelatte, *L'enlèvement du baron Empain* (Paris: Michel Lafon, 2006), 57.

26　**"We must set an example":** Silvana Empain police deposition, January 23, 1978; André Marcarof deposition, February 2, 1978; René Barough deposition, February 2, 1978.

26　**"The ransom is the family's problem":** Pierre Ottavioli, *Echec au crime* (Paris: Grasset, 1985), 169.

26　**be ready with the ransom money:** "Les Contacts avec les ravisseurs," investigative police document, copy provided to the author by André Bizeul.

26　**"There must be no police involvement":** Yvon Toussaint, *Les barons Empain* (Paris: Fayard, 1996), 375.

27　**Changing the earlier orders:** "Contacts avec les ravisseurs."

27　**"a nice Italian girl":** Empain interview with Gauthier De Bock, published on gauthierdebock.com, April 11, 2013, accessed April 11, 2020, http://www.gauthierdebock.com/la-vie-amputee-du-baron-empain/.

27　**Money had never been a problem:** Patricia Empain, interview with author, October 20, 2020.

27　**was better informed:** Diane Empain, interview with author, February 4, 2020.

27　**"My son has left":** Diane Empain, interview with author, February 4, 2020.

28   "roll out the red carpet": Toussaint, *Barons Empain*, 334.

28   phoned Wado's wealthy friends: Empain, *Vie*, 140.

28   no one actually opened a checkbook: Patricia Empain, interview with author, October 20, 2020; Silvana Empain, trial testimony, December 13, 1982, quoted in *France-Soir*, December 14, 1982.

28   Silvana even offered: Diane Empain, interview with author, February 4, 2020.

28   "If he comes back": Diane Empain interview, February 4, 2020.

28   "If she loves Wado": Diane Empain interview, February 4, 2020.

28   Shahnaz, then thirty-six, was no stranger: Rozell Empain police deposition, quoted in André Bizeul, *Empain, le rapt: Le récit de l'enquête* (Paris, Mareuil Editions, 2021), 88–89.

28   Shahnaz had telephoned Rozell: Bizeul, *Empain, le rapt*, 88–89.

29   "that I was dealing with a woman": Raymond Vuilliez police deposition, February 1978.

29   Vuilliez contacted René Engen: Raymond Vuilliez police deposition, February 1978; André Bizeul, telephone conversation with author, January 8, 2021.

29   "in the most revolting manner": Vuilliez trial testimony, December 3, 1982, quoted in *Le Monde*, December 6, 1982.

29   Shahnaz Arieh had a long history: André Bizeul, conversation with author, January 8, 2021.

29   "I don't want to answer that": Shahnaz Arieh police depositions, February 1 and 16, 1978; André Bizeul, conversation with author, January 8, 2021.

30   Engen drew up papers: Hondelatte, *Enlèvement*, 71.

30   signed off on the deal: Toussaint, *Barons Empain*, 380–381.

30   On the evening of Thursday, January 26: Hondelatte, *Enlèvement*, 69.

30   "You have the money?": Dialogue from Ottavioli, *Echec*, 177; Claude Cancès, *Histoire du 36 Quai des Orfèvres* (Paris: Editions Jacob-Duvernet, 2010), 291.

31   the kidnappers were seething: Caillol, *Lumière*, 171.

31   "After all, Empain": Dialogue from Caillol, *Lumière*, 71–72.

32   "Perhaps you have slept badly": Empain to Bierry, January 31, 1978.

32   "inscrutable": Claude Cancès, interview with author, November 16, 2018.

32   "I needed a man of my own": Empain, *Vie*, 61–68.

33   "slender, brown-haired": Empain, *Vie*, 67–68.

33   "All the problems are brought to me": Engen, quoted in *Le Monde*, January 30, 1978.

33   "a king in my kingdom": Empain, *Vie*, 118.

CHAPTER 3 ⟶ THE INVESTIGATORS

34 Belgium's King Baudouin: *Le Soir de Bruxelles*, December 2, 1982.

34 offered to share intelligence: *Le Monde*, February 2, 1978.

35 seventy-five novels: "Georges Simenon," Wikipedia, accessed July 4, 2019, https://fr.wikipedia.org/wiki/Georges_Simenon#Série_des _Commissaire_Maigret.

35 "No criminal band": Pierre Ottavioli, *Echec au crime* (Paris: Grasset, 1985), 178.

35 "the patience and tenacity": Jean-François Chaigneau, "Le Triomphe du Commissaire Ottavioli," *Paris Match*, April 7, 1978.

35 On quiet days: Claude Cancès, interview with author, November 16, 2018.

36 investigated the attempted assassination: Claude Cancès, *Commissaire à la Crim'* (Paris: Mareuil, 2017), 78.

36 Ottavioli had been visiting friends: Ottavioli, *Echec*, 169.

36 "We won't give in": Cancès interview with author, November 19, 2018.

36 Ottavioli was adamantly opposed: Ottavioli, *Echec*, 169–171.

37 headed up by Commissaire André Bizeul: André Bizeul, interview with author, January 23, 2020.

37 "five foot eleven": Quotes taken from Silvana Empain, police deposition, January 23, 1978, cited in André Bizeul, *Empain, le rapt* (Paris: Mareuil Editions), 27–28.

37 an ace detective: Bizeul interviews with author, January 23–24, 2020.

38 had just joined: Michel Desfarges, interview with author, January 29, 2020.

38 "the kind of pitiless, icy cop": Alain Caillol, *Lumière* (Paris: Cherche Midi, 2012), 85.

39 colleagues who accused him: Cancès interview, November 16, 2018.

39 leading the commando squad: Robert Broussard, *Mémoires du commissaire Broussard* (Paris: Nouveau Monde, 2012), chapter 21.

39 abduction of J. Paul Getty III: Details from Charles Fox, *Kidnapped: The Tragic Life of J. Paul Getty III* (New York: St. Martin's, 2018).

40 the case of Patty Hearst: Jeffrey Toobin, *American Heiress: The Kidnapping, Crimes and Trial of Patty Hearst* (New York: Profile Books, 2016).

40 "a caricature of the 'ugly capitalist'": "Schleyer, Key Figure in Industry, Once a Top SS Official in Prague," *New York Times*, October 20, 1977.

41 an armed band: "Red Army Faction," Wikipedia, accessed April 8, 2021, https://en.wikipedia.org/wiki/Red_Army_Faction.

41 Schleyer's chauffeured car: Details of Schleyer case from *New York Times*, October 20, 1977.

41 One of the most dramatic episodes: Details of Hazan case from Claude Cancès, *L'Affaire Hazan* (Paris: Mareuil, 2020).

42   The Hazan case was followed: Cancès, *Commissaire*, 86–101.

42   His method was simple: Ottavioli, *Echec*, 170–171.

42   "pay the bill": Robert Broussard, interview with author, August 30, 2018.

42   it took several weeks: Ottavioli's trial testimony, quoted in *Le Monde*, December 9, 1982.

42   any payment out of the question: Diane Empain, interview with author, February 4, 2020.

43   insisted on paying: Cancès, *Histoire*, 289; Robert Badinter, letter to author, June 13, 2018.

43   Ottavioli sent Commissaire Claude Cancès: Cancès, interview with author, November 16, 2018.

43   The purpose of the trip: Bierry trial testimony, quoted in *Le Monde*, December 9, 1982.

43   sought an international warrant: Ottavioli, *Echec*, 178.

43   As police later learned: Desfarges, interview with author, January 29, 2020.

44   more than 140,000 vehicles were stopped: *L'Humanité*, January 26, 1978.

44   Shortly after returning: Desfarges interview, January 29, 2020.

44   "Best not fall into his net": Bizeul, *Empain, le rapt*, 99.

44   "They didn't know anything": Desfarges interview, January 29, 2020.

45   Investigators speculated: Bizeul, interview with author, January 23, 2020.

45   four times the baron's annual salary: According to Jean-Jacques Bierry's January 25, 1978, police deposition, Empain's annual salary was 2.5 million francs.

45   Summoned by Desfarges: Bizeul, interview with author, January 23, 2020.

45   Under questioning: De Félix police deposition, February 1978.

45   11 million francs: De Félix police deposition, February 1978.

45   "When we entered the casino": Pierre Salik, quoted in Christophe Hondelatte, *L'enlèvement du baron Empain* (Paris: Michel Lafon, 2006), 63.

46   "he risked enormous sums": André Marcarof police deposition, February 2, 1978.

46   Empain eventually paid off: De Félix deposition, February 1978; Raymond Vuilliez deposition, February 1978.

46   gamblers could come into contact: Desfarges interview, January 29, 1978.

46   he funded his gambling addiction: Empain, *Vie*, 151–152.

46   One theory was: *Le Matin*, February 4.

46   "I immediately thought": Marcarof deposition, February 2, 1978.

47   Seeing Empain's picture: Gilles Malençon, "Empain-Caillol, le chemin du pardon," blog article, January 25, 2012, accessed January 4, 2020,

http://encetempslacom.blogspot.com/2012/01/empain-caillol-le
-chemin-du-pardon.html.

47 "secret garden": Empain, *Vie*, 149.

47 used it to tryst: Shahnaz Arieh police deposition, quoted by Bizeul, *Empain, le rapt*, 113–114.

47 she was never actually taken: Bizeul, *Empain, le rapt*, 113.

47 Giscard d'Estaing quietly sent an aide: Hondelatte, *Enlèvement*, 60; *Canard Enchaîné*, February 1, 1978.

47 "We knew he gambled": Bierry, quoted in Hondelatte, *Enlèvement*, 64.

48 "It is better that he not return": Diane Empain, interview with author, February 4, 2020.

48 "In all this discussion": Diane Empain, interview with author, February 4, 2020.

48 she had been courted: Cancès interview, November 16, 2018; André Bizeul interview, January 23, 2020; Diane Empain interview, February 4, 2020.

48 Engen had his own spy: Yvon Toussaint, *Les barons Empain* (Paris: Fayard, 1996), 377.

48 Fernet was: Ottavioli, *Echec*, 48.

49 "you must pay": Diane Empain interview, February 4, 2020.

49 police had tapped the phones: Ottavioli, *Echec*, 176–177.

49 Silvana complained to Ottavioli: Diane Empain interview, February 4, 2020.

49 "le beau Jean-Claude": Bizeul, *Empain, le rapt*, 113.

49 Diane was soon led: Details from Diane Empain interview, February 4, 2020; Hondelatte, *Enlèvement*, 77.

49 "My dear Patricia": Quoted in Hondelatte, *Enlèvement*, 77.

49 The envelope also contained: Bizeul interview, January 24, 2020.

50 no question of actually sending Patricia: Patricia Empain, interview with author, October 19, 2020.

50 "If you hear gunshots": Diane Empain interview, February 4, 2020; Diane Empain email to author, November 9, 2020.

50 The conversation was brief: Account of conversation from Diane Empain interview, February 4; "Contacts avec les ravisseurs," police investigative document.

50 They had loaded: Alain Caillol, email to author, March 25, 2020.

50 It would later wind up: *Paris Match*, April 7, 1978.

51 former colleagues suspect: Cancès, interview with author, December 14, 2018; Desfarges, interview with author, October 15, 2020.

51 But the news: Empain, *Vie*, 148.

CHAPTER 4 ∽ THE MAKING OF A GANGSTER

55   **Caillol was born:** Unless otherwise noted, all biographical details from Alain Caillol, interview with author, October 12, 2018.

57   **"She was hard":** Alain Caillol, *Lumière* (Paris: Cherche Midi, 2012), 132.

57   **"I was always afraid":** Alain Caillol, letter to Mireille Bonnelle, March 11, 1985, in Bonnelle and Caillol, *Lettres en liberté conditionnelle* (Paris: Editions Manya, 1990), 82.

59   **Arrested for a series of thefts:** André Bizeul, *Empain, le rapt* (Paris, Mareuil Editions, 2021), 337–339.

59   **Neighbors would see Caillol:** "Les Deux vies d'Alain Caillol," *Paris Match*, April 7, 1978.

59   **earned the equivalent of $50,000 a year:** Caillol trial testimony, December 3, 1982, quoted in *Libération*, December 4, 1982.

59   **"It was a way of life":** Caillol interview with Sonia Kronlund, broadcast on *France-Culture* radio, February 22, 2018.

59   **Among Caillol's underworld relations:** Unless otherwise noted, all details of Caillol's relations with Ardouin and Mesrine based on Caillol interview with author, October 12, 2018.

60   **"Let me go":** Description of Mesrine's courtroom escape from Robert Broussard, *Mémoires du commissaire Broussard* (Paris: Nouveau Monde, 2012), 402–404.

60   **"one of these criminal beasts":** Quoted in Broussard, *Mémoires*, 395.

60   **He once boasted:** Broussard, *Mémoires*, 401.

61   **2008 feature film:** *L'Instinct de mort*, directed by Jean-François Richet.

61   **Mesrine showed up:** Caillol interview with author, October 12, 2018.

61   **"It was a real Western":** Caillol interview, October 12, 2018.

61   **Caillol learned that firsthand:** Details of this episode from Caillol, *Lumière*, 77–80; Caillol interview, October 12, 2018.

62   **Though he specialized:** Caillol, interview with author, September 20, 2018.

62   **But before they could put:** Broussard, *Mémoires*, 404–414.

62   **Following Mesrine's arrest:** Caillol interview, September 20, 2018.

63   **he would later describe in a book:** Daniel Duchateau, *Sainte Anne, priez pour moi* (Paris: Pierre Belfond, 1974).

63   **"Duchateau is a mystic":** Quoted in *France-Soir*, March 29, 1978.

63   **"Money for me":** Duchateau, *Sainte Anne*, quoted in *Paris Match*, April 7, 1978.

63   **The reference to Champagne:** Caillol interview with author, November 19, 2018.

64   **One day at the Marché aux Puces:** Caillol, *Lumière*, 95–96.

64   **"an exceptional urban pilot":** Caillol, *Lumière*, 95.

65   "To plan a bank robbery": Caillol interview, November 19, 2018.

65   "Daniel was serious": Caillol interview, November 19, 2018.

65   "That's it, it's all over": Caillol interview, November 19, 2018.

CHAPTER 5   ∽   "MAKE THE MONEY COME TO US!"

66   "He must have read": Alain Caillol, interview with author, November 19, 2018.

66   Caillol's timeline: Alain Caillol, *Lumière* (Paris: Cherche Midi, 2012), 137.

67   "Watch the film first": Caillol interview, November 19, 2018.

67   serious behavioral problems: George Kiejman [Caillol's lawyer], interview with author, September 18, 2018.

67   "My life was rotten": Caillol, interview with Sonia Kronlund, broadcast on *France-Culture* radio, February 22, 2018.

67   But when the four comrades: Caillol, *Lumière*, 142.

67   "Instead of going after the money": Caillol, *Lumière*, 138.

67   "It was brilliant": Caillol, *Lumière*.

68   On the last point: Caillol, interview with author, September 20, 2018.

68   "Our main goal": Caillol, interview with Sonia Kronlund, February 22, 2018.

68   But the July 1977 bank job: Details on this bank robbery from Caillol, *Lumière*, 149–150; Caillol, interviews with author, September 20, 2018, and January 22, 2020.

69   "Willie the Crutch": Robert Broussard, interview with author, January 14, 2020.

69   "a key player in shock operations": André Bizeul, interview with author, January 24, 2020.

70   Caillol had helped him: Caillol, interview with author, January 22, 2020.

70   René Rigault: Caillol, interview with author, September 20, 2018.

70   a consigliere: Michel Desfarges, interview with author, January 29, 2020.

70   "Bertoncini was not like us": Caillol interview, January 22, 2020.

70   "limited intelligence": Alain Tincuff remark to trial judge, December 8, 1982, quoted in *Le Soir de Bruxelles*, December 9, 1982.

70   To help manage: Caillol, interview with author, January 22, 2020; Caillol, *Lumière*, 193.

71   Another recruit: *France-Soir*, December 10, 1982; *Le Monde*, December 4, 1982.

71   "a nice young guy": Caillol, quoted by Yvon Toussaint, *Les barons Empain* (Paris: Fayard, 1996), 412.

71   "Guillon was a big fish": Desfarges, interview with author, January 29, 2020.

71 **Caillol also called on his brother:** Details on François Caillol's criminal career from *Paris Match*, April 7, 1978; *Libération*, December 4, 1982.

71 **"odorless, colorless, and tasteless":** Pierre Caillol, quoted in *France-Soir*, December 11, 1982.

71 **but it's probable:** Alain Caillol, interview with author, September 20, 2018.

71 **Police later concluded:** Bizeul, interview with author, January 24, 2020.

72 **In the summer of 1977:** Bizeul, interview with author, January 24, 2020.

72 **On the Air France flight:** Caillol, interview with author, January 22, 2020.

CHAPTER 6 ⌒ PLANNING THE CAPER

73 **Hitler's "miracle weapon":** Details about the V-2 rocket program from Walter Dornberger, *V-2* (New York: Viking, 1954); Rowland Pocock, *German Guided Missiles of the Second World War* (New York: Arco, 1967).

73 **Of the six sites:** Details about French storage sites from "A-4/V-2 Hardened Bunkers in France," v2rocket.com, accessed January 14, 2020, http://www.v2rocket.com/start/deployment/bunkers.html.

75 **As Caillol's gang cogitated:** Caillol, interview with author, September 20, 2018.

75 **Alone behind the wheel:** Caillol, *Lumière* (Paris: Cherche Midi, 2012), 144.

76 **They considered the banker Guy de Rothschild:** Caillol interview, September 20, 2018; *Lumière*, 150–151.

76 **Another possible target:** Caillol interview, September 20, 2018.

77 **For all his megalomania:** Empain, *La vie en jeu* (Paris: Editions Jean-Claude Lattès, 1985), 109–110.

77 **That would change:** Nicolas Brimo, "Les Empain et les coquins," *Canard Enchaîné*, February 4, 1976; in subsequent issues, the *Canard* regularly pilloried Empain: January, 4, 1976; January 14, 1976; April 5, 1976; August 25, 1976.

77 **"Empain was the rising star":** Caillol interview, September 20, 2018.

78 **Most of the original planning:** Details from Caillol interview, September 20, 2018.

78 **The other big logistical task:** Caillol interview, September 20, 2018.

78 **"the mortuary room of a pyramid":** Description of tunnel and provisions, Caillol, *Lumière*, 159.

79 **A clean chop:** Caillol, email to author, April 14, 2021.

79 **Most of the supplies:** Caillol, *Lumière*, 83–158.

79 **Each member of the team:** Caillol interview, September 20, 2018.

79   **In mid-December:** Details from Caillol interviews, September 20, 2018, January 22, 2020; André Bizeul, interview with author, January 24, 2020; Michel Desfarges, interview with author, January 29, 2020.

80   **A champion skier in his youth:** Patricia Empain, interview with author, October 30, 2020.

80   **The maneuver unfolded:** Details of kidnapping operation from Caillol, *Lumière*, chapter 17; Caillol interview, September 20, 2018.

CHAPTER 7 ⟨⟨⟩ THE FOUNDER

85   **not an impressive man:** Details from Baron Empain, *La vie en jeu* (Paris: Jean-Claude Lattès, 1985), 14–18; Yvon Toussaint, *Les barons Empain* (Paris: Fayard, 1996), 34–37.

85   **"great man":** Caroline Suzor, *Le groupe Empain en France* (Brussels: Peter Lang, 2016), 4.

86   **Belgium was rapidly evolving:** Georges-Henri Dumont, *Le Belgique hier et aujourd'hui* (Paris: Presses Universitaires de France, 1991), chapter 5.

86   **Nothing predestined:** Details on Empain's family background from Suzor, *Le groupe Empain*, 5–6; J. A. Simar, "Édouard Empain: Intelligence créatrice, puissance industrielle," *Annales du Cercle royal archéologique d'Enghien* XLIII (2009–2011): 11–15.

86   **In the early 1860s:** Suzor, *Le groupe Empain*, 11.

87   **If young Édouard had:** Suzor, *Le groupe Empain*, 13.

87   **Though he would later:** Simar, "Édouard Empain," 13.

87   **That would change in 1873:** Toussaint, *Barons Empain*, 24–25; Suzor, *Groupe Empain*, 14.

88   **It was a propitious moment:** Suzor, *Groupe Empain*, 16–19; Simar, "Édouard Empain," 17.

88   **Windfall profits:** Details on Empain's first ventures from Suzor, *Groupe Empain*, 16–30; Simar, "Édouard Empain," 17–26; Toussaint, *Barons Empain*, 31–34.

88   **Empain was a visionary:** Details on Empain's style of capitalism from Toussaint, *Les barons Empain*, 30–31; Simar, "Édouard Empain," 16.

89   **inspired by the recent development:** Simar, "Édouard Empain," 25; Toussaint, *Barons Empain*, 70–71.

CHAPTER 8 ⟨⟨⟩ THE BIRTH OF THE MÉTRO

90   **They call it the Belle Époque:** Details on the period mainly from Maurice Culot, *Paris Belle Epoque: Architectures 1890–1914* (Paris: AAM Editions, 2005); Bernard Marchand, *Paris, histoire d'une ville* (Paris: Seuil, 1993), 159–171; Yvon Combeau, *Histoire de Paris* (Paris: Presses Universitaires de France, 1999), 76–79.

92   **Paris was saddled:** Marchand, *Paris*, 172–173; Philippe Enrico Attal, *La construction du métro de Paris, 1850–1940* (Paris: Soteca, 2017), 14–19; Roger-Henry Guerrand, *L'aventure du métropolitain* (Paris: La Découverte, 1999), 23–28.

92   **hardy souls:** Details from Attal, *Construction*, 47–48; André Mignard and Didier Janssoone, *L'histoire du métro parisien* (Paris: First Editions, 2014), 45.

92   **The problem was not new:** On Haussmann's transformation of Paris, Jean des Cars, *Haussmann: La gloire du Second Empire* (Paris: Perrin, 1988); Marchand, *Paris*, 172; Patrice Higonnet, *Paris, Capital of the World* (Cambridge, MA: Harvard University Press, 2002), 178–181.

93   **near-crisis proportions:** Marchand, *Paris*, 172–173.

93   **Paris was in fact far behind:** Combeau, *Histoire de Paris*, 41; Attal, *Construction du métro*, 13; Jean-Christophe Mabire, *L'exposition universelle de 1900* (Paris: L'Harmattan, 2000), 32.

93   **Faced with the prospect:** Guerrand, *Aventure*, 34.

93   **Over the years:** Guerrand, *Aventure*, 29–33; Attal, *Construction*, 23–26.

94   **Once the municipal council:** Attal, *Construction*, 26–28; Guerrand, *Aventure,* 34–35.

94   **"the Métro is anti-national":** Quoted in Guerrand, *Aventure*, 9.

94   **The council's pro-Métro majority:** Toussaint, *Barons Empain*, 79–83.

94   **"the dramatic choking of urban life":** Quoted in Toussaint, *Barons Empain*, 80.

95   **Waiting in the wings:** Toussaint, *Barons Empain*, 82–84.

95   **For that they turned:** Claude Berton and Alexandre Ossadzow, *Fulgence Bienvenüe et la construction du métropolitain de Paris* (Paris: Ponts et Chaussées, 2006); Monique Le Tac, *Fulgence Bienvenüe: Le père du métro de Paris* (Paris: Editions LBM, 2006).

96   **He laid out six initial lines:** On Bienvenüe's plan for the Métro, Attal, *Construction*, 36–37: Guerrand, *Aventure*, 40–41; Mignard and Janssoone, *Histoire*, 29–31.

97   **Under Bienvenüe's supervision:** Attal, *Construction*, 33.

97   **commission to the city of 5 centimes:** Guerrand, *Aventure*, 40.

97   **In March 1897:** On the choice of Empain as concessionaire and creation of CMP, Le Tac, *Fulgence Bienvenüe*, 96–97; Toussaint, *Barons Empain*, 85.

CHAPTER 9 ⤸ THE BIG DIG

99   **Early on the morning:** Roger-Henry Guerrand, *L'aventure du métropolitain* (Paris: La Découverte, 1999), 43; Philippe Enrico Attal, *La construction du métro de Paris, 1850–1940* (Paris: Soteca,

2017), 37; Monique Le Tac, *Fulgence Bienvenüe: Le père du métro de Paris* (Paris: Editions LBM, 2006), 85–88.

99   **Wherever possible:** On construction methods, André Mignard and Didier Janssoone, *L'histoire du métro parisien* (Paris: First Editions, 2014), 145–146; Attal, *Construction*, 39–40.

100   **On paper, these techniques:** Attal, *Construction*, 39; Guerrand, *Aventure*, 43–44; Yvon Toussaint, *Les barons Empain* (Paris: Fayard, 1996), 86–88.

100   **Some parts of the network:** Guerrand, *Aventure*, 44, 47–48; Bernard Marchand, *Paris, histoire d'une ville* (Paris: Seuil, 1993), 182; Le Tac, *Bienvenüe*, 93–94, 119–120.

101   **"The Métro worksites":** Jules Romains, quoted in Toussaint, *Barons Empain*, 87.

102   **the company invited architects:** Attal, *Construction*, 41; Guerrand, *Aventure*, 65–66.

102   **The winners had designed:** Georges Vigne, *Hector Guimard: Le geste magnifique de l'art nouveau* (Paris: Editions du Patrimoine, 2016), 87.

102   **It was at that point:** On Guimard's career and circumstances surrounding his choice, Vigne, *Guimard*, 87 and passim; Frédéric Descouturelle, André Mignard, and Michel Rodriguez, *Le métropolitain d'Hector Guimard* (Paris: RATP-Somogy, 2003), 21; Guerrand, *Aventure*, 66.

102   **Pressed for time:** Descouturelle et al., *Le métropolitain d'Hector Guimard*, 53–54, 67–72.

CHAPTER 10 ❧ OPENING DAY

104   **Fulgence Bienvenüe awoke:** Monique Le Tac, *Fulgence Bienvenüe: Le père du métro de Paris* (Paris: Editions LBM, 2006), 102–103.

105   **Leopold II was among those invited:** Amélie d'Arschot Schoonhoven, *Le Roman d'Héliopolis* (Waterloo: Avant-Propos, 2018), 58.

105   **Émile Loubet mounted the steps:** Description of opening ceremony from Le Tac, *Bienvenüe*, 102–104.

105   **The long-awaited event:** Overall description of 1900 Paris Exhibition from Jean-Christophe Mabire, *L'exposition universelle de 1900* (Paris: L'Harmattan, 2000); Pascal Varejka, *Paris 1900: La fabuleuse histoire de l'exposition universelle* (Paris: Prisma, 2015); Patrice Higonnet, *Paris, Capital of the World* (Cambridge, MA: Harvard University Press, 2002), 359–362.

106   **Loubet led a group of dignitaries:** Mabire, *Exposition*, 26–28.

106   **Grand Palais and its smaller neighbor:** Varejka, *Paris 1900*, 72–82.

107   **hailed by *Scientific American*:** Frank McCullough, *The Greater Journey: Americans in Paris* (New York: Simon & Schuster, 2011), 446.

107   **ephemeral exhibits were no less impressive:** Varejka, *Paris 1900*, 132–138.

107   The event offered a stunning array: Varejka, *Paris 1900*, 100–110; Mabire, *Exposition*, 39–43.

107   "serpentine dance": Varejka, *Paris 1900*, 62.

107   Palais de l'Électricité: Varejka, *Paris 1900*, 48–58; Mabire, *Exposition*, 116; Thierry Paquot, "Paris 1900 le Palais de l'Électricité," *Cahiers de Médiologie* 2000/2 (No. 10), 200–207, accessed June 8, 2020, https://www.cairn.info/revue-les-cahiers-de-mediologie-2000-2-page-200.htm#.

108   the builders missed that mark: André Mignard and Didier Janssoone, *L'histoire du métro parisien* (Paris: First Editions, 2014), 45; Philippe Enrico Attal, *La construction du métro parisien, 1850–1940* (Paris: Soteca, 2017), 45–46.

110   Only eight of the line's eighteen stations opened: Varejka, *Paris 1900*, 17.

110   "Along with the extraordinary coolness": Quoted in Varejka, *Paris 1900*, 20.

110   The public would have to wait another year: Frédéric Descouturelle, André Mignard, and Michel Rodriguez, *Le métropolitain d'Hector Guimard* (Paris: RATP-Somogy, 2003), 74.

111   "brilliant departure by a true artist": *Le mois littéraire et pittoresque*, September 1901, quoted in Philippe Thiébaut, *Guimard, l'art nouveau* (Paris: Gallimard, 1992), 116.

111   dark-green color: Georges Vigne, *Hector Guimard: Le geste magnifique de l'art nouveau* (Paris, Editions du Patrimoine, 2016), 88–89.

111   unconventional calligraphy: Descouturelle et al., *Métropolitain*, 98.

111   "contorted ramps and hunchbacked candelabra": Quoted in Yvon Toussaint, *Les barons Empain* (Paris: Fayard, 1996), 91.

111   "tortuous, with unhealthy lines": Quoted in Le Tac, *Fulgence Bienvenüe*, 99.

111   "works of art and symbols of Paris": Bernard Marchand, *Paris, histoire d'une ville* (Paris: Seuil, 1993), 169.

111   Once the Métro was up and running: Facts and figures from J. A. Simar, "Édouard Empain: Intelligence créatrice, puissance industrielle," *Annales du Cercle royal archéologique d'Enghien* XLIII (2009–2011): 41; Caroline Suzor, *Le groupe Empain en France* (Brussels: Peter Lang, 2016), 58; *Le métro parisien, 1900–1945* (Paris: Editions Atlas, 2011), 26–31; Toussaint, *Barons Empain*, 95.

112   topping 50 million francs: Suzor, *Le groupe Empain*, 303.

CHAPTER 11   IN LEOPOLD'S HEART OF DARKNESS

113   The first Baron Empain was ennobled: Yvon Toussaint, *Les barons Empain* (Paris: Fayard, 1996), 97–98.

114   purchased a magnificent home: Toussaint, *Barons Empain*, 158; Caroline Suzor, *Le groupe Empain en France* (Brussels: Peter Lang, 2016), 209.

114   **designed his own furniture:** Baron Empain, *La vie en jeu* (Paris: Jean-Claude Lattès, 1985), 17.

114   **"Petit pays, petits gens":** Quoted in Adam Hochschild, *King Leopold's Ghost* (New York: Mariner Books, 1999), 36.

115   **Casting a jealous eye:** Hochschild, *Leopold's Ghost*, 37–41; Maya Jasanoff, *The Dawn Watch: Joseph Conrad in a Global World* (New York: Penguin Press, 2012), 174.

115   **invited a handpicked assembly:** Hochschild, *Leopold's Ghost*, 43–44; Georges-Henri Dumont, *La vie quotidienne en Belgique sous Léopold II* (Paris: Hachette, 1974), 11–12.

115   **article in Britain's *Daily Telegraph*:** "Mr. Stanley's Mission," *Daily Telegraph*, November 22, 1877.

115   **Leopold hid his real design:** Hochschild, *Leopold's Ghost*, 58.

116   **"I am engaged by a foreign people":** Stanley, quoted in Dumont, *Vie quotidienne*, 12.

116   **Stanley's assignment was to build roads:** Hochschild, *Leopold's Ghost*, 71–72, 83.

116   **remained to obtain diplomatic recognition:** Details from Hochschild, *Leopold's Ghost*, 75–87; Dumont, *Vie quotidienne*, 13.

117   **"Only scientific explorations":** Leopold II, quoted in Hochschild, *Leopold's Ghost*, 65.

117   **"Without railroads, the Congo is not worth a penny":** Stanley, quoted in J. A. Simar, "Édouard Empain: Intelligence créatrice, puissance industrielle," *Annales du Cercle royal archéologique d'Enghien* XLIII (2009–2011): 70.

117   **The king agreed:** Dumont, *Vie quotidienne*, 13.

117   **By the time the Matadi–Léopoldville railroad:** Jasanoff, *Dawn Watch*, 233.

118   **The January 1902 agreement:** Simar, "Édouard Empain," 72–76; Toussaint, *Barons Empain*, 63.

118   **"my old master":** Toussaint, *Barons Empain*, 54.

119   **"Whoever doesn't know how to kill":** Toussaint, *Barons Empain*, 40.

119   **imposed a reign of terror:** Jasanoff, *Dawn Watch*, 209–213.

119   **"one must cut off hands, noses, and ears":** Hochschild, *Leopold's Ghost*, 165.

119   **"I could see every rib":** Joseph Conrad, *Heart of Darkness* (New York: Penguin Books, 1982), 22.

120   **"one of the more infamous international scandals":** "Report of the British Consul, Roger Casement, on the Administration of the Congo Free State," *British Parliamentary Papers*, 1904, LXII, Cd. 1933.

120   **It was followed by a blistering book:** Hochschild, *Leopold's Ghost*, 242.

120   **appointed his own commission of inquiry:** Hochschild, *Leopold's Ghost*, 251.

120 **Leopold agreed in 1908:** Hochschild, *Leopold's Ghost*, 160, 259.

120 **between 8 million and 13 million lives lost:** Hochschild, *Leopold's Ghost*, 233, 325.

121 **retained a direct role:** Simar, "Édouard Empain," 72.

121 **involved some sixty thousand workers:** Hochschild, *Leopold's Ghost*, 171.

121 **"as humanely as possible":** Hochschild, *Leopold's Ghost*, 171.

121 **Albert named Empain a major general:** Hochschild, *Leopold's Ghost*, 165–180; Simar, "Édouard Empain," 13.

122 **received an additional land grant:** Toussaint, *Barons Empain*, 65.

122 **Wado was given a VIP tour:** Empain, *Vie*, 215–217.

122 **"I didn't deserve all this deference":** Empain, *Vie*, 216.

123 **eight hundred European agents and fifty thousand local workers:** "Archives du Groupe Empain," Royal Museum for Central Africa (Brussels), accessed June 19, 2020, https://www.africamuseum.be /sites/default/files/media/docs/research/collections/archives/archives -empain-bck.pdf.

123 **Empain holdings were nationalized:** "Democratic Republic of the Congo," *Washington Post* Country Guide, accessed June 19, 2020, https://www.washingtonpost.com/wpsrv/world/countries /congodemocraticrepublicofthe.html.

CHAPTER 12 ⤜⤏ A PLACE IN THE SUN

124 **In the last week of January:** Marie-Cécile Bruwier and Florence Doyen, eds., "Héliopolis, la ville fondée par Édouard Empain," in *Héliopolis d'Egypte, la ville du soleil* (Brussels: Safran, 2019), 97.

124 **railroad and tramway operations:** Bruwier and Doyen, *Héliopolis*, 4, 104; Yvon Toussaint, *Les barons Empain* (Paris: Fayard, 1996), 110; Amélie d'Arschot Schoonhoven, *Le Roman d'Héliopolis* (Waterloo: Avant-Propos, 2018), 109.

125 **he was able to sign a contract:** J. A. Simar, "Édouard Empain: intelligence créatrice, puissance industrielle," *Annales du Cercle royal archéologique d'Enghien* XLIII (2009–2011): 56.

125 **Leopold II encouraged Belgian entrepreneurs:** Anne Van Loo and Marie-Cécile Bruwier, eds., *Héliopolis* (Brussels: Fonds Mercator, 2010), 89–90.

125 **counted on the advice:** On Pasha's background and links to Empain, Bruwier and Doyen, *Héliopolis*, 97; Toussaint, *Barons Empain*, 113–114; Schoonhoven, *Roman d'Héliopolis*, 61–63.

125 **Empain invited his friend:** Schoonhoven, *Roman d'Héliopolis*, 115.

126 **The first thing Boghos could do:** Schoonhoven, *Roman d'Héliopolis*, 117–119.

126 **riding on the back of a camel:** Photo from Empain family collection, courtesy Diane Empain.

127 **Empain in Bedouin robes:** Photo from Empain family collection, courtesy Diane Empain.

127 **Cairo itself was congested:** Toussaint, *Barons Empain*, 112.

127 **the vast tract of desert:** History and description from Van Loo and Bruwier, *Héliopolis*, 48–67.

127 **agreed to buy the land:** Details of land purchase from Van Loo and Bruwier, *Héliopolis*, 112–113; Toussaint, *Barons Empain*, 118–119.

128 **a young Belgian architect:** Van Loo and Bruwier, *Héliopolis*, 129.

128 **"I want to build a city here":** Marcel-Henri Jaspar, quoted in Toussaint, *Barons Empain*, 115–116.

128 **"Go back to Europe":** Toussaint, *Barons Empain*, 116.

129 **a vast real estate speculation:** Van Loo and Bruwier, *Héliopolis*, 115; Schoonhoven, *Roman d'Héliopolis*, 162.

129 **"an oasis rising over the ancient city":** Quoted in Simar, "Édouard Empain," 59.

129 **one of the world's biggest and most luxurious hotels:** Description of Heliopolis Palace Hotel from Van Loo and Bruwier, *Héliopolis*, 117–125; Simar, "Édouard Empain," 60.

130 **the bizarre Hindu Villa:** On the choice of architect and description of the villa, Van Loo and Bruwier, *Héliopolis*, 126–127, 131–145; Simar, "Édouard Empain," 60.

131 **Empain's other personal monument:** Toussaint, *Barons Empain*, 127–129; Bruwier and Doyen, "Héliopolis, la ville fondée par Édouard Empain," 4.

131 **"a fat Belgian lady":** Habib Ayrout, quoted in Toussaint, *Barons Empain*, 129.

131 **faced financial problems:** Van Loo and Bruwier, *Héliopolis*, 107; Simar, "Édouard Empain," 59–62.

132 **nationalized by Nasser:** Simar, "Édouard Empain," 52

132 **Palace Hotel was also taken over:** Simar, "Édouard Empain," 65; Bruwier and Doyen, "Héliopolis, la ville fondée par Édouard Empain," 38.

132 **left Heliopolis in 1913:** Toussaint, *Barons Empain*, 139.

132 **A touching set of photos:** Empain family photo collection, courtesy Diane Empain.

CHAPTER 13 ☙ OPERATION SNOWPLOW

135 **the snows started to fall:** Alain Caillol, interview with author, September 20, 2018.

135 **the men assigned to guard the prisoner:** Alain Caillol, *Lumière* (Paris: Cherche Midi, 2012), 165–168.

135 **"Make sure you're not tailed":** Caillol, *Lumière*, 167.

136   **snatches of conversation:** Baron Empain, *La vie en jeu* (Paris: Jean-Claude Lattès, 1985), 133–134.

137   **favorite ski resort of Europe's jet-setters:** Details and description from "Megève," Wikipedia, accessed February 22, 2020, https://fr.wikipedia.org/wiki/Megève.

137   **tried to avoid the flash-and-bling crowd:** Patricia Empain, interview with author, October 30, 2020.

137   **received an anonymous call:** André Bizeul, *Empain, le rapt* (Paris: Mareuil Editions, 2021), 135.

138   **"The baron will be executed the same day":** Bizeul, *Empain, le rapt*, 137.

138   **the group and the family had come around:** Pierre Ottavioli, *Echec au crime* (Paris: Grasset, 1985), 177.

138   **a fake ransom:** Jean Marc Mazzieri, interview with author, December 7, 2019.

138   **the perfect candidate:** Mazzieri interview, December 7, 2019.

139   **Mazzieri was not alone:** Details on police deployment and preparations from Marcel Leclerc and André Bizeul, report to Judge Louis Chavanac, February 24, 1978; Bizeul, interview with author, January 23, 2020.

139   **Broussard and Mazzieri headed from Paris to Geneva:** Mazzieri, interview with author, December 7, 2019.

140   **Broussard and his commando squad:** Robert Broussard, *Mémoires du commissaire Broussard* (Paris: Nouveau Monde, 2012), 346; Broussard, interview with author, August 30, 2018.

140   **Mazzieri checked into:** Mazzieri, interview with author, December 7, 2019.

140   **"You just woke me from my nap":** Mazzieri, interview with author, December 7, 2019.

140   **The team remained in place:** Mazzieri, interview with author, December 7, 2019; Leclerc and Bizeul, report to Chavanac, February 24, 1978.

141   **the police assumed that the news flash:** Broussard, interview with author, August 30, 2018.

141   **Caillol's band never intended to go to Megève:** Caillol, interview with author, November 19, 2018.

141   **"Fucking cops":** Quoted in Christophe Hondelatte, *L'enlèvement du baron Empain* (Paris: Michel Lafon, 2006), 96.

141   **Meeting in a parallel tunnel gallery:** Details from Caillol, *Lumière*, 179–181.

142   **"Shoot him in the head":** Caillol, interview with author, September 13, 2018.

142   **Caillol proposed to decide the matter:** Caillol, *Lumière*, 181–184.

143   **he would do the job himself:** Baron Empain trial testimony, December 13, 1982, quoted in *Le Figaro*, December 14, 1982; Caillol interview, January 22, 2020.

CHAPTER 14 ⌒ ON THE MOVE

144 **During the hiatus, he returned:** Caillol, interview with author, November 19, 2018; "Un honorable voisin," *Le Monde*, March 30, 1978.

144 **Duchateau was left in charge:** Caillol, interview with author, November 19, 2018; Caillol, email to author, March 23, 2020.

145 **Empain was blindfolded:** Caillol, interview with author, November 19, 2018; Baron Empain, police deposition, March 29, 1978.

145 **"I'm fed up":** Caillol, interview with author, November 19, 2018.

145 **Empain had the impression:** Empain police deposition, March 29, 1978.

145 **it was in fact an apartment:** Caillol, interview with author, September 20, 2018.

146 **"total improvisation":** Caillol, interview with author, September 20, 2018.

146 **an unhoped-for improvement:** Empain deposition, March 29, 1978; Empain, *La vie en jeu* (Paris: Jean-Claude Lattès, 1985), 144–145; Alain Caillol, *Lumière* (Paris: Cherche Midi, 2012), 186.

147 **nailed back in his wooden box:** Empain deposition, March 29, 1978; Caillol, *Lumière*, 187.

147 **Bertoncini told Empain that everything was on hold:** Christophe Hondelatte, *L'enlèvement du baron Empain* (Paris: Michel Lafon, 2006), 103.

147 **"Édouard, you are at home here":** Empain, *Vie*, 156.

147 **Bertoncini did what he could:** Empain, *Vie*, 155; Empain deposition, March 29, 1978.

148 **Wado's relationship with Bertoncini:** Empain, *Vie*, 136–139.

148 **showing him their own guns:** Empain, *Vie*, 157.

148 **"Empain joined our team":** Caillol, *Lumière*, 174.

148 **"When a hostage feels abandoned":** Robert Broussard, *Mémoires du commissaire Broussard* (Paris: Nouveau Monde, 2012), 355.

149 **police in Lyons received a strange phone call:** *Le Monde*, March 11, 1978; *Le Quotidien de Paris*, March 13, 1978.

149 **who should call the Lyons Judiciary Police:** André Bizeul, telephone conversation with author, January 8, 2021.

149 **One of Caillol's confederates:** Caillol, *Lumière*, 196.

CHAPTER 15 ⌒ THE FATAL RENDEZVOUS

150 **"Everything's okay":** Alain Caillol, interview with author, November 19, 2018; Alain Caillol, *Lumière* (Paris: Cherche Midi, 2012), 188.

150 **Caillol left Montgenèvre immediately:** Caillol, email to author, March 31, 2021.

151 **slammed the door on the project:** Caillol, *Lumière*, 188.

151 **Duchateau had contacted Engen:** Marcel Leclerc trial testimony, quoted in *Le Quotidien de Paris*, December 7, 1982.

151 **"The payer must know Paris well":** Baron Empain, handwritten letter dated March 22, 1978, copy provided to author by Jean Marc Mazzieri.

152 **again tapped for the job:** Mazzieri interview, December 7, 2019.

152 **Broussard mobilized a team:** Robert Broussard, interview with author, August 30, 2018.

152 **Ottavioli prepared to follow the action:** Claude Cancès, interview with author, November 16, 2018; Claude Cancès, *Histoire du 36 Quai des Orfèvres* (Paris: Editions Jacob-Duvernet, 2010), 292–293; André Bizeul, interview with author, January 24, 2020.

152 **"put our hands on a counter-hostage":** Pierre Ottavioli, *Echec au crime* (Paris: Grasset, 1985), 181.

152 **Mazzieri drove to Fouquet's:** Details of Mazzieri's movements and phone contacts with kidnappers from his handwritten notes on the operation and his interview with the author, December 7, 2019.

154 **Brainchild of Daniel Duchateau:** Caillol interview, November 19, 2018.

154 **"Listen to me!":** From Mazzieri's notes and interview of December 7, 2019.

154 **At 7:10 p.m., Mazzieri was instructed:** From Mazzieri's notes and interview of December 7, 2019.

155 **Duchateau, Caillol, and the man he calls Mathieu had been waiting:** Caillol, *Lumière*, 73.

155 **"We will cuff his hands":** Caillol, *Lumière*, 73.

155 **a formidable arsenal:** Caillol, *Lumière*, 189.

156 **When Mazzieri arrived at the Hilton:** Mazzieri interview, December 7, 2019.

156 **"The delivery of the ransom":** Baron Empain, *La vie en jeu* (Paris: Jean-Claude Lattès, 1985), 158.

156 **no longer believed in the operation:** Mazzieri interview, December 7, 2019.

157 **"Not a wink":** Details of this conversation from Mazzieri interview, December 7, 2019.

157 **The initial idea was to rendezvous:** Caillol interview, November 19, 2018.

158 **Mazzieri pulled into the breakdown lane:** Mazzieri notes and interview, December 7, 2019.

158 **Before Mazzieri could get out of the car:** Mazzieri notes and interview, December 7, 2019.

158 **Caillol slid in behind the wheel:** Caillol, interview with author, September 13, 2018; Caillol, *Lumière*, 40–43.

158 **"Mazeaud is safe":** Mazzieri interview, December 7, 2019.

158 **Broussard's command car:** Broussard interview, August 30, 2018.

159 **Caillol hit the brakes:** Caillol interview, September 13, 2018.

159 **at least three men began shooting:** André Bizeul, telephone conversation with author, January 29, 2021.

159 **"Hold your fire":** Mazzieri interview, December 7, 2019.

160 **"You asshole!":** Details of this exchange from Caillol, *Lumière*, 42; Alain Caillol, letter to Mireille Bonnelle, April 22, [1985], in Caillol and Bonnelle, *Lettres* (Paris: Editions Manya, 1990), 139.

160 **Police later found the vehicle:** Bizeul, interview with author, January 24, 2020.

160 **The firing had just ended:** Bizeul, interview with author, January 24, 2020; Broussard interview, August 30, 2018.

160 **Among the scattered police vehicles:** Mazzieri interview, December 7, 2019.

161 **Ottavioli and his colleagues had followed:** Michel Desfarges, interview with author, January 29, 2020.

161 **"Not exactly brilliant, Ottavioli":** Pierre Ottavioli, *Echec*, 187.

161 **the chief felt abandoned:** Michel Desfarges, email to author, January 16, 2020.

161 **When Ottavioli arrived on the scene:** Bizeul interview, January 23, 2020.

162 **"We have to interrogate the prisoner":** Bizeul interview, January 23, 2020.

162 **a "stormy" interrogation:** Ottavioli, *Echec*, 187.

162 **recruited by Duchateau:** Caillol trial testimony cited in *Libération*, December 8, 1982.

162 **Bizeul grabbed and twisted Caillol's wounded arm:** Caillol interview, September 13, 2018.

162 **"Duchateau is dead":** Bizeul interview, January 23, 2020; Caillol interview, September 20, 2018.

CHAPTER 16 ⤸ "CAN'T I CALL FROM HERE?"

163 **Caillol was a mess:** Alain Caillol, *Lumière* (Paris: Cherche Midi, 2012), 75.

163 **"The ballet of inspectors":** Caillol, *Lumière*, 76.

164 **"He's no fool":** Claude Cancès, *Commissaire à la Crim'* (Paris: Mareuil Editions, 2017), 72.

164 **Wado realized that the mood had changed:** Baron Empain, *La vie en jeu* (Paris: Jean-Claude Lattès, 1985), 158–159.

164 **"Listen. You've read what happened":** Empain, *Vie*, 160.

165 **Wado did not touch the meal:** Empain, *Vie*, 160.

165 **legend among French criminal lawyers:** Jean-Yves Dupeux [Empain's lawyer], May 28, 2018; physical description of Smadja-Epstein from André Bizeul, interview with author, January 23, 2029; Alain Caillol, interview with author, November 19, 2018.

165   **Smadja was the mistress of Michel Ardouin:** Caillol interview, November 19, 2018.

165   **She had been involved in an abortive plot:** Bizeul interview, January 23, 2020.

165   **quasi-official lawyer of the *milieu*:** Georges Kiejman, interview with author, September 18, 2018.

165   **When she entered Caillol's hospital room:** Caillol, *Lumière*, 85–86.

166   **"only concern":** *L'Aurore*, March 30, 1978.

166   **Fingerprints lifted from his corpse:** André Bizeul, *Empain, le rapt* (Paris: Mareuil Editions, 2021), 204.

166   **Desfarges was dispatched to Grenoble:** Michel Desfarges, interview with author, January 29, 2020.

166   **Irène Caillol told him her husband had left home:** Irène Caillol, police deposition, March 26, 1978, quoted in Bizeul, *Empain, le rapt*, 222–223.

166   **"The more I think about it":** Bizeul, *Empain, le rapt*, 222–223.

167   **"I'm in Italy":** Bizeul, *Empain, le rapt*, 223; Desfarges interview, January 29, 2020.

167   **Other detectives went to question Alain's wife:** Bizeul, *Empain, le rapt*, 221.

167   **the cops continued talking to his wife:** Caillol interview, September 20, 2018; Bizeul confirms that Pierrette Caillol told them about Palma, interview with author, January 24, 2020.

167   **"Look—you go to Cusco":** Information from a former detective who wishes to remain anonymous in order to discuss internal police matters.

168   **"a chickpea for a brain":** Cancès, *Commissaire*, 75.

168   **"What were you doing in Palma?":** Caillol, *Lumière*, 83; Caillol interview, September 20, 2018.

168   **That's when Caillol decided to take the initiative:** Caillol, *Lumière*, 86.

168   **he would need the judge's authorization:** Pierre Ottavioli, *Echec au crime* (Paris: Grasset, 1985), 188.

168   **dressed in his hospital gown:** Details from Caillol, *Lumière*, 86–87.

169   **large office with cream-colored walls:** Description from "Au 36 quai des Orfèvres, le bureau des légendes," *M le magazine du Monde*, April 16, 2017.

169   **"you will bear the sole responsibility":** Quoted by Cancès, *Commissaire*, 73. That Caillol risked the death penalty is confirmed by his lawyer, Georges Kiejman, interview with author, September 18, 2018; also by Jean-Yves Dupeux [Empain's lawyer], interview with author, May 28, 2018.

169   **"I squinted as hard as possible":** Dialogue from Caillol, *Lumière*, 87–88. Other officers present (Cancès, Bizeul) tell a different version of the story, claiming Ottavioli offered his own phone in order to trick Caillol, but

Ottavioli himself confirms that it was Caillol who "considered it expedient to use my telephone." Ottavioli, *Echec*, 189.

170   "The baron must be liberated": Ottavioli, *Echec*, 189.

170   "It's good at ninety-nine percent": Ottavioli, *Echec*, 189.

170   the conspirators had voted earlier in the day: Empain, *La vie en jeu* (Paris: Jean-Claude Lattès, 1985), 161.

170   "After all, that was the only thing you could do": Bizeul, *Empain, le rapt*, 211.

170   "Because he was the easiest": Bizeul, interview with author, January 23, 2020.

171   "he talks too much to be a leader": Robert Broussard, interview with author, August 30, 2018.

171   Ottavioli's phone was linked to a tape recorder: Bizeul interview, January 23, 2020.

171   Desfarges is convinced: Desfarges, interview with author, January 29, 2020.

172   "Empain just called from the Opéra": Bizeul, *Empain, le rapt*, 213.

172   "Voilà!": Bizeul, *Empain, le rapt*, 213.

CHAPTER 17   ☙   FROM ONE PRISON TO ANOTHER

173   Guillon had good news and bad news: Baron Empain, *La vie en jeu* (Paris: Jean-Claude Lattès, 1985), 160–162.

174   "Why aren't you dressed?": Empain, *Vie*, 8.

176   "I'd like to speak to Silvana, please": Dialogue from Empain, *Vie*, 11–12.

177   "Where are we going?": Dialogue from Empain, *Vie*, 11–12.

177   He wrenched open the rear door: Empain, *Vie*, 12.

177   "Since Papa's phone call": Patricia Empain, interview with author, October 19, 2020.

178   "We need to move as fast as possible": Empain, *Vie*, 164.

178   "Empain was visibly relieved": Robert Broussard, interview with author, August 30, 2028.

178   in no mood to sit through an interrogation: Empain, *Vie*, 64–65, 137.

178   he had never seen the kidnappers: Bizeul, interview with author, January 24, 2020.

178   "strange, totally lacking in warmth": Empain, *Vie*, 164.

179   "like the return of Monte Cristo": Empain interview in Christophe Hondelatte, *L'enlèvement du baron Empain* (Paris: Michel Lafon, 2006), 136.

179   "I hugged him and kissed him": Patricia Empain, interview with author, October 19, 2020.

180   "I understood that I was now a prisoner": Empain, *Vie*, 164.

180   found in a Brussels garbage dump: "Abducted Belgian Industrialist Is Found Dead," *New York Times*, April 11, 1978.

CHAPTER 18   ⌒   THE BARON'S PROGENY

183   a man who commanded respect: Details on Empain from Yvon Toussaint, *Les barons Empain* (Paris: Fayard, 1996), 34–38.

184   fell in love with a certain Jeanne Becker: Toussaint, *Barons Empain*, 104–105.

184   one writer hypothesized: Amélie d'Arschot Schoonhoven, *Le Roman d'Héliopolis* (Waterloo: Avant-Propos, 2018), 50.

184   daughter of a Brussels distiller: Toussaint, *Barons Empain*, 105–106.

184   François made an excellent match: On François's marriage, education, and barony, Toussaint, *Barons Empain*, 106–107; Caroline Suzor, *Le groupe Empain en France* (Brussels: Peter Lang, 2016), 38, 44; Oscar Coomans de Brachène, ed., *Etat présent de la noblesse belge* (Brussels: Collection Etat Present, 1974), 33.

185   François began to nurture the secret hope: Toussaint, *Barons Empain*, 107; Suzor, *Groupe Empain*, 44.

185   married Jeanne Becker in April 1921: Toussaint, *Barons Empain*, 189.

185   asked François to take his oldest son under his wing: Toussaint, *Barons Empain*, 190.

185   The general finally realized what was going on: Toussaint, *Barons Empain*, 191.

185   Jean Empain married: Toussaint, *Barons Empain*, 193; Coomans de Brachène, *Noblesse belge*, 31–32.

186   Along with female flesh: Toussaint, *Barons Empain*, 193–194.

186   On July 21, 1929: Details of funeral from Toussaint, *Barons Empain*, 205–206; Suzor, *Groupe Empain*, 309; "Baron Empain Dies Near Brussels at 77," *New York Times*, July 23, 1929.

186   Cairo had never seen such a funeral: Description of funeral based on news clips cited in Toussaint, *Barons Empain*, 206–207, and photographs from the Empain family collection, courtesy of Diane Empain.

187   mistress of the moment: Toussaint, *Barons Empain*, 208.

187   inherited an immense fortune: Toussaint, *Barons Empain*, 213–215.

187   wasted no time seizing control: Toussaint, *Barons Empain*, 216–217; Suzor, *Groupe Empain*, 45, 347–348.

188   "cousin fausse-couche": Toussaint, *Barons Empain*, 264.

188   a somber introvert: Details from Louis Empain's obituary in *Le Soir de Bruxelles*, June 4, 1976; Toussaint, *Barons Empain*, 253–256; Suzor, *Groupe Empain*, 350.

188   competent if not brilliant businessman: Toussaint, *Barons Empain*, 229.

188   **famous for hosting nonstop parties:** Toussaint, *Barons Empain*, 224–226; photos from Empain family collection, courtesy Diane Empain.

189   **The château itself:** Description of château from Diane Empain, interview with author, February 25, 2020; photos from Empain family collection, courtesy Diane Empain.

189   **Johnny would head out to sea:** Toussaint, *Barons Empain*, 222.

189   **Shipboard photos:** From Empain family collection, courtesy Diane Empain.

189   **In addition to Josephine Baker:** Toussaint, *Barons Empain*, 220–221.

189   **a beautiful young Swedish woman:** Details on Knudsen's affair with Jean Empain from Paul Bringuier, "La Ronde des Gogos," *Détective*, May 28, 1938; *L'officiel de la Mode*, October 13, 1930.

CHAPTER 19   GOLDIE

191   **The lady in gold was Rozell Rowland:** Details from Betty Jane Rowland, interview with Leslie Zemeckis in "Minsky Stripper Turns 100," *Huffington Post*, January 25, 2016, accessed July 20, 2020, https://www.huffpost.com/entry/minsky-stripper-turns-100_b_9065388.

191   **"skin like satin":** Undated, unsigned newspaper clipping in Diane Empain's collection.

192   **Their devout Christian Scientist parents:** Betty Jane Rowland, "Minsky Stripper"; Diane Empain interview, February 25, 2020.

192   **"Dad ended up keeping scrapbooks":** Undated, unsigned newspaper clipping in Diane Empain's collection.

192   **recruited the girls to perform:** Betty Jane Rowland interview, "Minsky Stripper."

192   **The Swedish-born Granlund:** Abel Green, "Memoirs of a Broadway Drum Beater," *New York Times*, February 10, 1957; Granlund obituary, *New York Times*, April 22, 1957.

193   **A promotional picture:** Photo from Empain family collection, courtesy Diane Empain.

193   **"This dainty little eyeful":** "Gilt Girl Makes Hotel Debut," *Kings County News*, undated clipping [probably July 1935] in the Diane Empain collection.

193   **Rozell jumped at the chance:** Details on Rozell's London engagement from Yvon Toussaint, *Les barons Empain* (Paris: Fayard, 1996), 231–232.

193   **"Johnny arrived":** Rozell Rowland, quoted in Toussaint, *Barons Empain*, 232.

194   **"Well, go ask him":** Toussaint, *Barons Empain*, 232.

194   **"I'm sick of scuffling around":** Toussaint, *Barons Empain*, 233.

194   **on the deck of the *Héliopolis*:** Toussaint, *Barons Empain*, 233–234.

194   **"I have the best place":** Toussaint, *Barons Empain*, 233.

194   "I realized that everything belonged to the baron": Toussaint, *Barons Empain*, 233.

194   "The Baron owns this hotel too": Postcard from Empain family collection, courtesy Diane Empain.

195   president of the Heliopolis Racing Club: *Le livre d'or du turf* (Paris: Nouvelle Edition, 1932), 109–112.

195   Photos show them bundled up: Photos from Empain family collection, courtesy Diane Empain.

195   "If it's a boy": Toussaint, *Barons Empain*, 234.

196   "the longest months of my life": Toussaint, *Barons Empain*, 235.

196   On October 7, 1937: "U.S. Dancer Wed to Baron," *New York Times*, November 11, 1937; Toussaint, *Barons Empain*, 235–236; Diane Empain, interview with author, February 24, 2020.

196   Wado in the care of his nanny: Diane Empain, telephone conversation with author, April 26, 2021.

CHAPTER 20   DISGRACE

197   Electrorail, did quite well: Caroline Suzor, *Le groupe Empain en France* (Brussels: Peter Lang, 2016), 335.

197   According to "friends": "Baron Empain a Prisoner," *New York Times*, July 25, 1940.

198   Perhaps the *Times* confused him: "Louis Empain, tel que nous l'avons connu," *Vers l'Avenir*, June 3, 1976.

198   uniformed German officers: Suzor, *Groupe Empain*, 427.

198   extravagant Champagne dinners: "Enquête en Belgique depuis la date du 26-1-46 de MM. Massoulier & Vacher sur l'activité du Baron Empain," Archives Nationales (France), Empain-F/12/9582, folder 7.

198   a bear escaped from Johnny's zoo: Marie-France Fondère [adopted granddaughter of Jean Empain], interview with author, November 14, 2020.

198   Johnny abhorred the rise of bolshevism: Yvon Toussaint, *Les barons Empain* (Paris: Fayard, 1996), 271.

199   befriended Reichsmarschall Hermann Göring: Annie Lacroix-Riz, *La non-épuration en France de 1943 aux années 1950* (Paris: Armand Colin, 2019), 472.

199   "she had been the mistress of a German captain": Lacroix-Riz, *Non-épuration*, 472.

199   not a collaborator: Diane Empain, telephone conversation with author, December 13, 2020.

199   Among the collaborators in the Empains' circle: Lacroix-Riz, *Non-épuration*, 472.

199 **"elite of the artistic, literary, and political world"**: Corinne Luchaire, *Ma drôle de vie* (Paris: Sun, 1949), as quoted by Toussaint, *Barons Empain*, 275.

199 **Corinne and her father fled**: "Corinne Luchaire," Wikipedia, accessed July 28, 2020, https://en.wikipedia.org/wiki/Corinne_Luchaire.

199 **threats from the French Resistance**: Toussaint, *Barons Empain*, 278.

200 **"clearly pro-German attitude"**: Letter from the Secrétariat d'Etat à la Production Industrielle to the Commission Nationale d'Epuration [1944], Archives Nationales, Z-45, folder 7, 2080.

200 **"miserable personage"**: Massoulier and Vacher, "Enquête en Belgique," Archives Nationales, F/12/9582, folder 7.

200 **"very badly considered"**: Massoulier and Vacher, "Enquête en Belgique."

201 **important financial interests**: Massoulier and Vacher, "Enquête en Belgique."

201 **sanction one key piece**: Details on Métro under the Occupation from Suzor, *Groupe Empain*, 409–411; Roger-Henri Guérrand, *L'aventure du métropolitain* (Paris: La Découverte, 1999), 80–84.

201 **assassinated a German naval cadet**: Robert Paxton, *Vichy France* (New York: Columbia University Press, 1972), 223.

201 **The conduct of the company officials**: Guerrand, *L'aventure*, 82; Suzor, *Groupe Empain*, 433–435.

201 **Jews wearing the yellow star**: Guerrand, *Aventure*, 82.

202 **"total cooperation"**: CMP report of May 28, 1942, cited in Toussaint, *Barons Empain*, 275.

202 **took a more sinister form**: Details from Suzor, *Groupe Empain*, 435–436.

202 **CMP's leadership was targeted**: Suzor, *Groupe Empain*, 457–459; Guerrand, *Aventure*, 85; Toussaint, *Barons Empain*, 276–277.

202 **the group lost its position**: Suzor, *Groupe Empain*, 441.

202 **Johnny Empain was fighting for his life**: Toussaint, *Barons Empain*, 286.

203 **"He spoke to me"**: Baron Empain, *La vie en jeu* (Paris: Jean-Claude Lattès, 1985), 21.

203 **announced that he had to return to France**: Details on Jean Empain's return to France from Toussaint, *Barons Empain*, 282, 285–291.

204 **"since you're here"**: Empain interview in *Les barons Empain: La dynastie fracassée*, documentary by Tanguy Cortier and Alice Gorissen, aired on Arte, April 13, 2016.

204 **Jean Empain expired**: Obituary in *New York Times*, February 12, 1946; Toussaint, *Barons Empain*, 291.

204 **"perfect and unalterable"**: Empain, *Vie*, 23.

204 **The reading of Jean Empain's will**: Details from Toussaint, *Barons Empain*, 281.

205 **"Who do you think you are?"**: Toussaint, *Barons Empain*, 290.

205   **perhaps it was Goldie:** Baron Empain (Wado), interview in Cortier and Gorissen, *La dynastie fracassée*; Baron Empain, *Vie*, 24–25.

205   **"pigeon-toed and droopy-mouthed":** Toussaint, *Barons Empain*, 265.

205   **effectively assumed command:** Suzor, *Groupe Empain*, 47–48.

205   **"I was surprised when he proposed":** Rozell Empain, interviewed by Toussaint, in *Barons Empain*, 299.

206   **The wedding took place:** Oscar Coomans de Brachène, ed., *Etat présent de la noblesse belge* (Brussels: Collection Etat Present, 1974), 31.

206   **Photos of the event:** Empain family collection, courtesy Diane Empain.

206   **"From time to time":** Rozell Empain, interviewed by Toussaint, *Barons Empain*, 318.

CHAPTER 21   THE INHERITOR

207   **Wado's childhood was one of privilege:** Baron Empain, *La vie en jeu* (Paris: Jean-Claude Lattès, 1985), 26–27.

207   **"I was frightened to death":** Rozell Empain, quoted in Yvon Toussaint, *Les barons Empain* (Paris: Fayard, 1996), 321.

208   **The real maternal figure:** Empain, *Vie*, 26–27.

208   **a boy named Bernard Moine:** Empain, *Vie*, 26–27.

208   **sent to a Catholic boys' school:** Empain, *Vie*, 28; Empain interview in *Le Monde*, November 4, 1985.

209   **perhaps more:** Hervé Bierry interview with author, June 26, 2020.

209   **a "perfect man":** Empain, *Vie*, 29–31.

209   **affair with Jacques Doyasbère:** Diane Empain, interview with author, February 4, 2020.

210   **"born of an unknown and unnamed mother":** Diane Empain interview, February 4, 2020.

210   **a thoroughbred mare:** Jean Delannoy, "Flicka, à livre ouvert," *L'Eperon*, May 2015.

210   **she trained obsessively:** Delannoy, "Flicka"; Diane Empain interviews, December 13 and 14, 2020.

210   **"No one told him":** Diane Empain interview, February 4, 2020.

210   **photos show Wado giving her a ride:** Empain family collection, courtesy Diane Empain.

211   **"Darling Wado":** Postcard dated August 4, 1957, courtesy Diane Empain.

211   **"He was a wonderful man":** Baron Empain, quoted in Toussaint, *Barons Empain*, 320.

211   **left Bouffémont and took his daughter:** Diane Empain interview, February 4, 2020.

211   **"Jacques Doyasbère was kindness":** Diane Empain interview, February 4, 2020.

211   **she wanted her daughter back:** Diane Empain interview, February 4, 2020.

212   **"Your father is no longer your father":** Diane Empain, email to author, December 15, 2020.

212   **"He was always fantastic with me":** Diane Empain interview, November 13, 2020.

212   **"just the sweetest man":** Isabelle de Montagu, interview with author, January 19, 2021.

212   **Wado completed his *baccalauréat*:** Empain, *Vie*, 32.

213   **In August 1957:** Details on Empain's vacation and meeting with Silvana, Empain, *Vie*, 33–34.

213   **agreed to accompany Wado to Milan:** Empain, *Vie*, 34.

213   **Aldina de Ambrosis was:** Details from Patricia Empain, emails to author, April 24 and May 8, 2021.

214   **The wedding took place:** Empain, *Vie*, 35.

214   **they flew instead:** Diane Empain interview, February 4, 2020.

214   **A photo taken just before their departure:** Empain collection, courtesy Diane Empain.

215   **After a brief stopover in New York:** Empain, *Vie*, 35.

215   **Rozell's sister Betty Jane:** Details on Betty Jane Rowland's dancing career from Leslie Zemeckis, "Minsky Stripper Turns 100," *Huffington Post*, January 25, 2016, accessed July 20, 2020, https://www.huffpost.com/entry/minsky-stripper-turns-100_b_9065388; Betty Jane Rowland interview, November 6, 2012, on youtube.com, accessed April 29, 2020, https://www.youtube.com/watch?v=ETWe5zMhcrA.

215   **queen of the "femme trade":** "Burlesque Notes," *Billboard*, March 28, 1942.

215   **the same mannerisms:** Diane Empain interview, February 2, 2020.

216   **died of a heart attack in 1944:** *Detroit Free Press*, July 13, 1944.

216   **lived a quiet life:** Alvah Werner [Lorraine's stepson], interview with author, November 27, 2020.

216   **settled into a Brussels apartment:** Empain, *Vie*, 39–42.

216   **some unsettling news:** Details of Empain's confrontation with Édouard and seizure of power, Empain, *Vie*, 42–52.

218   **"pity for this man":** Empain, *Vie*, 52.

218   **Wado had much to learn:** Empain, *Vie*, 52–54.

218   **began to raise a family:** Empain, *Vie*, 35–36.

218   **"I can see them now":** Jean-François Empain, interviewed in *L'affaire du Baron Empain*, documentary by Cyrielle Galliot-Nahon, Carson Productions, March 2019.

219   **an abrupt end in November 1967:** Empain, *Vie*, 55–56.

219   **Wado was the fourth president:** Empain, *Vie*, 61.

219   **named director general:** Empain, *Vie*, 69.

220   **"to be pitiless":** Empain, *Vie*, 69.

220   **offering to sell a preponderant share:** Jacqueline Grapin, "Le baron Édouard-Jean Empain," *Le Monde*, February 5, 1974.

220   **"Trojan horse":** "L'industrie nucléaire va-t-elle passer sous contrôle étranger?" *France-Soir*, November 20, 1973; Empain, *Vie*, 141–142.

CHAPTER 22   ☙   WADO'S TRIUMPH

221   **crown jewel of French industry:** History of Schneider from Baron Empain, *La vie en jeu* (Paris: Jean-Claude Lattès, 1985), 73; Yvon Toussaint, *Les barons Empain* (Paris: Fayard, 1996), 340–341; "Schneider et Cie," Wikipedia, accessed October 21, 2020, https://fr.wikipedia.org/wiki/Schneider_et_Cie.

222   **Charles Schneider slipped and fell:** "Mort de M. Charles Schneider," *Le Monde*, August 8, 1960; Toussaint, *Barons Empain*, 342.

222   **hide Jewish children:** "Juste parmi les nations: Liliane Schneider," ajpn.org website, accessed May 15, 2020, http://www.ajpn.org/juste-Lilian-Schneider-4186.html.

222   **a senior banking official was parachuted in:** Toussaint, *Barons Empain*, 342.

222   **Charles Schneider's sister decided to sell:** Empain, *Vie*, 75–76.

223   **"The Schneider affair is too important":** Charles de Gaulle to Georges Pompidou and Valéry Giscard d'Estaing, July 26, 1963, Archives Nationales, Michel Poniatowski papers, 340 AP III/131, folder 2.

223   **"the Schneider group holds":** Pompidou to Giscard d'Estaing, October 24, 1963, Archives Nationales, Poniatowski papers, 340 AP III/131, folder 2.

223   **his wife was a descendant of Eugène Schneider:** "Valéry Giscard d'Estaing: Le président qui aimait les femmes!" *France Dimanche*, December 24, 2020.

224   **began courting Liliane Volpert:** Empain, *Vie*, 85–88.

224   **"precious elderly lady":** Empain, *Vie*, 89.

225   **When the time was ripe:** Takeover details in Empain, *Vie*, 89–95.

225   **finance minister even threatened:** René Tendron, "Pourquoi Empain," *Nouvel Economiste*, January 30, 1978, 38.

225   **took over the presidency of Schneider:** Empain, *Vie*, 98.

225   **frenzy of takeovers and acquisitions:** Empain, *Vie*, 116–117.

226   **secret contempt for Baron Empain:** Toussaint, *Barons Empain*, 350–351.

226   **"master of the universe":** This and following quotes from Empain, interviewed for *Paroles d'otages*, documentary by Jean-Claude Raspiengeas and Patrick Volson, TF1 Vidéo, 1990.

CHAPTER 23 ∽ AFTERSHOCKS

229 **Desfarges drove up:** Details from Michel Desfarges, interview with author, January 29, 2020.

230 **"That was an incredible find":** Desfarges interview, January 29, 2020.

230 **Wado insisted on going to the American Hospital:** Baron Empain, *La vie en jeu* (Paris: Jean-Claude Lattès, 1985), 169.

231 **Ottavioli, Bizeul, and Desfarges showed up:** André Bizeul, interview with author, January 24, 2020.

231 **neighbors had not noticed anything:** Desfarges interview, January 29, 2020.

231 **the job of Judge Louis Chavanac:** Desfarges interview, January 29, 2020.

231 **corps of** *juges d'instruction*: On the role of these special magistrates, Jean-Claude Farcy and Jean-Jacques Clère, *Le juge d'instruction: Approches historiques* (Paris: Editions Universitaires de Dijon, 2010).

232 **"difficult in his dealings":** Desfarges interview, January 29, 2020; Desfarges, telephone conversation with author, December 19, 2020.

232 **Chavanac immediately got Wado's back up:** Empain, *Vie,* 166; Empain interview in *Paris Match,* June 12, 1981; Jean-Yves Dupeux [Empain's lawyer], interview with author, May 28, 2018.

232 **Chavanac's hostile questioning:** Empain, *Vie,* 137, 166.

233 **"I was already divorced":** Empain, interview with Christophe Hondelatte, *L'enlèvement du baron Empain* (Paris: Michel Lafon, 2006), 135–136.

233 **all he got from Silvana:** Empain interview in *Paris Match,* March 20, 1981.

233 **"if there is lipstick on his collar":** Yvon Toussaint, *Les barons Empain* (Paris: Fayard, 1996), 421.

233 **Engen had scolded Silvana:** Toussaint, *Barons Empain,* 173.

234 **"Madame, I don't know":** André Bizeul, interview with author, January 23, 2020.

234 **was there to help:** Diane Empain interview, February 4, 2020; Patricia Empain, email to author, February 17, 2021.

234 **"With Patricia and Christine":** Diane Empain interview, February 4, 2020.

234 **Braly hailed from a wealthy family:** Obituary of Joyce Booth [Braly's mother], *Houston Chronicle,* June 16, 2019. Details of Patricia's relationship and marriage with Braly from Patricia Empain, interview with author, October 19, 2020.

235 **"I knew from her voice":** Patricia Empain interview, October 19, 2020.

235 **"When they told him":** Patricia Empain interview, October 19, 2020.

235 **"In their eyes":** Empain interview in *Paroles d'otages,* documentary by Jean-Claude Raspiengeas and Patrick Volson, TF1 Vidéo, 1990.

236 **"I had to choose":** Patricia Empain interview, October 19, 2020.

236 **Wado decided to return:** Empain, *Vie*, 170.

236 **Empain's erstwhile protégé briefed him:** Empain, *Vie*, 170–171.

237 **overall sales were up by 17 percent:** Toussaint, *Barons Empain*, 428.

237 **"an image inside the group":** Empain interview in Raspiengeas and Volson, *Paroles d'otages*.

237 **"I will keep you informed":** Toussaint, *Barons Empain*, 426.

237 **"I wiped the slate clean":** Empain, *Vie*, 175.

237 **"both my nurse and my mistress":** Empain, *Vie*, 175.

237 **"This woman loved everything about me":** Empain, *Vie*, 173.

238 **signed over the powers of the presidency:** Empain, *Vie*, 174.

238 **"He's finished":** Toussaint, *Barons Empain*, 427–428.

238 **Bierry reluctantly agreed:** Hervé Bierry, interview with author, June 26, 2020.

238 **"definitive eclipse":** Claude Pierre-Brossolette, quoted in Toussaint, *Barons Empain*, 428.

238 **nursed hopes of one day becoming its CEO:** Gilles Malençon, "Empain-Caillol, le chemin du pardon," encetempsla.com, January 25, 2012, consulted December 5, 2019, http://encetempslacom.blogspot .com/2012/01/empain-caillol-le-chemin-du-pardon.html.

238 **"two roosters on the same manure pile":** Empain, quoted in Toussaint, *Barons Empain*, 372.

238 **Some even speculated:** Echoing widespread press speculation on this point, lawyer Georges Kiejman suggested during the December 1982 trial that "high level" officials might have organized the kidnapping "to damage a man with extremely important responsibilities in France's economic and military arsenal." *Le Monde*, December 6, 1982.

239 **Wado and Shahnaz settled into a grand hotel:** Empain, *Vie*, 175–177.

239 **may actually have gotten "married":** Patricia Empain, email to author, January 18, 2021.

239 **Their California idyll was interrupted:** Empain, *Vie*, 177–178.

240 **"After his liberation":** Rozell Empain, quoted in Toussaint, *Barons Empain*, 431.

240 **summoned him to a tête-à-tête:** Empain, *Vie*, 177.

240 **"I can assure you":** Hondelatte, *Enlèvement*, 150–151.

241 **Raymond Barre decorated Engen:** "René Leopold Alexis Engen," *World Biographical Encyclopedia*, consulted October 29, 2020, https://prabook .com/web/rene_leopold_alexis.engen/1302118.

241 **"Engen was a remarkable captain of industry":** Desfarges, interview with author, January 6, 2021.

241 **questioning Wado's lack of "assiduity":** François de Witt, "Qui dirige chez Empain-Schneider?" *L'expansion*, September 21–October 4, 1979.

242   "His mother is American": Empain, *Vie*, 178.

242   As soon as Moine arrived: Empain, *Vie*, 178–179.

242   "You really intend not to return?" Empain, *Vie*, 179.

243   he and Shahnaz boarded the **Queen Elizabeth 2**: Toussaint, *Barons Empain*, 431.

CHAPTER 24 ⤙ EXILE'S RETURN

244   Empain's first stop was London: Baron Empain, *La vie en jeu* (Paris: Jean-Claude Lattès, 1985), 180.

244   "I intended to smash everything": Empain, *Vie*, 180.

244   Relations between the two men had become strained: Empain, *Vie*, 168.

245   "we have instructions": Empain, *Vie*, 181.

245   "Of course, Baron": Empain, *Vie*, 181.

245   He called a press conference: *Le Monde*, September 9, 1978.

246   "a conquering gladiator": Quoted in Toussaint, *Barons Empain* (Paris: Fayard, 1996), 432.

246   "I am the principal shareholder": Empain, *Vie*, 182.

246   Wado's return occurred at a difficult moment: Empain, *Vie*, 182–194; Toussaint, *Barons Empain*, 434–445.

247   a role like the queen of England: Empain, *Vie*, 114, 190.

247   offered to resign: Empain, *Vie*, 183.

247   The baron's candidate to replace him: Empain, *Vie*, 184.

247   not a man to play prime minister to Empain's monarch: Empain, *Vie*, 190.

248   The final straw was the perfidious trick: Empain, *Vie*, 191.

248   decided to sell all his shares: Empain, *Vie*, 192–194; "Paribas rachète au baron Empain sa participation dans le groupe Empain-Schneider," *Le Monde*, February 27, 1981.

248   The Empain-Schneider group itself soon disappeared: Bruno Dethomas, "La triste fin d'une aventure industrielle," *Le Monde*, June 23, 1984.

248   was liquidated in 1984: Dethomas, "La triste fin."

248   pursued a slash-and-burn policy: "Didier Pineau-Valencienne," *Le Monde*, December 12, 1987.

249   denounced as an "industrial gravedigger": "L'Establishment s'étonne du sort réservé à Didier Pineau-Valencienne," *Le Monde,* May 29, 1994.

249   spent twelve days in a Brussels prison: *Le Monde*, "L'Establishment s'étonne." (Didier Pineau-Valencienne did not respond to the author's multiple requests for an interview.)

249   a spiral of self-destructive drift: Empain, *Vie*, 192–194.

249   ended his longtime affair with Shahnaz Arieh: Patricia Empain, email to author, January 16, 2021.

249 **One woman who encountered Wado:** Marie-France Fondère [Empain's niece], interview with author, November 14, 2020.

CHAPTER 25 ⟡ THE DRAGNET

251 **immediately fled the country:** Alain Caillol, *Lumière* (Paris: Cherche Midi, 2012), 71–74.

251 **Chavanac issued arrest warrants:** André Bizeul, interview with author, January 24, 2020.

251 **The first one they nabbed was Le Gayan:** Bizeul interview, January 24, 2020; "Une deuxième arrestation," *Le Monde*, April 1, 1978.

252 **François Caillol and Bernard Guillon had driven:** Bizeul interview, January 24, 2020; *Le Figaro*, December 10, 1982.

252 **Otta dispatched Claude Cancès:** Michel Desfarges, interview with author, January 29, 2020, and telephone conversation with author, October 14, 2020.

252 **compromising items in his car:** Desfarges interview, January 29, 2020; *France-Soir*, December 10, 1982.

252 **Police also suspected:** Desfarges interview, January 29, 2020.

253 **Desfarges led a team:** Desfarges interview, January 29, 2020; Bizeul interview, January 24, 2020.

253 **Bertoncini had initially fled to Italy:** Details from Bizeul interviews, January 23 and 24, 2020; Bizeul to Pierre Ottavioli, report on Lisbon mission, June 14, 1978, photocopy provided to the author by André Bizeul.

253 **Bertoncini flew to Lisbon:** Bizeul report on Lisbon mission; André Bizeul, *Empain, le rapt* (Paris: Mareuil Editions, 2021), 294.

254 **Bizeul warned Portuguese authorities:** Bizeul, *Empain, le rapt*, 296.

254 **Bertoncini's flight to freedom ended:** Desfarges interview, January 29, 2020.

254 **"After two days":** Desfarges interview, January 29, 2020.

254 **they went to search Bertoncini's apartment:** Desfarges interview, January 29, 2020; "L'instigateur présumé du rapt du baron Empain est arrêté à Paris," *Le Monde*, November 23, 1978.

255 **Among the papers:** Details on Desfarges's mission to Lausanne from Desfarges interview, January 29, 2020.

256 **Brunet was shot dead:** Robert Broussard, interview with author, August 30, 2018.

256 **Rigault died of cancer:** *France-Soir*, December 3, 1982.

256 **According to Caillol:** Alain Caillol, *Lumière*, 48; Caillol interview, January 22, 2020.

256 **Lawyers for Caillol and Guillon petitioned:** "Trois mises en liberté," *Le Monde*, May 27, 1981; *France-Soir*, May 22, 1981.

257   "Go buy a newspaper": *France-Soir,* May 27, 1981; *Le Figaro,* May 28, 1981.

CHAPTER 26   THE RECKONING

258   "He was like Gary Cooper": Catherine Tardrew, quoted in Christophe Hondelatte, *L'enlèvement du baron Empain* (Paris: Michel Lafon, 2006), 32.

259   the top joint of his own finger: Baron Empain, *La vie en jeu* (Paris: Editions Jean-Claude Lattès, 1985), 195.

259   "someone you wouldn't want to meet": Michel Desfarges, interview with author, January 29, 2020.

259   "They looked tiny": Empain, interviewed by Hondelatte, *Enlèvement,* 169–170.

259   Versini and his two associate judges: Opening trial description from Jean-Yves Dupeux [Empain's lawyer] email to author, September 16, 2020; Empain, *Vie,* 195–196; Hondelatte, *Enlèvement,* 161–165; *Le Monde,* December 4, 1982.

260   Alain Caillol was the first to take the stand: *Le Monde,* December 9, 1982.

260   François Caillol claimed to know nothing: *Le Figaro,* December 11, 1982; *France-Soir,* December 11, 1982.

260   "I'm not alone in believing": Georges Kiejman, quoted in *Le Figaro,* December 4, 1982; *Le Matin de Paris,* December 6, 1982.

260   Kiejman returned to this theme: *Le Matin,* December 18, 1982; *Le Figaro,* December 18, 1982.

261   force Empain to sell his shares: Georges Kiejman, interview with author, September 18, 2018.

261   not a "shred of concrete evidence": Kiejman interview, September 18, 2018.

261   "not the greatest plea of my career": Kiejman interview, September 18, 2018.

261   one of the most respected and eloquent members: On Kiejman's career, *Georges Kiejman, autoportrait,* documentary by Michaël Prazan, Talweg Production, 2019, consulted December 5, 2020, http://www.film-documentaire.fr/4DACTION/w_fiche_film/17254_1.

261   "Smadja was good for pimps and hustlers": Alain Caillol, interview with author, November 19, 2018.

261   "thought he had a right": Kiejman interview, September 18, 2018.

262   knocked a huge hole: André Bizeul, interview with author, January 23, 2020.

262   "Don't put it in the investigative file": Bizeul interview, January 23, 2020.

262   "That was just idle chatter": *Libération,* December 7, 1982.

262   "It's inadmissible": Bizeul interview, January 23, 2020.

263   "The commissaire may continue his testimony": Bizeul interview, January 23, 2020.

263   "He was looking at twenty years": Bizeul interview, January 23, 2020.

263   "The baron must be released immediately": *Libération*, December 8, 1982; *Le Monde*, December 9, 1982.

263   "It was Brunet and Duchateau": Georges Bertoncini testimony, quoted in *Le Figaro*, December 9, 1982.

263   "They were no friends of mine": Georges Bertoncini testimony, quoted in *Le Figaro*, December 9, 1982.

264   "Baron Empain can tell you": Georges Bertoncini testimony, quoted in *Le Figaro*, December 9, 1982; *Soir de Bruxelles*, December 9, 1982; *Le Monde*, December 13, 1982.

264   claimed to know nothing: *Le Figaro*, December 11, 1982; *France-Soir*, December 11, 1982.

264   "police would look for the brother of Alain Caillol": François Caillol testimony, quoted in *Le Figaro*, December 11, 1982.

265   suspected that François was one of the shooters: André Bizeul, telephone conversation with author, January 29, 2021.

265   Bernard Guillon likewise denied any part: *Le Figaro*, December 10, 1982; *France-Soir*, December 10, 1982.

265   On Monday, December 13: Details of Empain's testimony from *Le Monde*, December 15, 1982; *Le Figaro*, December 14, 1982; *Le Matin de Paris*, December 14, 1982; *Libération*, December 14, 1982; Hondelatte, *Enlèvement*, 192–194.

265   "There were five of them": Empain testimony, quoted in Hondelatte, *Enlèvement*, 195.

265   "For me, that meant the end": Empain testimony, quoted in Hondelatte, *Enlèvement*, 194.

266   "Not all of my jailers": Empain testimony, quoted in *Le Monde*, December 15, 1982.

266   "I intended to say as little as possible": Empain testimony, quoted in *Le Monde*, December 15, 1982.

266   "This is the voice that I heard": Empain testimony, quoted in *Le Monde*, December 15, 1982.

266   "That's false!": Guillon, quoted in *Le Monde*, December 15, 1982.

266   "Monsieur Guillon is mistaken": Empain testimony, quoted in *Libération*, December 14, 1982.

267   "When I finished speaking": Empain, *Vie*, 99, 201.

267   "Put yourself in his place": Dupeux closing argument, quoted in *Le Monde*, December 16, 1982; *Le Quotidien de Paris*, December 15, 1982.

268   "punishments justice hands out are too severe": Kiejman closing argument, quoted in Hondelatte, *Enlèvement*, 202.

268   "What do you think of a society": Hondelatte, *Enlèvement*, 202–203.

268   All eight defendants were found guilty: *Le Monde*, December 20, 1982.

269   "My faith helped me resist": *Le Monde*, December 20, 1982.

CHAPTER 27 ⟨⟩ AFTERLIVES

270   **a kidney stone:** Baron Empain, *La vie en jeu* (Paris: Jean-Claude Lattès, 1985), 220.

270   **a voodoo image on the wall:** Patricia Empain, email to author, January 18, 2021.

270   **"enriched":** Empain, interviewed by Josyane Savigneau, *Le Monde*, November 11, 1985.

271   **he started a business:** Empain, *Vie*, 202.

271   **Air Matériel had been bombed:** Empain, *Vie*, 203; *Libération*, December 27, 1982.

271   **sold his share of the business:** Empain, *Vie*, 206–207.

271   **harassing calls:** Empain, *Vie*, 210–211.

272   **"As my colleagues and I":** Robert Broussard, interview with author, August 30, 2018.

272   **"He needed to talk":** Broussard interview, August 30, 2018.

273   **uncontested divorce in 1990:** Jean-Yves Dupeux [Empain's lawyer], email to author, October 5, 2020.

273   **"I didn't see him":** Jean-François Empain, interviewed in *L'affaire du Baron Empain*, documentary by Cyrielle Galliot-Nahon, Carson Productions, March 2019.

273   **"She was not moved by my kidnapping":** Empain, interviewed in *Les barons Empain: La dynastie fracassée*, documentary by Tanguy Cortier and Alice Gorissen, aired on Arte, April 13, 2016.

274   **he had fallen in love:** Yvon Toussaint, *Les barons Empain* (Paris: Fayard, 1996), 361–362.

274   **Goldie exacted a hefty settlement:** Diane Empain, interview with author, December 14, 2020.

274   **Édouard and Rosmarie were married in 1975:** Toussaint, *Barons Empain*, 362–364.

274   **a monthly stipend of 115,000 Belgian francs:** "Protocole d'accord transactionnel," May 7, 1993, photocopy provided by Diane Empain.

274   **revoked his adoption of Wado:** "Révocation d'adoption," September 30, 1981, Tribunal de Première Instance de Bruxelles, RG. No. 128.566.

275   **stepfather's management was "catastrophic":** Baron Empain, interviewed in *Paris Match*, March 20, 1981.

275   **"After the kidnapping":** Diane Empain interview, November 14, 2020.

275   **Wado did not contest the action:** Diane Empain interview, November 14, 2020.

275   **11 percent of the Empain-Schneider group:** Diane Empain interview, December 10, 2020.

275 **sold it to the local municipality:** Figure cited in Toussaint, *Barons Empain*, 364, and confirmed by Diane Empain, interview with author, December 10, 2020.

275 **sold the stock back to the group:** Diane Empain interview, December 10, 2020.

276 **"I don't have any great needs":** Empain, interviewed by Josyane Savigneau, *Le Monde*, November 11, 1985.

276 **"For me, it's normal":** Diane Empain, interview with author, February 4, 2020.

276 **decided to sell the château:** Diane Empain interview, February 4, 2020.

276 **When relatives from Ohio visited:** Alvah Werner [son of Diane Empain], interview with author, November 2, 2020.

276 **sold the building to a mason:** Diane Empain interview, April 26, 2021.

277 **Goldie moved in with her daughter:** Diane Empain interview, February 4, 2020.

277 **her mother once tried to run her over:** Diane Empain, email to author, December 16, 2020.

277 **baroness built a large traditional-style country house:** Maguy Tran [friend of Rozell], interview with author, May 30, 2018.

277 **she was hospitalized in Saint-Tropez:** Diane Empain interview, October 12, 2020.

277 **"She had become unmanageable":** Diane Empain interview, February 4, 2020.

277 **"She knew she was trapped and muzzled":** Diane Empain interview, October 12, 2020.

277 **Diane received a phone call:** Details and quotes about Rozell Empain's suicide from Diane Empain interview, February 4, 2020; Sylvain Henry, "Rozell Rowland, baronne Empain, se suicide en se défénestrant," *Oise Hebdo*, April 5, 2006.

278 **The other members of Wado's family:** Details from Patricia Empain, interview with author, October 23, 2020.

278 **"It changed everybody's lives":** Patricia Empain interview, October 23, 2020.

279 **Jean-François lives in Lausanne:** Patricia Empain interview, October 23, 2020.

279 **"I'd tell him":** Jean-François Empain, interviewed by Cyrielle Galliot-Nahon in *L'affaire du Baron Empain*.

279 **François Caillol returned to his home:** Alain Caillol, email to author, March 4, 2021.

279 **sliced off the top joint:** "Automutilation collective à Fleury-Mérogis," *Le Monde*, August 11, 1984.

279 **Guillon was the one police suspected:** Michel Desfarges, interview with author, January 29, 2020.

279   **still living somewhere in France:** Alain Caillol, email to author, March 4, 2021.

279   **arrested in Brittany five years later:** Alain Lallemand, "Bertoncini tombe pour trafic de stupéfiants," Associated Press, September 28, 1994; *Libération*, June 20, 2020.

280   **found dead in his cell:** "L'ex-ravisseur du baron Empain meurt en prison," *Libération*, February 20, 2001.

280   **a severe asthma attack:** Caillol interview, December 14, 2018.

CHAPTER 28 ❧ LIGHT AND TWILIGHT

281   **"complex and interesting personality":** Baron Empain, *La vie en jeu* (Paris: Jean-Claude Lattès, 1985), 200.

281   **"cultivated man with social pretensions":** Georges Kiejman, interview with author, September 18, 2018.

281   **"a piece of filth":** Michel Desfarges, interview with author, January 29, 2020.

281   **"I look more like a little boy grown old":** Alain Caillol, letter to Mireille Bonnelle, April 29, [1985], in Bonnelle and Caillol, *Lettres en liberté conditionnelle* (Paris: Editions Manya, 1990), 153.

282   **"When we called Bierry":** Alain Caillol, interview with author, September 13, 2018.

282   **"We refused to compromise":** Alain Caillol, quoted in *Le Figaro*, January 13, 2012.

283   **"First of all":** Caillol interview, October 12, 2018.

283   **"*Risques du métier*":** Caillol interview, November 19, 2018.

283   **"Restaurants, travel, ski vacations":** Caillol interview, September 20, 2018.

283   **"The idea was to create a shock":** Caillol interview, January 22, 2020.

284   **"cleanly and not damage the flesh":** Caillol email to author, April 21, 2021.

284   **"There were only two solutions":** Caillol interview, January 22, 2020.

284   **"without hesitation":** Caillol interview, January 22, 2020.

284   **"Quickly, so he wouldn't even know":** Caillol interview, January 22, 2020.

284   **"Empain had become almost like a friend":** Caillol interview, January 22, 2020.

284   **"We would have been so enraged":** Caillol interview, November 19, 2018.

285   **"We killed him":** Caillol interview in *Baron Empain, trahison et pardon*, documentary by Dominique Rizet, 17 Juin Média, 2015.

285   **Arrested again in 2000:** Caillol, interview, September 20, 2018.

285   **a pension of €1,000 a month:** Caillol interview, February 7, 2019.

285 **Caillol developed a rich intellectual life:** Details from Bonnelle and Caillol, *Lettres en liberté conditionnelle*; Georges Kiejman, interview with author, September 18, 2018; author's various interviews and conversations with Caillol.

286 **"The curtains, the bedspreads":** Alain Caillol, quoted by Patricia Tourancheau, "Remords postbaron," *Libération*, January 12, 2012.

286 **When he was first released from prison:** Caillol interview, September 13, 2018.

286 **"It was like with my father":** Alain Caillol, *Lumière* (Paris: Cherche Midi, 2012), 205.

286 **They had a more substantive exchange:** Details of Caillol's meeting with Empain from Gilles Malençon, "Empain-Caillol, le chemin du pardon," encetempsla.com [Malençon's blog], January 25, 2012, consulted December 5, 2019, http://encetempslacom.blogspot.fr/2012/01/empain-caillol-le -chemin-du-pardon.html. (Caillol confirmed the accuracy of this account in an email to the author, December 3, 2020.)

287 **"We talked about this and that":** Caillol interview, January 22, 2020.

288 **"I was one of the first to talk to him":** Caillol interview, January 22, 2020.

288 **"Everything that Alain Caillol has written":** Baron Empain, interviewed in *Le Figaro*, January 13, 2012.

289 **"Each one of us saw in him":** Caillol, quoted in "Un acte manqué," *Charente Libre*, January 25, 2012.

289 **"Maybe he will reach out his hand":** Caillol, *Lumière*, 205.

289 **Pierre Caillol had suffered:** *France-Soir*, March 29, 1978; *Paris Match*, April 1–7, 1978.

289 **"He was too ashamed of me":** Caillol, *Lumière*, 133.

290 **"I had absolutely no moral education":** Caillol interview, October 12, 2018.

290 **"prime candidate for psychoanalysis":** Georges Kiejman, interview with author, September 18, 2018.

CHAPTER 29   ∽   WADO'S ADIEU

291 **Under its steep thatched roof:** A detailed description and video tour of La Chaumière is available online: https://youtu.be/PVHlHirM3P8.

291 **"Rozell was fun":** Patricia Empain, interview with author, October 19, 2020.

292 **obtained Monegasque citizenship:** Diane Empain, interview with author, November 13, 2020.

292 **As his debts mounted:** Diane Empain, email to author, June 1, 2021.

292 **"I would tell him":** Diane Empain interview, February 4, 2020.

292 **the subject of a remarkable 2016 documentary:** *Les barons Empain: La dynastie fracassée,* documentary by Tanguy Cortier and Alice Gorissen, aired on Arte, April 13, 2016.

294 **Wado fainted:** Dr. Raymond Abadji, interview with author, July 13, 2020.

295 **"like a second kidnapping":** Abadji interview, July 13, 2020.

295 **"He won't live long":** Abadji interview, July 13, 2020.

295 **"Every morning when he woke up":** Diane Empain interview, February 4, 2020.

295 **he seemed to rally for a time:** Patricia Empain interview, October 30, 2020.

295 **"I am just an old cardiac case":** Baron Empain, email to Patricia, January 29, 2018.

295 **"Alone in my Chaumière I cry":** Baron Empain, email to Diane Empain, February 1, 2018.

296 **Toward the end of May:** Diane Empain interview, February 4, 2020.

296 **"Monsieur wants me to call an ambulance":** Diane Empain interview, February 4, 2020.

296 **"I don't want to die":** Diane Empain interview, February 4, 2020.

296 **Wado had always said:** Patricia Empain, email to author, May 17, 2021.

296 **"It was like the Dead Poets Society":** Diane Empain interview, February 25, 2020.

EPILOGUE

301 **"I can't stand to look at myself":** Diane Empain, interview with author, February 4, 2020.

301 **"My mother was diabolical":** Diane Empain interview, February 4, 2020.

302 **"she would wake me up at five a.m.":** Diane Empain interview, February 4, 2020.

302 **her "little thing":** Diane Empain, email to author, December 12, 2020.

302 **underwent years of psychoanalysis:** Diane Empain, telephone conversation, December 14, 2020.

302 **When Diane became pregnant:** Diane Empain, email to author, January 17, 2021.

302 **The boy didn't know Diane was his real mother:** Alvah (Al) Werner, telephone interview with author, November 27, 2020.

302 **Goldie tried to derail the whole thing:** Werner telephone interview, November 27, 2020.

303 **"nasty person who always wanted to control":** Werner telephone interview, November 27, 2020.

ABOUT THE AUTHOR

Tom Sancton, author of *The Bettencourt Affair* and five other non-fiction books, was a longtime Paris bureau chief for *Time* magazine, where he wrote more than fifty cover stories. A Rhodes scholar who studied at Harvard and Oxford, he is currently a research professor at Tulane University in New Orleans, where he spends part of the year. In 2014, the French government named Tom Sancton a Chevalier (Knight) of the Order of Arts and Letters.